DATE DUE

DEMCO 38-297

An Introduction to

Vietnamese Literature

An Introduction to
VIETNAMESE
LITERATURE

Maurice M. Durand
and
Nguyen Tran Huan

Translated from the French by
D. M. Hawke

COLUMBIA UNIVERSITY PRESS
NEW YORK   1985

Library of Congress Cataloging in Publication Data

Durand, Maurice M.
An introduction to Vietnamese literature.

Translation of: Introduction à la littérature
vietnamienne.
Bibliography: p.
Includes index.
1. Vietnamese literature—History and criticism.
I. Nguyen, Trân Huân. II. Title.
PL4378.D813 1985   895.9′22′09   84-12754
ISBN 0-231-05852-7

Columbia University Press
New York   Guildford, Surrey

Printed in the United States of America

Clothbound editions of Columbia University Press Books are Smyth-sewn and
printed on permanent and durable acid-free paper.

CONTENTS

Preface vii

Translator's note ix

Synopsis of the History of Vietnam xi

I: General 1

II: Folk Literature 29

III: Vietnamese Poetry Before Nguyen Trai 51

IV: Nguyen Trai and *Quoc-am thi-tap* 58

V: Le Thanh Tong and *Hong Duc quoc-am thi-tap* 65

VI: The Sixteenth Century and Nguyen Binh Khiem 70

VII: The Seventeenth and Eighteenth Centuries: Growth and Flowering of *Nôm* Poetry and Narrative Verse 75

VIII: *Kim Van Kieu* and Narrative Verse 86

IX: The Nineteenth Century 95

X: The Twentieth Century 107

XI: Journalism in Vietnam 156

XII: The New Poetry 165

XIII: The Contemporary Vietnamese Novel 177

Bibliography 192

Index 201

PREFACE

This book represents a collaborative effort: Professor Durand undertook the section on Vietnamese literature from the earliest times up to the "pre-French" period, while I was responsible for the two later periods, the French (1862–1945) and the contemporary (1945–1975).

Unhappily Professor Durand, after a long illness, died in April 1966, when the French edition of the book was in proof. In seeing it through the press I of course scrupulously respected his original text, making only such very few alterations as were needed to take account of later information. Thus the real name of Ba Huyen Thanh quan ("wife of the *sous-préfet* of Thanh quan") was not known until 1965, when it came to light as the result of research carried out by the Hanoi research team. Similarly with the great nineteenth-century poetess Ho Xuan Huong, only her surname (Ho) and pseudonym (Xuan Huong) were known; but thanks to the work of North Vietnamese scholars such as Tran Thanh Mai and Nam Tran, what may be her real given names became known at the end of 1964.

N.T.H.

TRANSLATOR'S NOTE

In this translation, as in the original French edition, the diacritical marks of Vietnamese have necessarily been for the most part omitted in the body of the book to save printing costs. Thus no distinction is made in the text between Vietnamese letters represented by a single letter in the Latin alphabet (e.g., between D and $\underline{Đ}$ or a and $â$), nor are the tones marked. The only exceptions are those few passages (pp. 19–20, 23, and 50) where diacritics are essential to differentiate between two otherwise identical transliterations. The alphabetical index at the end of the book does, however, include the diacritics of Vietnamese.

Words and phrases likely to be unfamiliar to English-speaking readers are briefly explained in a note the first time they occur.

The surviving co-author, Dr. Nguyen Tran Huan, has added sections to chapters 10 and 12 to update them to 1975 (the year in which Vietnam was reunified), and would have gone further had he not been prevented by ill health. In any case, however, a complete and balanced perspective on Vietnamese literary history can probably only be achieved after a certain lapse of time.

D.M.H.

SYNOPSIS OF THE HISTORY OF VIETNAM

From the earliest times to 257 B.C.
Legendary period. Hong Bang dynasty ruled over the kingdom
of Van Lang (approximately North Vietnam).

257–111 B.C.
Prehistoric period. According to tradition, the kingdom of Au
Lac was first ruled by King An-Duong-Vuong (257–207 B.C.),
and subsequently subjugated by the Chinese general Ch'ao-T'o
(Trieu Da), founder of the Ch'ao (Trieu) dynasty.

111 B.C.–A.D. 43
Beginning of the historic period: first Chinese colonization. In
A.D. 39–43, revolt of the two Trung sisters, Vietnam's national
heroines.

A.D. 43–543
Second Chinese colonization. Vietnam under Chinese influence. Formation of Lin-yi (later to become Champa).

544–602
Vietnamese Early Ly dynasty.

603–938
Third Chinese colonization. Vietnam under increasingly strong
Chinese influence.

939–1407
Independent Vietnamese dynasties: the Ngo (939–967), Dinh (968–980), Early Le (980–1009), Late Ly (1010–1225); Tran (1225–1400), and Ho (1400–1407). Continuing struggle against China and the Mongols. Military, administrative and economic reorganization of the country. Buddhism and Confucianism flourish.

1407–1427
Colonization by the Chinese Ming dynasty; struggle for independence led by Le Loi.

1428–1788
Late Le dynasty, initiated by Le Loi's victory over the Chinese. Development of literature, history and geography, and triumph of Confucianism. Internecine strife between the great lords of the North and the South. Introduction of Christianity; first contacts with foreign merchants and explorers; invention of the *quoc-ngu* system of transliteration, codified by Fr. Alexandre de Rhodes. Final defeat of Champa: South Vietnam occupied by Vietnamese forces and colonized.

1788–1802
Nguyen Tay-Son dynasty.

1802–1945
Nguyen dynasty. For the latter part of this period (1862–1945) Vietnam was a French colony, and French culture was the preponderant influence.

1945
August Revolution, followed by declaration of independence and proclamation of the Democratic Republic of Vietnam.

1946–1954
First Indochina war, ending with the 1954 Geneva agreements, under which the country was partitioned at the 17th parallel into the Democratic Republic of Vietnam in the North and the Re-

public of Vietnam in the South. The Geneva agreements also provided for elections to be held by 1956 in order to reunify the country.

1955–1963

Ngo Dinh Diem in power as first president of the Republic of (South) Vietnam. In 1956 his government refused to carry out the provisions for holding elections; it became increasingly unpopular, and was eventually overthrown by a *coup d'état* in November 1963. Meanwhile Ho Chi Minh's government in the North set out with help from the USSR and China to build a socialist state.

1964–1975

The United States gave increasing economic and military aid to South Vietnam, and in March 1965 started sending in combat troops and bombing North Vietnam. But though the number of U.S. combat troops in early 1968 reached half a million, and enormous areas of Vietnam were devastated, Washington finally came to realize that military victory was impossible; and in January 1973 it signed a cease-fire agreement providing for the withdrawal of its forces and recognition of a Provisional Revolutionary Government in the South. On May 1, 1975, the country was formally reunified under a Vietnamese government for the first time since 1802, with its capital at Hanoi.

I: GENERAL

The history of Vietnam is dominated by a succession of events which influenced literature in different ways. The country was a province of China from the second century B.C. to the tenth century A.D., under Chinese suzerainty from then until the end of the nineteenth century, and under French rule from then until 1954, when the Communist régime took over in North Vietnam. After so many centuries of Chinese rule, the country is steeped in Chinese influence. The French contributed Western material civilization, new ways of thinking, modern technology, and social revolutionary ideas. The latter, reinforcing the urge for national liberation, paved the way for independence. Unhappily, however, the Geneva agreements divided the country into two; the two halves moved in politically opposite directions, and until April 1975 were engaged in hostilities against each other.

LEGENDARY ORIGINS

The early history of Vietnam is obscure. Our only sources of information about it are legends and tales in Chinese amplifying passages in the old Chinese official history, and accounts of the country and its customs by Chinese authors.

According to legend the first rulers of Vietnam were of supernatural origin. They were supposedly descended on the one hand from the legendary Chinese emperor Than Nong, and on the other from the dragon ruler or Water King of Lake Dong Dinh, in southern China; and in general the prehistory of Vietnam is bound up with that of the early peoples of China south of the Blue River. The first Kingdom of Vietnam was known either as Van Lang (if we accept the traditional spelling) or as Da Lang (if we assume a mistake in the characters); it comprised southern China, present-day North Vietnam and also part of Laos.

The following is the account of its origins given in *Linh-nam trich quai,* a collection of fables in Chinese dating from the late fifteenth century. Lac Long Quan was its first king, after he parted from his consort, Queen Au Co:

Long Quan[1] lived with Au Co. A year later the latter gave birth to a membranous pouch; they regarded this as an ill omen, and abandoned it in the wilderness. Five or six days later there appeared in the pouch a hundred eggs, from which there hatched a hundred menchildren. They returned to their parents' house and were fed by them, and they all grew up without needing to be suckled. Their intelligence and courage were noteworthy, and they were feared and respected by all. These brothers, it was said, were no ordinary men.

By this time Long Quan had long since returned to the Water Palace. The children and their mother wished to return to the Northern Kingdom (China). When they reached the border, Hoang De[2] got to hear of it: he placed himself at the head of his troops and drove them out of the confines of his kingdom. The children and their mother, unable to return to the Northern Kingdom, came home again and appealed to Long Quan, saying: "Father, where are you, that you leave us, mother and children, widowed and orphaned? We are all stricken with sorrow and distress."

Long Quan came quickly and found them abandoned in the wilderness. Co said to him: "I am from the Northern Kingdom: I lived with you and brought forth a hundred sons. I have not the wherewithal to feed them or bring them up. Now you desert me and go away, so that

1. I.e., "Dragon Lord." Lac Long Quan means "Dragon Lord of the Lac." Lac is apparently the name of a tribe: it occurs again in Au Lac, the kingdom that succeeded Van Lang.
2. The legendary Chinese emperor Huang Ti (2697–2597 B.C.).

we are people without father and without husband, and nothing is left for us but to bewail our lot. I beg leave to follow you."

Long Quan replied: "I am of the race of dragons, and chief of the watery breed. You are of the race of immortals[3] sprung from the earth. Water and fire are opposing elements, and their perfect union is difficult indeed. Even though the female element *(yin)* and the male element *(yang)* mate and produce children, nevertheless they are of different breeds, and it is hard for them to remain together for long."

So he bade fifty of his sons follow their mother back to the mountains, and the other fifty he bade follow him back to the Southern Sea (Nam Hai). He bade them govern each one his own district, and enjoined them as follows: "Whether you go up to the mountains or down to the sea, you shall let one another know if you are in difficulties, and you shall by no means desert one another." The hundred sons agreed, each for himself; and then they separated and went their ways. It is they who are the ancestors of the Hundred Yue (Viet). Co and her fifty children lived on Mount Phong, the present-day Bach Hac area, in Son Tay (North Vietnam). The bravest among them they raised to the rank of king, giving him the title Hung Vuong (Brave King). So he succeeded Long Quan and ruled over the kingdom, which became known as Van Lang. The kingdom was divided into fifteen provinces *(bo)*. It was bounded by the sea on the east, by the kingdom of Ba Thuc[4] to the west, by Lake Dong Dinh in the north, and by the kingdom of Ho Ton Tinh[5] to the south.

Hung Vuong bade his younger brothers govern the provinces. At first the people did not have what they needed for survival. They made clothes out of the bark of trees and wove mats out of grass; they distilled spirits from the sap of trees; they lived on coconuts and breadfruit, and salted birds, animals, insects, and fish. They preserved root ginger, and used knives to turn the soil and fire to clear the ground. The earth produced rice and glutinous rice in plenty, and they cooked it in bamboo pipes. They built houses on piles, for safety from tigers and wolves. They cut their hair short, for easier movement in the upland forests. When a child was born, they laid it on a banana leaf. When boys and girls contracted marriage, they used areca nut. . . .

3. I.e., the *tien* (Chinese *hsien*). The components of the character denote "mountain people."
4. Corresponding roughly to Szechuan.
5. The name used in Vietnamese mythology for Champa, the kingdom which in ancient times formed the southern portion of North Vietnam: its northern border was north of Hué.

This extremely fruitful and important text illustrates the imaginative process by which details from Chinese texts found their way into Vietnamese history. The name of the country, Viet Nam, indicates a link with the Viet peoples, branches of which took root in southern China while the main body settled down in what is now North Vietnam. Though this text is doubtless incomplete as an historical account, the Vietnamese do nevertheless preserve a very ancient folk-memory of a time when a branch of the Viet living south of the Blue River migrated: they came and settled in the delta of the hilly region of Tonkin, with their center of gravity in the Bach Hac area. The Vietnamese storyteller, basing himself on early Chinese ethnography, describes a primitive people at a cultural level equivalent to that of present-day minorities in Vietnam.

A whole series of etiological and other tales has been set against the background of this early period and the first dynasty of kings: they make up what we propose to call the Hung Vuong cycle.

The Hung Vuong apparently reigned until the third century B.C. They were succeeded in 257 B.C. by Au Lac, a short-lived kingdom which lasted only until 207 B.C., when it was overthrown by the then king of Kwangtung, Trieu Da. The Au Lac kingdom was founded by a Thuc prince who conquered Van Lang and reigned under the name of An Duong Vuong. His capital was not far from Hanoi, at Co Loa—today one of the main archeological sites of Vietnam. An echo of this period survives, both in Chinese literature and in oral tradition, in the shape of a touching story about the end of the city of Co Loa. An Duong Vuong had a daughter, Mi Chau; and following an early clash between Trieu Da and An Duong Vuong, the latter gave her in marriage to Trieu Da's son, Trong Thuy. Now An Duong Vuong had a magic crossbow with a trigger made from the claw of a turtle-spirit, the Golden Turtle: a single bolt from this crossbow would put the enemy to flight, and thanks to it An Duong Vuong held out triumphant in his capital, Co Loa. The wily son-in-law Trong Thuy coaxed the secret of the crossbow out of his wife, and then:

He secretly made another trigger and substituted it for the magic claw of the Golden Turtle. When he had got what he wanted, he sought leave of Mi Chau to go home and see his parents, saying: "The mutual love of husband and wife is unforgettable; love of one's parents calls for the severance of worldly ties. I am leaving today to go back and see them, and it is hard for me to set a date for my return. If by any chance our two kingdoms were no longer at peace, so that we were separated, one in the north and the other in the south, I would come and look for you. It were well that you appoint a sign, so that I may know where you are."

Mi Chau replied: "Though we were separated far from one another, yet our love would not fade. I have a blanket embroidered with goose-feathers, that I generally carry with me: if strife were to break out, I would pull feathers off it and drop them at the turnings of the road, to guide you; when you saw them, you could set about coming to my rescue."

Trong Thuy set off with the magic trigger. Da rejoiced when he received it, and raised an army to attack the king.[6] The latter took up his magic crossbow and went on with his game of chess as though nothing had happened. "So Da is not afraid of the magic crossbow?," he said, laughing. Da came on: the king drew his bow, but the magic trigger had gone and there was nothing he could do about it; so he hurriedly took to flight. Setting Mi Chau behind him on his horse, he fled southwards.

Trong Thuy recognized the goose-feathers and set out in pursuit of the fugitives. When An Duong Vuong reached the sea, his way was blocked and his plight became parlous. There was no boat to take him across the sea. The king lamented and cried out: "Heaven has undone me! Messenger of the Clear River,[7] where are you? Come speedily and save me!"

The turtle leapt up above the waters of the river[8] and called mockingly: "Your enemy is behind you!"

The king drew his sword to cut off Mi Chau's head, and she wept and said: "I am a child. If my heart is a traitor's and I have plotted to harm you, father, may I turn to fine dust when I die. But if I have been ever loyal and full of filial piety, and have been deceived by a man, then when I die may I turn into a precious pearl, beyond compare even with the snow for purity."

6. I.e., An Duong Vuong.
7. I.e., the Golden Turtle. In another legend it helps in the building of Co Loa, and gives An Duong Vuong the claw used in the mechanism of his crossbow.
8. Where it flows into the sea: the fugitives had reached the mouth.

Mi Chau died beside the sea. Her blood ran down into the water, was swallowed by an oyster, and turned into a gleaming pearl. The king, holding in his hand a seven-inch rhinoceros horn, went down to the bottom of the sea, while the Golden Turtle went on ahead and made a way for him. Da's army arrived at the spot to be faced by the rising tide, and found nothing but Mi Chau's body. Trong Thuy carried it away in his arms and buried it at Loa Thanh,[9] and she turned into jadestone. Trong Thuy fell ill, and constantly pined for her. He haunted the spot where she used to wash and bathe, thinking that she was there with him in the wind and the colored clouds. Eventually he committed suicide by throwing himself down the well.

Here we see a Vietnamese trait which we shall come across again: a tendency, that is, to draw no sharp line between the natural and the magical. Historical events are intermingled with myth, and reality with the world of dreams. Much of Chinese literature delights in themes in which mortals form relationships with immortals.

CHINESE RULE

Vietnam was a province of China from the second century B.C. until the 10th century A.D. Power was exercised by governors appointed by the Imperial Chinese court—or, during the disruption of the Chinese Empire, by whatever dynasty was in power in southern China.

These eleven centuries saw the moulding of ancient Vietnam. Gradually it emerged from the primitive stage and developed a political and administrative structure. Meanwhile on the intellectual and ethical plane Vietnamese thought was influenced by religious and philosophical ideas brought from China—though the old animistic beliefs still survived to some extent. The teaching of Chinese spread, and education was organized on an

9. I.e., "city shaped like a shell"—the old name for Co Loa, so called on account of its tall spiral shape.

official basis. Vietnamese who wished to achieve public office (and with it an affluent life) needed to learn Chinese, both for the purpose of their dealings with the representatives of the ruling power and for the sake of contact with Chinese civilization—which at that time led the world.

The Vietnamese pronounced Chinese characters with an accent of their own, which has led some to speak of Sino-Vietnamese characters—an absurdity, since the characters are the same whether pronounced with a Chinese or a Vietnamese accent. Indeed, the so-called Sino-Vietnamese pronunciation is probably no more than the Ancient Chinese pronunciation current during the Han and T'ang dynasties, preserved and subsequently modified during the period of Vietnamese independence. This Ancient Chinese pronunciation was passed on by Vietnamese teachers from one generation to another, and either became frozen or evolved in accordance with specifically Vietnamese phonetic trends; whereas in China it evolved along lines of its own. A rough parallel is to be found in Canadian French, which has evolved on different lines from the French spoken in France: it now appears archaic and provincial by comparison.

Chinese learning and culture seem to have been enthusiastically welcomed by the Vietnamese. Some passed the Chinese public examinations, or achieved distinction as men of letters. Others held important posts in their own country or even in China. A class of literati grew up, and rapidly became the dominant class: its members were sufficiently erudite to feel themselves in no way inferior to the Chinese literati. On the achievement of independence one of the earliest Vietnamese dynasties, the Ly (1010–1225), in 1075 instituted triennial public examinations on the Chinese model.

Chinese education had a profound effect on Vietnamese culture. Students and scholars spent their youth learning Chinese and studying the authors included in their examination syllabuses. The set texts were generally either the great classics of Chinese antiquity (the *Book of Poetry, Spring and Autumn,* the *Four*

[7]

Books, Annals, etc.), or else the works of later great Chinese writers. Purely literary works occupied first place; but official instruments such as decrees, petitions etc. were added to the curriculum to test candidates who would later become civil servants under the Empire and be expected to draft such documents themselves. Even these official instruments, instead of being couched in an appropriately flat and impersonal style, were embellished by examination candidates with all manner of academic and rhetorical flourishes.

All Vietnamese writing from the earliest beginnings right up to the eighteenth century betrays this overwhelmingly strong Chinese influence. The vast majority of extant works, whether handwritten or printed with wood blocks, are in Chinese. Indeed, the literature of Vietnam's early period would have amounted to no more than an appendage of Chinese literature, were it not for a rich tradition of popular narrative—and the introduction of *nôm* transcription for writing Vietnamese, which produced some major works in the seventeenth and eighteenth centuries. Starting in the twentieth century there is of course a plethora of modern works in Roman transcription *(quoc-ngu).*

BUDDHISM

During the first ten centuries Buddhism, which probably reached Vietnam in the second century A.D., spread side by side with Confucianism. Buddhist priests were an object of veneration, and the kings, especially the Ly dynasty (1010–1225), were either true believers or great respecters of religion. Buddhism inculcates an attitude of gentle resignation in face of the transience of this world. Its ethic is founded on the belief that good deeds and thoughts in this life lead, if not to everlasting salvation, at any rate to better existences in the future. Some of the Ly and Tran emperors of Vietnam chose to retire to a pagoda and end their days in meditation, repentance for their misdeeds, and the practice of good works. This served both a religious end, to improve their own personal prospects, and a political one, to secure the orderly succession of the royal house—for it meant that the heir apparent was actually enthroned and ruling during the recluse Emperor's lifetime.

The first independent Vietnamese dynasty, the Dinh (968–980), granted the Buddhist priesthood an official hierarchy like the civil and military mandarins; and Buddhist priests such as Ngo Chan Luu and Dang Huyen Quang later held high political posts. Their power reached its zenith under the succeeding dynasties, the early Le (980–1009) and the Ly (1010–1225). They were the emperors' confidants, and their amanuenses and ambassadors. They were the custodians of culture. They were indispensable to the nobles, who needed to devote their time to waging war and administering their fiefs. But above all, until the days of the Tran the emperors and their court seem to have subsisted in an atmosphere in which superstition was rife. Buddhist and Taoist priests revolved around them like satellites in orbit, vying with each other and enjoying royal favor in proportion to the extent of their supposed magical powers. Thus Tu Dao Hanh, a priest of the Zen[10] school in the days of the emperor Ly Nhan Tong (1072–1127), enjoyed an established reputation as a magician. He was himself the son of a Buddhist grandee, which may itself give grounds for suspecting the purity of Vietnamese Buddhism at that time. In addition to foreign Buddhists domiciled in Tonkin, and monks leading an ascetic life in the various pagodas, we are dimly aware from history and even more from mythology of the existence of magician-priests, living a life partly worldly and partly monastic. Taoist and other magicians were still powerful, and the efforts of the Buddhist priesthood were aimed at undermining their authority and propagating Buddhist doctrines.

The genuine monks have left us poetry in Chinese on typical Buddhist themes: the vanity of human existence, joy and tranquillity through solitude, the merits of good deeds. Few texts

10. Zen: the practice of mind-control used in Buddhist meditation. The word is the Japanese form of the Sanskrit *dhyāna* (Chinese *Ch'an*).

from the Ly period have survived except as quotations in historical and biographical works. The great encyclopedist Le Qui Don (1726–1784), in his *Kien van tieu luc* (Account of Things Learnt), tells us in chapter 4, on literature, that research on the literature of the Ly era is impossible for lack of source material. All he gives is a few short pieces in Chinese five-syllable verse from a work called *Thien uyen tap anh thu*[11] (Book of the Great Monks of the Garden of *Dhyāna*), i.e., the collected lives of the great Zen monks, among them nineteen Vietnamese friars. They are poems by the emperor Ly Nhan Tong (1072–1127) and various ministers of the Ly in honor of this or that Buddhist priest. Thus there is a five-syllable octet addressed to the Indian friar Tī-ni-da (i.e., Vinītaruci), who came to Tonkin in the sixth century and started the teaching of the law at Phap Van pagoda (Bac Ninh district). It may be translated as follows:

You took up your pilgrim's staff and came to the Southern Kingdom.
I know that you have long practiced *dhyāna,*
And that you have undertaken to open the way of Buddha for believers
So that they may commune deeply in spirit, fountainhead of all things.
The Lankā sutra[12] appears like a gleaming moon;
But aboard the boat of illumination you have attained lotus-scented shores.[13]
So when can I see you again
To talk with you of the deep mysteries of Buddhism?

Ly Nhan Tong also wrote poems dedicated to the Buddhist priests Giac Hai and Van Hanh (d. 1018), to the latter of whom we owe the following charming quatrain:

11. On this work (whose title varies slightly in different manuscripts) see Tran Van Giap, "Le bouddhisme en Annam des origines au XIIIe siècle," *Bulletin de l'École Française d'Extrême-Orient* 32, pp. 13f.
12. The Lankāvatāra sutra is a philosophical disquisition supposedly delivered by Buddha Shākyamuni on Mount Lankā, in Sri Lanka: it is one of the texts adopted by the Zen sect.
13. I.e., Nirvana.

The body is like a lightning-flash, which appears briefly and vanishes.
In spring the trees are thriving; in autumn, lo! they are withered.
Beyond fear, beyond dread, let prosperity and hard times pass by;
Prosperity and hard times are fleeting as the dew spread out upon the
grass.[14]

A seven-syllable quatrain by the high mandarin Doan Van Kham
is addressed to the Zen priest Khong Lo Quang Tri (d. between
1085 and 1091):

You planted your pilgrim's staff on the High Mountain, and left be-
hind the six earthly illusions.[15]
In your secret retreat you indulge in irresolute dreams, and question
the floating clouds.
As for me, I zealously exert myself in countless futile matters,
And am bogged down in my mandarin's duties at the Imperial court.

But Buddhism, being an imported religion, did not and never
will completely supplant the old superstitions or the worship of
local spirits. Much of Vietnamese literature in Chinese and *nôm*
is devoted to tales about spirits. The majority are of no great
literary interest, though valuable from the point of view of the
anthropology, and indeed also the history, of Vietnam. But some
of the *nôm* texts, hymns to spirit deities set in a rhythmical verse
form designed to be sung to a musical accompaniment, have
aesthetic and literary merit.

THE INFLUENCE OF COURT LIFE ON LITERATURE

Under the various Vietnamese dynasties power was highly cen-
tralized, and everything revolved around the Emperor and the
court. The ambition of every Vietnamese was success in the literary examinations, which led at worst to a provincial mandar-

14. See M. Durand, "Littérature vietnamienne," *Encyclopédie de la Plèiade: Histoire des littératures*, vol. 1 (Paris: Gallimard, 1955), p. 1322.
15. *Luc tran:* the illusions of sight, hearing, smell, taste, touch and thought.

in's post and at best to high office at court. Emperors and ministers were very often men of culture, and encouraged creative writing. Much of the official material commissioned by the Emperor was written in Chinese: e.g., annals such as *Dai Viet su ky toan thu* (Complete History of the Great Viet), published in 1697 but actually a conflation of earlier official annals by Le Van Huu (1272) and Ngo Si Lien (1479), with additions up to 1662 by Pham Cong Tru and Le Hi; and *Kham dinh Viet su thong giam cuong muc* (Universal History of the Viet, Text and Commentaries, by Imperial Command), printed in 1884. These two works, usually referred to for brevity as *Toan thu* and *Cuong muc*, represent the official histories of the Le (1428–1789) and the Nguyen (1789–1945) respectively. In addition to annals the various dynasties commissioned geography books, pilots' guides, legal compendia, and so forth. All this Chinese material is utilitarian rather than literary in character: much of it has been analyzed by Émile Gaspardone in his *Bibliographie annamite (Bulletin de l'École Française d'Extrême-Orient, 34)*.

Some emperors were of a literary bent, and had pretensions as writers themselves. Some became the centers of literary salons, or else merely liked having sound scholars around them. The emperor Le Thanh Tong (1442–1497) has gone down in Vietnamese literary history as the founder of a learned society, the Tao Dan ("Altar of Poetry"); it consisted of 28 members whom he likened to the 28 constellations, with himself at their head. His personal intervention gave great impetus to writing, and part of his reign, the Hong Duc period (1470–1497), was one of the most brilliant in early Vietnamese literature.

Life at court, with its entertainments and festivities, afforded great scope for writers, composers, and actors, and thereby contributed to the flowering of literature. We have some details of the songs and dances performed by young men and girls at banquets in the Imperial palace under the Tran (1225–1400): the subject matter is taken from Chinese literature. The classical Vietnamese theater, which is entirely Chinese in inspiration, seems to have been introduced into Vietnam by a Chinese actor captured in 1285 when the Yuan armies were defeated by the forces of the Tran at Tay Ket, in Hung Yen province, North Vietnam. His name was Ly Nguyen Cat, and he was a notable singer. Le Qui Don writes in *Kien van tieu luc:*

> His singing classes were attended by the sons and daughters of the best families. Nguyen Cat wrote plays on themes from classical antiquity, such as the story of the Queen Mother of the West presenting the peach of immortality. The characters in this play are the mandarin Chu Tu Dan. . . . There is a cast of twelve in all. They wear brocade gowns and embroidered robes. There is music from drum, flute and guitar, hand-clapping and loud strumming on wooden sounding-boxes, entrances and exits, and miming. The audience are easily moved: the idea is to melt the soft-hearted and amuse the gay. This marks the origin of the theatre in our country.

At palace entertainments there was some story-telling in the vernacular, but songs certainly seem to have been sung in Sino-Vietnamese.

Many writers found court life repugnant. The nervous strain of maintaining their position, the intrigue, the cliques, the unscrupulous behavior of the courtiers, the fickleness of the Emperor's favor—all these factors drove them to seek their happiness away from the capital and the court and to savor the delights of *otium*. The finest of the *nôm* poems by Nguyen Trai (1380–1442), Nguyen Binh Khiem (1491–1585) and many other poets consist of denunciations of the artificiality and superficiality of life in society and eulogies of solitary communion with nature.

Vietnamese public opinion was always acutely sensitive to the policies of the Imperial court. So long as the Emperor and the nobles showed the will to defend the country's good name and territorial integrity, the common people and the writers who spoke for them sang their praises and acclaimed their warlike deeds. There are legends and tales, stories and lays, featuring the heroes who triumphantly resisted the various Chinese invasions. The battles won by the Trung sisters (A.D. 43), Emperors Dinh Tien Hoang (968–979), Le Thai To (1428–1433) and Nguyen Hue (1788–1792), and General Tran Hung Dao (thirteenth century) against mighty Chinese armies, and their successful defence of the country's independence, prompted many later Vietnamese poets and prose writers to celebrate their exploits in patriotic vein.

Conversely, when the Nguyen emperors after Gia Long (1802–1819) perforce capitulated to the French, and collaborated with them following the capture of Tourane[16] in 1858, they provoked a chorus of literary execration. Poems in shocked accents inveighed vociferously against a Court which could neither organize a defence against the invader nor yet support the guerrilla resistance. The crusading zeal of men like Phan Van Tri (who took his Second Degree in 1849), Nguyen Dinh Chieu (1822–1888), and later patriotic writers is directed not only against the French but even more against the Hué court and the ministers—who in 1862 surrendered the three western provinces and in 1884 recognized the French protectorate over Central and North Vietnam.

From the days of the first Chinese conquest (111 B.C.) there were trading links between Tonkin and southern China, and they became closer as time went on. Later came contacts with France and the establishment of the French presence in Vietnam, which caused a considerable economic and social upheaval. With the reorganization carried out by the Chinese authorities, and the establishment later of relative peace and unity under the various Vietnamese dynasties and then under the French administration, trade and cottage crafts grew up, and then the first industries. New social classes came into being, with some awareness of their own importance. Vietnamese society had originally consisted only of the nobility and its satellite groups (mandarins and officials) on the one hand, and the common people (principally peasants, but later also craftsmen, laborers, and small tradesmen) on the other. Now it acquired a bourgeoisie, sprung from the common people, whose relative prosperity allowed it

16. Now better known as Da Nang.

to play the part of an educated middle class. Villages and urban centers expanded: a working class came into being, and the urban population increased in size. These people were avid readers, which tended to foster the expansion of literature and the press; and they were fertile ground for the growth and interaction of new ideas and theories in every field, especially in politics. The abolition by the French of public examinations (the last to be held in Hanoi were in 1876 and 1879) led to a gradual decline in the influence of the literati. Conservative and slow to adapt to changing circumstances, most of them turned either to revolution or to despair.

Chinese influence slowly relaxed its grip on literature. Books in Chinese were gradually superseded by books in the vernacular, written first in *nôm* and then in *quoc-ngu*. Today all Vietnamese writing is in *quoc-ngu*. With the growth of the population and the spread of education, literature is no longer the exclusive preserve of men with Second or Third Degrees in the old examinations: writers come from all social classes, and literature is written for ordinary people. This is possible because *quoc-ngu* is an easy system to learn and has been widely and efficiently disseminated. Illiteracy has been largely eliminated. Indeed, a taste for reading is very widespread, and even a Vietnamese who cannot read enjoys being read to and likes quoting passages and sayings he knows by heart.

NÔM

Leaving aside purely Chinese texts, native Vietnamese works were written in *nôm* until the twentieth century. Classical works now current in *quoc-ngu* should therefore not be mistaken for original editions. The early editions of *Kim Van Kieu*, for instance, were printed in *nôm* characters. The word *nôm* is usually translated "vulgar" or "demotic": thus *nôm* characters are demotic characters as distinct from Chinese characters. Others regard it as cognate with *nam*, i.e. denoting Vietnamese characters as distinct from Chinese characters. In either case the sense is the same.

Nôm characters are formed out of Chinese characters either by using them singly with a different pronunciation and meaning from the Sino-Vietnamese, or by combining them, usually in pairs side by side. In such combinations one character, the "phonetic," gives the sound, and the other, the "significant," the meaning. Early *nôm* is more difficult to read than that used by scholars and copyists of the late nineteenth and early twentieth centuries. In early *nôm* (up to the beginning of the nineteenth century) the significant is often omitted and only the phonetic written, which can lead to confusion between homophones.

Let us take as an example of a *nôm* character the word *nôm* itself. This character exists in Chinese, and is pronounced *nan* (Sino-Vietnamese *nam*), meaning "chatter, whisper, speak indistinctly, twittering of swallows." In *nôm* it is pronounced *nôm,* and is differentiated in modern usage from *nam* meaning "chatter, whisper." Now it is interesting to note that the pronunciation of Ancient Chinese as reconstructed by Karlgren[17] gives this character a vowel value intermediate between *a* and *o*. Hence we may surmise that originally the same character denoted for the Chinese both "babbling, indistinct mumbling" and the language of the Vietnamese. Later sound changes resulted in *nôm* for "Vietnamese language" and *nam* for "whisper, speak indistinctly."

Nôm characters often help to clarify the meanings of words that otherwise, i.e., without the *nôm* significant, would be vague. Conversely some characters are conventionally pronounced in a particular way, e.g., the character which combines "sky" and "above" is always read as *troi,* "sky," and is *nôm:* Sino-Vietnamese uses *thien* for "sky."

A *nôm* text contains, in addition to *nôm* words properly so-called, a considerable admixture of Sino-Vietnamese words: indeed, to make out original early Vietnamese texts a knowledge

17. *Grammatica serica recensa,* 650 a–c.

both of Ancient Chinese and of Sino-Vietnamese is essential. The choice of a particular *nôm* character to represent a given sound can often be explained by reference to Ancient Chinese: to take a simple example, in the Vietnamese word *muoi* the significant has the meaning "ten" and the phonetic is abridged from the Chinese *mai*, "to go, walk." In Ancient Chinese the latter was pronounced mwai or muoei—the latter approximating to the modern *muoi*.

Thus the analysis of *nôm* texts is of linguistic as well as literary and philological interest. They throw light on Vietnamese semantics and the comparative phonetics of Southeast Asian languages in relation to Chinese, and have an important role to play in research. A great deal of work is at present being done in this huge field, both in North and South Vietnam and also in Paris.

QUOC-NGU

The origins of *quoc-ngu,* or the transliteration of Vietnamese in Roman characters, are bound up with the history of Roman Catholic missions in Southeast Asia and Vietnam. When they exchanged notes about the language, the early missionaries naturally put down the sounds they heard in an alphabet familiar to them. They also had to preach to their congregations and give exegesis in Vietnamese. So they wrote out their sermons, and their translations of the Catechism and the Lives of the Saints, in the notation used in their mother tongues. Most of the missionaries were French, Italian, Spanish, or Portuguese, so that these four languages determined the transliteration used. The habit gradually grew up in the various communities of using romanized transliteration instead of Chinese or *nôm,* and more and more documents came to be written in Catholic *quoc-ngu.* But it is noteworthy that *quoc-ngu* did not gain currency outside Catholic circles until the end of the nineteenth century. Non-Catholic Vietnamese (Buddhists and Confucians) and the administration, having neither happened nor needed to learn the Catholic system, seem to have ignored or disdained it. Official documents, books, and literary works were written in Chinese or *nôm* right up to the end of the nineteenth century. This is an interesting case of a system of transliteration peculiar to a limited social group being first boycotted by the education authorities and the populace on political grounds (i.e., the hostility of Vietnamese ruling houses to Christianity[18]), and then, again as the result of political factors (i.e., the advent of French colonial rule and the dominance of Western culture), gaining ground and becoming the standard system throughout the country.

The system of Roman transliteration was in use since the seventeenth century, and is generally reckoned to have been devised and popularized by a French Jesuit, Fr. Alexandre de Rhodes. Such of the early romanized writings as survive are, apart from a few archaisms, still relatively easy to read today. Actually Fr. de Rhodes made use of work done by two other priests, Fr. Gaspard de Amaral and Fr. Antonio Barbosa, who spent the years 1635 to 1639 in Tonkin and died in 1646 and 1647 respectively. The former compiled a *Dictionarium Annamiticum Lusitanum* and the latter a *Dictionarium Lusitanum Annamiticum*—both since lost.

The starting point of the new system of writing is marked by

18. Christians were in general mistrusted and hated by Vietnamese officialdom and the non-Christian population, being regarded as traitors to their country and lackeys of the French. The Hué court officially decreed the designation of Christians as *diu dan* ("weed people"), the comparison being with weeds that grow among crops *(luong dan,* i.e., "good people"); and it was not until 1866, in response to pressure from the Catholic clergy, supported by the French authorities, that the expression was amended to *giao-dan,* "religious people," as opposed to *binh-dan,* "ordinary people." This mistrust was due partly to deliberate Vietnamese Government propaganda and partly to the help given by Christians to the French: thus in 1883 the citadel of Son Tay, garrisoned by Vietnamese troops and Black Flags, fell to the French supposedly as the result of treachery by a Catholic herb-peddler, Luong Van Dat (see *Van Su Dia,* no. 32, pp. 39–40).

two works by Fr. de Rhodes which appeared in 1651. The first is *Dictionarium Annamiticum, Lusitanum et Latinum* (Annamese-Portuguese-Latin Dictionary), to which was appended *Linguae annamiticae seu tunchinensis brevis declaratio* ("Short Statement on the Annamese or Tonkinese Language"), consisting of a synopsis of Vietnamese grammar. The second is *Catechismus pro iis, qui volunt suscipere Baptismum in octo dies divisus (Phep giang tam ngay cho ke muon chiu phep rua toi ma vao dao Thanh Duc chua bloi)*, i.e., "The Catechism Explained in Eight Days for Persons Wishing To Be Baptized and Received into the Christian Faith." An excellent new edition of this work with introduction and notes was brought out by Fr. André Marillier, of the French Overseas Missions (Saigon: Groupe littéraire Tinh-Viêt, 1961). In this catechism Fr. de Rhodes relates his writing to a Vietnamese background, brings in Vietnamese proverbs and jokes, and generally goes out of his way to cater for a Vietnamese readership.

It is obvious from a perusal of these two works that the *quoc-ngu* system was influenced by the notation used in certain Romance languages. The influence of Italian, Spanish, and Portuguese is apparent in the representation of monosyllabic vowel clusters, which are diphthongized in pronunciation. For instance, the *ai* in *mai* (Viet. "tomorrow") is pronounced as in the Italian *mai* ("ever") or the Portuguese *mai* ("more"); *voi* (Viet. "elephant") is pronounced like the Italian *voi* ("you"), etc. The groupings *qua, que,* and *qui* are pronounced as in Italian, being thus assimilated to words such as *cui* ("firewood"), *cuon* ("to roll"), *cuoc* ("to dig"), etc., in which the *u* is really a vowel as in Italian *cuore* ("heart"), *cui* ("to whom"), or Spanish *cuando* ("when"), *cuanto* ("how much") etc.

The Vietnamese notation *gh* before *e* or *i,* as against *g* before *a, o, ó, u,* or *ú,* reflects the fact that in Italian *gh* is used before *e* or *i* to denote a hard *g*. For instance, in Vietnamese *ghermire* ("to catch") the initial consonantal group has the same value as in English "ghetto"—the analogy being with words such as Ital-

[19]

ian *ghirlanda* ("garland"). In other words, *gh* before *e* or *i* denotes the same sound in Vietnamese as *g* before *a, o, ó, u,* or *ú.* In Italian *ge* and *gi* the *g* is soft, for instance in *gemere* ("to groan") the initial consonant has the same value as in English "gentle." Hence in *quoc-ngu* the series is *ga, go, gó, gu, gú, ghe, ghi* rather than *ga, go, gó, gu, gú, ge, gi.* In some early texts, however, *ge* and *gi* are found in place of *ghe* and *ghi.*

Gi, on the other hand, is used in *quoc-ngu* to represent a sound close to that of the Italian, as for instance Vietnamese *gia* ("family"), *già* ("old"), *gie* ("stuff"), *gio* ("wind"), etc.

The influence of Portuguese shows itself, for instance, in the notation used for nasal final vowels. Early *quoc-ngu* has *a, o,* and *u* with *tilde* instead of the modern spelling *-ang, -ong,* and *-ung,* while hooked *o* and *u* are written *-ong* and *-ung.* In Fr. de Rhodes's *Catechism* we find *tlaõ* for *trong* ("inside"), *cũ* for *cung* ("bow"), *saõ* for *song,* etc.

These writings also throw light on the original pronunciation of certain words, and when the whole corpus of early *quoc-ngu* texts has been examined it should be possible to some extent to trace the evolution of Vietnamese phonetics. Thus they contain examples of *mloi* for *loi* ("word"), *mle* for *le* ("reason"), *bloi* for *troi* ("sky"), *tlau* for *trau* ("water buffalo"), *tlaõ* for *trong* ("inside"), *tluoc* for *truoc* ("before"), and so on.

Fr. de Rhodes's system underwent but little change during the seventeenth and eighteenth centuries. Such eighteenth-century texts as we have been able to examine[19] are still somewhat difficult to read; the conventions adopted in Fr. de Rhodes's dictionary are for the most part still maintained in them.

There are many early *quoc-ngu* texts and Catholic writings in the Vatican which have not yet been published. They need to be examined if we are to understand the evolution of *quoc-ngu* between Fr. de Rhodes's time and Mgr. Taberd's (early nineteenth century). A Vietnamese Jesuit, Fr. Philippe de Rosario (or in Vietnamese Fr. Binh), spent the years 1796 to 1830 in

---

19. Professions of faith by Catholic priests, and letters. These documents were made available to us by courtesy of Professor Boxer, of London University.

Europe, including thirty years in Lisbon; and an interesting conspectus of his *quoc-ngu* writings is given in *Panorama de la littérature moderne (Bieu nhat lam van-hoc can-dai)*[20], by Professor Thanh Lang of Saigon University.

It was not until the nineteenth century, and more especially the late nineteenth century, that *quoc-ngu* assumed its present form. A comparison of dictionaries such as those of Taberd (1838), Le Grand de la Liraÿe and Caspar (both 1877), Paulus Cua (1895), and Génibrel (1898) with de Rhodes's shows how the language and the system evolved in the intervening period.

The French administration encouraged the use of *quoc-ngu* by the non-Catholic press and printing industry; and so too did the efforts of some first-rate Vietnamese men of letters such as Nguyen Truong To (1827–1871), Truong Vinh Ky (1837–1898) and Huynh Tinh Cua, otherwise known as Paulus Cua (1834–1907). These three men were all Roman Catholics, so it is not surprising to find them helping to popularize the romanization of Vietnamese.

The first, Nguyen Truong To,[21] was one of the first convinced reformers in Vietnam. He was anxious to see peace between Vietnam and France so that his countrymen might learn modern science and technology. He campaigned for the reform of traditional education, and for the inclusion in the public examinations of subjects such as science, mathematics, law, agriculture, and astronomy. He pressed for students to be sent

20. Saigon: Tu Do, 1958, pp. 40f.
21. A remarkable man for a Vietnamese, and for his time. A native of Nghe An, he met Mgr. Gauthier, who took him with him to Italy and France. Returning to Cochin-China, he was frustrated in his plans to bring about peace between France and Vietnam, and retired to Nghe An, where he helped the local inhabitants with land-clearance and improvement schemes. In 1866 he was invited to join a purchasing and staff-recruitment mission to France, but in the event it was unable to leave because of hostilities between Vietnam and France. In the same year he prospected for minerals in Nghe An and Ha Tinh. In 1871 he was due to take a party of students to France, but had to stand down on grounds of ill health; and he died in the same year. He was famous for the fifteen memoranda on proposed reforms which he submitted to the emperor Tu Duc.

to France, and advocated the expansion of printing and the dissemination of books and newspapers in *quoc-ngu*.

The second, Truong Vinh Ky,[22] was the first to bring Nguyen Truong To's ideas to fruition. He romanized a number of popular *nôm* texts such as *Kim Van Kieu* (1875), *Dai Nam quoc-su dien-ca* (1875), *Gia huan ca* (1882), *Luc Van Tien* (1889), *Phan Tran* (1889), etc., and so aroused the interest of all classes of society in reading *quoc-ngu*. He also wrote prolifically in *quoc-ngu* himself. The development of modern Vietnamese *quoc-ngu* prose can be said to date from Truong Vinh Ky.

The third, Huynh Tinh Cua,[23] proceeded on the same lines as Truong Vinh Ky. Among other things he compiled volumes of collected tales, which he published in *quoc-ngu* under the titles *Truyen giai buon* ("Stories To Dispel Sadness") (1880) and *Truyen giai buon cuon sau* ("More Stories To Dispel Sadness") (1885). His main claim to fame, however, in the context of the advancement of Vietnamese, is the compilation of the first dictionary to show the state of the language in his day: *Dai-nam quoc-am tu-vi* (Dai-nam National Language Dictionary) (vol. 1, 1895; vol. 2, 1896). This was a major contribution to the crystallization of the vocabulary and the standardization of the spoken language, and remained the standard work of reference for Vietnamese until the publication in 1931 of the dictionary of the *Association pour la Formation Intellectuelle et Morale des Annamites (Hoi Khai tri tien duc: Viet-nam tu dien)*—the AFIMA Dictionary for short.

22. An extremely brilliant man and a gifted linguist. Born in Vinh Long province in Cochin-China, he was singled out by the missionaries for study at the seminaries at Pinhalu (Cambodia) and Penang, and learned Thai, Cambodian, Chinese, Burmese, Laotian, Greek, Latin, Spanish, Italian, Japanese, Portuguese, and French. In 1863 he went as interpreter with Phan Thanh Gian's mission to France, which was aimed at securing the return of the three eastern provinces of Cochin-China ceded to France the year before. On his return he held teaching posts at the Collège des Interprètes and then at the Collège des Stagiaires. In 1886, after a brief spell with the Council of the Royal Family at Hué, he retired from public life to devote himself to scholarship and writing.

23. Also known as Paulus Cua (1834–1907). Born in Baria province, in 1861 he was accorded the rank of provincial governor *(doc phu-su)*. He was on the staff of the journal *Gia-dinh Bao,* and is the author of several books.

The influence of these three writers originated in Cochin-China and gradually spread from there to the rest of Vietnam. Compared with modern writers their style seems to us abrupt, heavy, and somewhat turgid: but in their own day, when Chinese influence was still predominant, it was easy for ordinary people to understand, being largely free from Sino-Vietnamese locutions. Thanks to them, *quoc-ngu* spread outwards from its foothold in the South. The North was slower to outgrow Sino-Vietnamese, and it was not until the beginning of the twentieth century that it took the lead in the process of change.

Meanwhile in the light of advances in Indochinese linguistics and linguistics in general, French and Vietnamese linguists felt that the *quoc-ngu* system needed improving. From the time of Aymonier[24] onwards many reforms were put forward, but they all came to nothing. Improvements were suggested by Vietnam's first Transliteration Board, at the time of the First International Congress of Far Eastern Studies held at Hanoi in 1902, but to no purpose. The chairman was Chéon, an experienced Vietnamese specialist, and the members of the Board included such reputable scholars as Pelliot, Finot, and Cadière. Their suggestions for reform were as follows. *G* should be kept for the series *ga, ge, gi, go, gó, gu, gú; gi* should be replaced by *j;* the unvoiced guttural should be represented by *k* throughout, in order to avoid having *ca* and *co* on the one hand and *ke* and *ki* on the other; *â*, the sound of which is close to that of *o*, should be replaced by hooked *a; y* should not be substituted for *i* in *ly, ky, my*, etc.; *ch* should instead be written *č* or *c, h* being kept to denote aspiration—thus *co* for *cho* ("market"), *khac* for *khach* ("guest, foreigner"); *d* should be replaced by *z; n* should be used in place of *nh (ban* for *banh* ["cake, bread"]); *w* should be used to denote the semi-vowel *(kwa* rather than *qua* ["to pass"]); retroflex *s* should take the place of *s;* and *x*, the sound of which is close to that of the palatal sibilant, should be replaced by *ç*. All these proposals are in line with the principles of phonetic notation, but they did not gain acceptance. Inertia and force of

24. *Nos transcriptions* (Saigon, 1886).

habit are supposedly the reasons, plus the difficulty of altering printers' fonts. In 1906 the Council for the Advancement of Native Education expressed the hope that the current notation *ay* could be replaced by *ei,* as being closer to the actual pronunciation—and furthermore Fr. de Rhodes used *ei.* The hope was also expressed that the vowel *a* should carry a short marking wherever it was short, even by position. On May 16, 1906, a decree by the Governor-General of Indochina announced a competition for textbooks written in accordance with the guidelines laid down by the Development Council in 1906. But despite all this *quoc-ngu* remained unchanged. In 1928 Nguyen Van Vinh proposed the replacement of *d* by *y* and of the diacritics by letters added at the end of the word; but neither this nor attempts at reform launched by individuals or groups of writers made any headway against the established system. It became nationwide, and is now in use both in the North and in the South.

Today *quoc-ngu* is fairly well standardized. Admittedly there are dialectal variations in pronunciation, which are reflected in the spelling. In Cochin-Chinese, for instance, the endings *-at,* *-ang, -ong,* and *-ieng* are pronounced *-ac, -an, -on,* and *-ien,* and they are so spelled in Cochin-Chinese texts: e.g., *mac* for *mat* ("eye"), *van* for *vang* ("to resound"), *don* for *dong* ("heap"), *cuon* for *cuong* ("mad") (but *phung* for *phun* ["to blow"], *hang hoi* for *han hoi* ["well ordered"]) and *bien* for *bieng* ("lazy"). But otherwise the spelling is more or less uniform throughout the length and breadth of Vietnam.

The development of *quoc-ngu* since the French occupation has been summarized by Nguyen Hien Le[25] as follows. First, there was a period from 1866 to 1914 which saw the shaping of *quoc-ngu* prose under the lead of Truong Vinh Ky and Huynh Tinh Cua. *Quoc-ngu* did not keep very close to Chinese, nor had it yet absorbed much in the way of French influence; and the consequence was some untidiness and loose syntax and a ten-

25. *Tieng Viet ngay nay,* vol. 64, no. 5, pp. 38–43.

dency to be repetitive and obscure, with ill-balanced and disjointed sentences. The next period, which extended from World War I to 1930, was remarkable for the part played by North Vietnamese periodicals such as *Dong duong tap chi, Huu Thanh,* and *Nam Phong.* Staffed by literati of good background and experience such as Nguyen Huu Tien, Nguyen Don Phuc, Phan Ke Binh, and Tan Da, they were exposed to the powerful influence of Chinese. Vietnamese prose grew loftier and more flowing, and the vocabulary richer; but the language was far removed from common parlance. The two best prose writers of the time were Phan Ke Binh and Pham Quynh.

In the third period, from 1930 to World War II, *quoc-ngu* finally broke away from Chinese and came closer to everyday speech. It became livelier, clearer, more vivid, and more natural as it was exposed to the influence of French. Among those in the vanguard of this development was Hoang Tich Chu; the *Tu-luc* group also played a major part in the molding of *quoc-ngu* as we know it today. The vocabulary of Vietnamese was enriched by additions from French, and many more disyllabic words were borrowed from Chinese. Since 1945 *quoc-ngu* has spread into all fields of thought and all literary media.

WESTERN INFLUENCE ON VIETNAMESE LITERATURE

From the nineteenth century onwards Vietnam, like China, sought to absorb Western learning and habits of mind. Its access to them was at first indirect, through the medium of progressive Chinese writers; and later at first hand from the fountainhead of French culture provided for it on the spot by the occupying power—or else in metropolitan France, in the case of those Vietnamese able to go and study there.

In China the defeats suffered at the hands of the West in 1840–42 (the Opium War) and of Japan in 1894–95 had given many intellectuals food for thought. They decided that the time had come for them to give up their traditional scholarly ideals and learn from the West. Some of them traveled to Europe and America and acquired a knowledge of Western philosophy, letters, and technology; and on their return they campaigned for the abandonment of the old-style classical education and a greater orientation towards Western culture.

A great effort was required before classical Chinese was superseded by the spoken usage, or *pai-hua*. The latter was simpler, more discursive, clearer, and more universally known, and it made translation from Western sources easier. Gradually writers began to imitate the style of such translations, and in every field a renaissance took place. The literary media were revolutionized. Short stories, novels, and plays on Western lines proliferated. The classical compositions dear to the hearts of the old literati were abandoned. Ancient Chinese literature written in the vernacular became all the rage, and enjoyed widespread success.

Vietnam felt the effects of these changing trends in China. It had itself capitulated to France and been compelled to give up Cochin-China (which became a French colony) and accept French protectorates in Annam and Tonkin. Intellectuals saw that if they were to regain their national independence and defeat the occupying power they would first need to learn from it; and this would mean the abandonment of traditional Confucian scholasticism, which bore no relation to a changing world and led only to a mandarin's post under a backward, outworn social and political system.

Some of these would-be innovators went and studied abroad, in China, Japan, Europe, and America. Those who stayed at home worked with the help of letters from them, of translations of European works by Chinese reformers, and of articles in avant-garde Chinese journals. Vietnamese intellectuals were much influenced by the Chinese writer K'ang Yu-wei (Khang Huu Vi) (1858–1927), and still more by Liang Ch'i-ch'ao (Luong Khai Sieu) (1873–1929). The latter was a pupil of the former, and as a young man was a brilliant scholar. After the defeat of China by Japan in 1894 he campaigned for constitutional reforms and was forced to go into exile in Japan. He returned to China when the Republican régime came to power, and died in Peking in 1929.

Through the intermediary of China, Vietnamese intellectuals were introduced to French eighteenth-century philosophical ideas, in particular to Rousseau's *Contrat social* and Montesquieu's *Esprit des lois,* and to English philosophers such as John Stuart Mill and Herbert Spencer. They became familiar with concepts such as racial equality, individual freedom, political organization, universal suffrage, democracy, etc. French education saw to it that the noble ideals of the French Revolution were brought prominently to the notice of the younger generation. The influence of Western writing led writers to turn their backs on the Sino-Vietnamese hybrid, and also to concern themselves with a living society rather than with the dead world of the Chinese classics. It occurred to people that Vietnamese needed to be improved before it could be fully expressive; and also that writers ought to escape from their obsession with the ancient world and the heroes of yore and concentrate instead on the lives and feelings of ordinary people. Gradually Vietnamese gained the upper hand and became the sole language. From contact with French prose its style became simpler and clearer and better adapted for realism. In French poetry Vietnamese poets discovered new forms such as the sonnet, *vers libre,* etc. The influence of French writing, both prose and poetry, encouraged a critical approach, the analysis of feelings in depth, and a self-conscious outlook.

A new vocabulary was now needed to describe the novelties, both abstract and concrete, imported from the West: and the result was a remarkable enrichment of Vietnamese, partly by borrowing from the new Chinese vocabulary, partly by spontaneous invention, and partly by the adoption of French words phonetically transcribed into *quoc-ngu.*

There was also an abrupt shift in the ratio of prose and poetry produced. Before the nineteenth century poetry was written in Chinese or *nôm,* prose almost always in Chinese. From the end of the nineteenth century, with the advent of *quoc-ngu,* prose works began to proliferate. First came translations of Chinese cloak-and-dagger novels such as *Story of the Three Kingdoms,* and then translations of French school textbooks. The press grew in stature, and played an important part in popularizing the national language and influencing public opinion. Journalists of drive and ability worked unstintingly in support of the new trend, collecting foreign material on every subject under the sun and printing translations of it with explanations for the edification of their fellow countrymen. Among these popularizers the best-known names are those of Pham Quynh and Nguyen Van Vinh. The former was the moving spirit of the famous periodical *Nam Phong* (July 1917–December 1934), which printed numerous translations from Chinese and French and so opened a door on Western science and literature for the whole literate public unacquainted with those languages.

The literati on the staff of *Nam Phong* also devoted time to translating the early Vietnamese texts in Chinese and *nôm* and publishing them in *quoc-ngu;* so that this journal not only enriched the language but also increased public awareness of Vietnam's literary heritage. In addition to translations of Descartes's *Discours de la Méthode,* Epictetus's *Manual,* and Corneille's poems, its publications included *Hong Duc quoc-am thi-tap* (Collected Poems of the Hong Duc Period) and *Lich trieu hien chuong loai chi* (Regulations Made by the Various Dynasties, Arranged in Categories), by Phan Huy Chu.

[28]

II: FOLK LITERATURE

FOLKTALES

The richness of Vietnamese folklore is evident from the multiplicity and diversity of folktales current in both North and South. They are of varied origin. Some represent adaptations or popularizations of ancient fables, written in Chinese and contained in classical anthologies such as *Viet-dien u linh tap* (Anthology of the Unseen Powers of the Land of Viet) (1329), *Linh-nam trich quai* and *Truyen ky man luc* (Giant Anthology of Wondrous Legends) (early sixteenth century). Others are based on the *jātakas*[1] of Buddhist literature, or on events in Vietnamese history. Some represent local legends associated with particular shrines, others Chinese folktales taken over *en bloc*. All the universal folklore themes are found: Cinderella, the ransoming of the wedding procession, frogs as sons-in-law,[2] riddles, wives who are really fairies, grateful animals and ungrateful human beings, inexhaustible treasures, thieves betrayed, etc. Hence quite apart from the pleasure of reading them they offer scope for research which could contribute to our anthropological knowledge.

Some of the folktales are etiological myths: i.e., they purport to explain the derivation of place-names, the genesis of moun-

1. *Jātakas:* stories of the Buddha's former births.
2. See P. Serruys, *Folklore ordos,* Han Hiue, vol. 3, fasc. 1–2, p. 132 (Publications of the Centre Sinologique Français, Peking).

tains, rivers, and particular features of the terrain, and the origins of expressions, sayings, customs, and household objects. Thus there are stories explaining why Buddhists regard dog meat and plants of the onion family as unclean; why the water buffalo can no longer talk; why particular birds have the names they do and sing the songs they do; why the crow is black but the peacock brightly colored; why the ape has a red behind; and so on.

Why the Ape Has a Red Behind

Once upon a time there was a monkey who kept teasing the Buddha. At length the Buddha got annoyed; he tried playing tricks on the ape, but to no avail. Then he got so cross that he decided to catch him and strike him dead.

The ape and his family lived in the mountains, and by day they always used to come and sit on a rock at the foot of the mountain, above the pagoda. The rock was known as Flat Rock.

One day the Buddha played the following trick on him. He took away the rock and heated it until it was red-hot, and then put it back again. The monkey came and sat on the rock; its behind went all red, and it became known as the ape with the red behind *(con do dit)*.

(Landes, *Contes et légendes:* ms. B.1 of the Société Asiatique)

Here is another story explaining why rice, which once upon a time in the earthly paradise of Vietnam grew wild and had great big grains, took on its present form:

Story of the Rice Grain

Once upon a time rice had huge grains, as big as a cup or a pot, and no-one cultivated it. At harvest-time people lit lamps, burnt incense and said a few prayers, and the rice grain went into whichever house it wished.

One day there was a man's wife who was very lazy. Her husband had bidden her sweep the floor clean in order to say prayers and welcome in the rice grain, but being lazy she did not do so. Her husband said his prayers, and the rice grain hastened to his house: but the woman was still bending down sweeping. The rice grain burst into the house, and the goodwife picked up her broom and hit it so hard that it was smashed to smithereens.

The rice grain was angry, and said: "Because of this misdeed, men must harvest with the sickle, and cultivate rice if they are to have any to eat; and the grain will be small because the woman hit it and it flew into smithereens."

(Landes, *Contes et légendes*)

Many beliefs in the fields of mythology and cosmogony can be deduced from Vietnamese folktales. For instance, that in the beginning men, animals, and spirits could communicate one with another: they all spoke the same language and could understand one another, and animals and human beings thought similar thoughts and had similar needs. The idea of human beings and spirits having to do with each other is widespread in Southeast Asia: thus the Meos believe that ancient peoples lived in the dense forests and in caves on the cliffs, and had social intercourse with demons.[3]

The supreme being in the Vietnamese pantheon is the Jade Emperor or Celestial Emperor, borrowed from Chinese mythology. His court is made up of spirits of all kinds who are in touch with human beings, and it is on the strength of their reports that he decides to punish or reward them. He sends his sons to be reincarnated on earth, usually in the persons of the great (heroes, princes, Premier Scholars,[4] etc.), and recalls them if they behave extortionately or reach the end of their terms of exile.

One important feature of Vietnamese folktales is the Water Kingdom, already mentioned above in connection with the early history (see p. 2). In mythology snakes are the Water King's children, and announce floods and deluges to come. The Water King is the possessor of inexhaustible treasures and magic talismans, and men who are brave and good may on occasion re-

3. David Crockett Graham, *Songs and Stories of the Ch'uan Miao*, Smithsonian Institution, April 8, 1954, p. 135: "Two Brothers Bewitched by a Frog Demon."
4. The *trang-nguyen*, i.e., those who came first in the national (Third Degree) examinations.

ceive gifts from him. The water spirits (the Water King, dragons, and snakes) are often in love with mortals, and sometimes disguise themselves as mortal men in order to seduce and dishonor their wives (cf. the Amphitryon legend). These spirits commonly take the form of snakes, and when they wish to appear in human form they shed their snakeskins. The ruler of the underworld is Diem Vuong, the King of Hell in Chinese mythology. Human beings can go down into Hell and come back to earth again provided they are equipped with amulets or charms specifically associated with underworld spirits, such as cauls or dragon skins. Some confusion exists between Hell and the Water Kingdom, and the way to the former often seems to lie through the latter. In general there are no clear-cut borders between the various worlds of this mythology, either between Hell and the Water Kingdom or even between them and the mortal world.

In the beginning, when heaven and earth had just appeared, there lived Khong Lo and the lady Giat Hai. Khong Lo is credited in mythology with the molding of the earth's contours: he travels the world, raising up mountains, and the Cochin-Chinese legend of the creation of Mount Ba Den is part of his cycle.

Many of the stories and folktales show the influence of Buddhism; e.g., often an earlier legend is taken over and the Buddha introduced in the role of a deus ex machina.

Buddhism is based on belief in the futility of worldly goods. Wealth such as gold is an illusory possession that passes from hand to hand: hence salvation lies in getting rid of one's wealth and dedicating oneself to religion. When eighteen thieves repent of spending their lives appropriating other people's property, they commit suicide and become eighteen *arahats*.[5]

---

5. *Su-tich 18 ong la-han* (Story of the Eighteen *Arahats*), in Nguyen Dong Chi, *Kho tang truyen co tich Viet-nam* (Treasury of Ancient Vietnamese Stories) (Hanoi, 1958). *Arahat* (Vietnamese *la-han*) is the Pali word for a stage in the progress toward Buddhist perfection.

Salvation without suicide is possible through strict adherence to the precepts of Buddhism: kindness, humanity, and piety. Any trade practiced at the expense of life, either human or animal, must be given up. The trade of butcher appears in a bad light in Buddhist tales because of the slaughter of animals, and one of the best conversions is that of a butcher who gives up his trade.[6]

The Buddhist paradise, Nirvana, is attained after passing through a number of transmigrations and reincarnations, these being determined by the amount of merit earned in each of our existences (or acquired by our ancestors). Pious deeds may take many forms. But in rewarding them the Buddha has regard more for the good intentions of a believer seeking to acquire merit than for the outward appearance of his actions.

A single misdeed or evil thought cancels out a lifetime of meritorious living: thus a Buddhist priest who, impelled by desire and curiosity, sleeps with the pagoda-keeper's wife[7] loses all the benefit of his prayers and acts of devotion. Another priest loses the benefit of twenty years of pious living for desiring to touch a comely young woman.[8] The hermit Bat Nhan endured all the discomforts of his condition without once losing patience: though festooned with insects, parasites, and bird-droppings, he showed no sign of irritation until the day when two birds nesting on his head started to quarrel about something silly. He lost his temper and pulled off their nest, and this action robbed him of the chance of entering Nirvana.[9]

The Buddha rewards or punishes human beings according to the purity of their intentions. In "The Wicked Brother and the Golden Axes" (Landes ms., 1, 12, 15), the wicked brother kills and dismembers the Buddha, who has been like a guardian angel to him; but the severed limbs turn into snakes and

6. *Su-tich cay huyet du* (Story of the Dragon-tree), Nguyen Dong Chi, *Kho tang*, pp. 88–90.
7. *Su-tich con ech* (Story of the Frog), *ibid.,* pp. 110f.
8. *Su-tich con nhai* (Story of the Tree-frog), *ibid.,* pp. 110f.
9. *Su-tich chim tu hu* (Story of the Cuckoo), *ibid.,* p. 94.

crocodiles and bite the wicked grasping brother to death. Conversely the Buddha often appears in the guise of an old man or an old beggar and gives genuinely pious men their reward immediately in this life. He may simply help his protégés with advice.[10] He rewards those who give him food and shelter without ulterior motive. In "Charity Rewarded" (Landes ms., 1, 12, 19), every time the beggar who is really the Buddha spits, his spittle turns into blobs of gold.

One very curious story is entitled "Retribution for a Previous Life" (Landes ms., 1, 12, 16). It is reminiscent of stories in the *Dhammapada*,[11] for instance, in which an existing situation is explained by reference to events in the heroes' earlier existences. Surprisingly, a good and upright man is caught in a trap set by a friend of his, who owes him everything and yet sets out to kill him. The Buddhist explanation of such strange situations is that the doomed man had committed an identical sin in a previous life: i.e., the rich good man in the story had in an earlier existence killed a friend of his. But the story ends happily thanks to the intervention of a spirit, who reveals to the rich man the reasons why he has been under threat. The two friends, enlightened as to the causes of their own conduct, demonstrate their free will and get rid of fatalistic ideas about retribution: they make up their quarrel and live in harmony, happy and wealthy. Though supposedly a Buddhist story, this may be read as an attack on Buddhism.

In addition to these Buddhist stories about anonymous priests or believers, there are also cycles of legends about various deities, some of whom, such as the goddess Quan Am (Chinese Kuan-yin) and the spirit Dai Thanh, are extremely popular. The story of the latter is known from the version given in *Tay du ky* (*Hsi yü chi*), a Chinese tale which has also been rendered into

10. *Su-tich con muoi, ibid.,* p. 114.
11. See *Buddhist Legends Translated from the Original Pali Text of the Dhammapada Commentary,* by Eugène Watson Burlingame (Cambridge: Harvard University Press, 1921).

six- and eight-syllable *nôm* verse.[12] The following episodes are
preserved in Landes ms., 1, 12, 25 under the title "Story of Dai
Thanh and the Buddha Quan Am." Dai Thanh was the Buddha's servant, and one day she bade him go and throw away a
blob of her spittle. Instead of doing as he was bidden, Dai Thanh
ate it, and by so doing acquired supernatural powers almost equal
to the Buddha's. The latter, to punish him, made her fingers
into five mountains and imprisoned him under them. Dai Thanh
was set free by the monk of the T'ang, and from then on helped
the monk whenever he ran into difficulties. He fought many
battles against demons and evil spirits, and hence is venerated
in Sino-Vietnamese mythology as a giant-killer.[13] He appears as
the enfant terrible of the Vietnamese pantheon, launching attacks out of anger or spite against Heaven itself: none can daunt
him save the Buddha.

As regards Quan Am, one of the most popular tales sets out
to explain why she has a thousand eyes and hands:

The Goddess with a Thousand Eyes

There was a female Buddha called Buddha Shākya *(Duc Phat Thich Ca)*.
When she was small she took the vows and entered a pagoda as a serving-maid. It had five hundred priests, five hundred priestesses and five
hundred novices, and they asked Buddha Shākya: "You are the only
serving-maid: will you be able by yourself to wait on five hundred priests,
five hundred priestesses and five hundred novices?" Buddha Shākya
said: "Yes, I shall be able to wait on them all."

Thenceforward she lived most virtuously; she did all she could to
lead a perfect life from her youth until the time when she became
Buddha Shākya. Then Heaven bestowed upon her its most precious
gift: a hundred feet, a hundred hands and a hundred eyes. Each fin-
ger had an eye on it which had grown there quite naturally. That is

12. *Tay du dien ca,* Library of the École Française d'Extrême-Orient, Text AB
81 and *quoc-ngu* transcription, published by Xuan Lan, Imprimerie Van Minh,
Hanoi-Haiphong; and Library of the École Française d'Extrême-Orient, Text
Q.8.118(9).
13. Maurice Durand, *Imagerie populaire vietnamienne* (Publications de l'École
Française d'Extrême-Orient, 1960).

why people called her "Buddha with a thousand hands and a thousand eyes" *(Duc Phat Ba thien thu thien nhan)*. Heaven gave birth to this woman; she was the reincarnation of the Buddha who is the most precious of all Buddhas.

(Landes ms., 1, p. 669)

Vietnamese folktales are concerned with many other themes besides Buddhism. In *Chang Lia*[14] we have the character who was nicknamed "the Gentleman-Robber" *(Ke trom quan-tu)*, because he attacked only the rich and spared the poor. Likewise Co Bu in "The Story of Co Bu,"[15] who was reputed to be a great soothsayer and man-at-arms: when he rose in rebellion and looted villages, he plundered only the rich. The theme of Gargantua and Pantagruel occurs: historical figures such as Le Nai, son-in-law of Vu Quynh (1452–1497), Le Nhu Ho, Dai Vuong Hai,[16] Ong O,[17] etc. are portrayed in folktales as having insatiable appetites and Herculean strength. Another very common theme is transformation: we find men turning into tigers, fish turning into dragons, priests turned into frogs, wicked priestesses turned into lime-cauldrons, a priest or a swindling woman into a porpoise, wicked misers into apes with red behinds, the miser Thach Sung into a grey lizard, and so forth. The story of Thach Sung, taken from Chinese folklore, comes to us in this impish Vietnamese version:

How Thach Sung Was Turned into a Grey Lizard

Thach Sung was the richest man in the world: he had everything. One day a person came to him and said: "You reckon yourself the richest man in the world; I challenge you to a contest to see which of us is the richer. What will you do if it turns out that there is something you have not got?" Thach Sung, thinking that he was very rich and had everything, said to this person: "You wish to compete against me. Very

14. Nguyen Dong Chi, *Kho tang*, pp. 155f.
15. Landes ms, 1, p. 629.
16. Nguyen Dong Chi, *Kho tang*, pp. 189–93.
17. *Ibid.*, pp. 193–96.

well: if there is anything whatever that I have not got, I will give you everything I possess."

At this the person asked: "Have you any rice-weevils pickled in brine *(me kho)*?" Thach Sung had none, and was at a loss. He had to resign himself to keeping his promise and giving away all his wealth. Then he died heartbroken and was turned into a grey lizard *(than lan)* with an incessantly clicking tongue. Hence the saying "To be Thach Sung and have no pickled weevils" *(Thach Sung con thieu me kho).*

Riddles and puzzles constitute a well-worn theme in Vietnamese as in all other folktales. Set by an evil spirit or a foreign ruler (in Vietnamese folktales the Emperor of China), the riddle is so difficult that the King's subjects and ministers alike confess themselves baffled, and only the hero of the tale can solve it. Sometimes the puzzles or riddles to be solved form part of a judgment pronounced by the King or some mandarin. Vietnamese ambassadors to China and Premier Scholars often appear as the heroes of all kinds of testing situations, and show such ingenuity that they make laughingstocks of the malicious Chinese.

An Ambassador in China

Once upon a time there was a very gifted man, and the King sent him as ambassador to China. There the Chinese put his cleverness to the test by inviting him to a banquet held at the top of a tower. He climbed the tower, but down below at the foot of the tower they took the ladder away. The man was at a loss; then he picked up two parasols and let himself fall. His extreme cleverness was extolled by all.

The Chinese made another attempt, and said to him: "Go into the pagoda to see Buddha." He went into the pagoda, and when he was inside they locked the door. Our friend, on the inside, was at a loss. Some statues of Buddha made of flour and icing sugar had been put there, and our friend ate them all. Ten days later the Chinese unlocked the door, and saw that the statues of Buddha had all gone. They asked where they were, and our friend replied that the Buddhas were in his heart.

(Landes ms., 10, 7, 7).

Heroic labors and ordeals form the subject of a splendid story, "The Five Twin Brothers" (Landes ms., I, I, VIIb). The King subjects one of the five brothers to a series of ordeals, never suspecting that for each one his place is taken by one of his twins. The first brother, Manh Me ("The strong"), carries away the King's entire stock of rice in two sacks. The second, Kho ("The dry"), survives punishment by drowning. The third, Uot ("The moist"), comes unscathed through ordeal by fire, and the fourth, Minh dong gan sat ("Bronze-bodied and steel-livered"), through ordeal by beheading. In the end it is the last brother, the one who can read the clouds and foretell the future, who marries the King's daughter and succeeds to the throne.

The famous story of Tam and Cam, known abroad as "The Vietnamese Cinderella," incorporates many familiar fairy-tale themes (rivalry between elder and younger sisters, the spiteful stepmother, transformation scenes, etc.), as well as labors and trials.

The Story of Tam and Cam
(1st version from Landes ms.)

A man and his wife each had a daughter by an earlier marriage: the husband's daughter was called Cam and the wife's Tam. They were the same size, and which was the elder and which the younger was unknown. The couple discussed the matter and came to a decision: "Enough said: let us give them each a fish-trap and send them off to catch fish. The one who catches the most will be the elder and the one who catches the least the younger."

Cam caught the most and Tam the least. Tam, furtively seeing that Cam had caught more fish than her, treacherously induced her to cross the river and pick water-lilies so that they could each enjoy themselves in turn. Cam crossed the river and picked the flowers, but meanwhile Tam, who had stayed on her side, took all Cam's fish and went home. Cam came back to find only one fish, a gudgeon;[18] and she sat down and cried. An Immortal came down from Heaven and appeared to her, and asked her why she was crying; and she told the Immortal about Tam's deceitfulness in sending her to pick flowers. The Immortal asked

18. *Ca bong mu,* "gudgeon" or "goby."

her to look and see whether she had no fish left, and she replied that she had only one, a gudgeon. The Immortal told her to take it home, release it in the well and feed it. At mealtimes she should call it and give it something to eat. When she called it to feed it she should say: "Ahoy there, gudgeon, some boiled rice and fresh fish! There is some rice and fish left,[19] come and eat." So each day when Cam came back from taking the water buffaloes to pasture, she called it and fed it.

Then Tam began to spy on her and watch her, and she saw that Cam liked doing this and took pleasure in it. One day when Cam had gone off with the water buffaloes and Tam was left at home, she mimicked her and called the fish, using the same words that Cam always used. The fish, thinking Cam was calling it to feed it, came up to the surface to feed; and Tam caught it and killed and ate it. When Cam came home from taking the water buffaloes to pasture, she called the fish to come for its food, but in vain: there was no sign of it. Cam sat down and cried.[20] The cock went "cock-a-doodle-doo," and said: "Give me three grains of rice and I will show you the fish-bones." Cam fed the cock, and the cock showed her the fish-bones in a corner of the verandah. Cam saw the fish-bones and picked them up and held them in her hands and cried. The Immortal came down and questioned Cam, and Cam told the Immortal the story. The Immortal said to her: "Tomorrow, go to the market and buy four jars: put the fish-bones into them and bury the jars at the four corners of your bed. In three months and ten days exactly, dig up your jars and you will see. Everything you have wished for will be in the four jars: dresses, trousers, and shoes." And that is just what she found: and after a long time she took them out to put them in the sun.[21]

A passing crow snatched up a shoe, and flew away and dropped it in the Crown Prince's palace. Now the Crown Prince was not yet married, and when he found the shoe he organized a public contest to choose himself a wife. Whosoever could put the shoe on would be chosen by the Crown Prince to be his wife. The Crown Prince had the month and day of the contest proclaimed in every province and county, and let it be known that the young woman whom the shoe fitted would be chosen as his wife.

Tam's mother would not let Cam be the first to go to the contest.

19. *Com thua ca can: can* means the dregs, lees, or remains of a liquid. The usual expression is *com thua canh can;* so here the narrator (or the copyist) may have confused *ca* and *canh.*

20. The text reads *con Cam noi khoc,* "Cam said tearfully," which does not make sense here.

21. The train of thought is not entirely clear here.

Tam went first, but the shoe would not fit her foot, and she came home again and said that the shoe would not fit her. Cam kept on asking her stepmother: "Let me go and see whether the shoe is the right size for me"; but her stepmother would only let her go if she first sorted out a pile of beans mixed with sesame seeds. "When you have finished that, I will let you go," she said. The Immortal, seeing that the stepmother had her knife into Cam in this way, turned into a flock of pigeons,[22] which came and helped her with the sorting so that her stepmother would let her go. But when the job was done she still would not let her go: she said that the pigeons had eaten all her beans and sesame, and that she was not willing to let her go.[23] The Immortal then appeared and emptied the pigeons' gizzards, and the beans and sesame were restored in full as they were before. Only then would the stepmother let her go. Cam went to the contest and tried on the shoe, and it fitted: so the Crown Prince took her to wife.

Now it happened that Cam's father fell ill. Cam's stepmother sent for her, and bought some biscuits[24] and put them under the father's back. Then she lied and said to Cam: "Your father is very ill: when he tosses and turns his bones make a loud cracking noise, like that." Then Tam induced Cam to climb an areca palm to pick some of the nuts as a tonic for her father; and when she was up the tree picking the areca nuts, Tam cut through the tree at the foot so that it fell and Cam was killed. After Cam's death the Crown Prince pined for her and was very sorrowful. Tam's mother took Tam and gave her to the Crown Prince as a replacement for Cam; but he did not want Tam, and kept his hopes pinned on Cam's return.

One day Tam was washing the Crown Prince's clothes. Now when Cam died she had turned into a *hoanh hoach*.[25] She flew off to the Prince's palace, and seeing Tam washing the Prince's linen she called out to her: "Hoanh hoach! Hoanh hoach! Wash my husband's linen properly! Hang it out on a pole, not on a hedge to get torn, my husband's linen!" The Crown Prince, who had come out, saw the *hoanh hoach* and said: "If that is my wife, she will creep up my sleeve; if not, she will go away." The bird came and crept up his sleeve, and the Prince took it in and fed it. But one day, when the Prince was not there, Tam

22. *Bo cau.*
23. There seems to be a lacuna in the text here. The stepmother must have refused to let Cam go even when the beans and sesame had been sorted out, and the pigeons must then have eaten them.
24. *Banh trai.*
25. Perhaps a canary.

[40]

caught the *hoanh hoach* and killed and ate it. When the Crown Prince came home, he asked where the bird had gone. Tam said: "I am pregnant and had a craving, and I killed and ate it." The Prince said to her: "You killed it, but where did you leave its feathers?" Tam showed the Prince where she had put them, close to the hedge. The Crown Prince went to look, and saw that a lovely tender young bamboo-shoot[26] had sprung up. One day when the Prince had gone hunting, Tam, who had stayed at home, cut the bamboo-shoot and cooked and ate it. She threw away the rind, and from it there grew up a persimmon tree[27] which bore a single fruit, very fine and large. Tam tried to pick the persimmon, but could not break the stalk. Now there was an old beggar-woman who used to come and sit at the foot of this persimmon tree. Observing how beautiful the persimmon looked, she coveted it, and made a wish: "Please Heaven, let that persimmon fall into my bag." The persimmon fell into the old woman's bag, and she took it home and hid it in her stock of rice.[28] When she went out begging, Cam would creep out of the persimmon and cook the rice and sweep the house for the old woman. One day the old woman lay in wait for her and caught her coming out of the persimmon. She surprised her as she was coming out of the persimmon, and Cam told her her story. Then the old woman realized that she was Cam; and she took her as her adopted daughter.

When it was nearly the day of the rice offering[29] to her husband, the old woman said to Cam: "The day of the rice offering to your father is nearly here, and we have not a penny piece to make him an offering." Cam replied: "There is no need to worry, Mother. When the day comes all the proper dishes will be there." On the day itself, at nightfall, Cam laid a table in the open air and prayed that the Immortal would come down from Heaven and help her to obtain all the dishes for the offering. When the offering had been duly performed, Cam asked her foster-mother to go and invite the Crown Prince. The Prince laughed and made fun of the old beggar-woman: "What wonderful things have you made, then, that you think to invite me?" Then he added: "If you want me to accept your invitation, hang the roadway with brocade and your front door with gold, and then I will go." The old woman went home and reported the Prince's wishes to Cam. Cam replied: "There is no difficulty about that: go and tell the Crown

26. *Mut mang (muc mang).*
27. *Cay thi.*
28. *Ghe gao.*
29. *Quai com.*

Prince to come, and that everything will be as he wishes." Then Cam begged the Immortal to come down, and he arranged for the roadway to be hung with brocade and the door overlaid with gold. The Crown Prince arrived, and as he went into the house he noticed a box of most beautifully made betel-leaf quids. He asked the old woman who had made the quids. The old woman went inside and asked Cam what she should say, and Cam told her to say that she, the old woman, had made them. The Prince asked the old woman to make some in front of him, so that he might see her do it. Cam turned into a fly, and by flying this way and that showed the old woman how to go about it. The Prince noticed the fly's gyrations, and realized that it was the fly that was enabling the old woman to make the quids; so he took out his fan and drove the fly away, and the old woman could no longer make the quids. The Prince questioned the old woman, and she was seized with fear and confessed that it was her daughter that had made them. The Prince asked the old woman to send for her daughter and introduce her to him. How could he have any idea that it was Cam, his first wife? Then Cam told him her story, and the Prince took Cam home with him.

When Tam saw Cam again she pretended to be delighted, and asked her: "Where have you been all this time, that you have stayed so beautiful? Tell me, that I may do the same." Cam said to her: "If you want to be beautiful, boil a big cauldron of water and jump in and wash in it, and then you will be beautiful." Tam heeded this piece of advice, thinking that Cam was telling the truth. She jumped right into the boiling water, and died with her teeth bared and her mouth twisted up into a snarl. Cam bade some soldiers cook Tam's body, salt it, and send it to Tam's mother to eat: and Tam's mother, thinking it was pork, ate it. One day when she was eating some, a crow alighted on a tree and called to her: "The crow knows;[30] you are eating your daughter's flesh: is it not crisp and gamy?" Tam's mother, hearing the crow say this, railed at it and said: "This is some meat which my daughter sent me to eat; why do you say that I am eating my daughter's flesh?" But when she had almost finished the barrel and saw her daughter's face, she realized that Tam was dead.

Société Asiatique, Landes ms. B.1 (corresponds to Text 22 in *Contes et légendes annamites*)

There are fables and folktales galore about Chinese and Vietnamese historical figures, many of them local celebrities associated with particular districts. They are commonly credited

30. *Qua lau lau.*

with miraculous birth: i.e., they are reincarnations of spirits or immortals, which goes to explain their physical and intellectual superiority and their valorous deeds. The national heroes most frequently featured in story-cycles are Dinh Tien Hoang (Emperor from 968 to 979), Trung Trac and Trung Nhi, the two Vietnamese Joan of Arc figures (first century A.D.) and Nguyen Trai, the statesman and writer (1380–1442).

Here is the story of Dinh Tien Hoang's boyhood, as portrayed in popular mythology:

The Story of King Dinh Tien Hoang

Dinh Tien Hoang's parents died while he was still a boy. He lived with his uncle and herded water buffaloes. One day, when he had taken his water buffaloes to graze on the hillside, he persuaded those of his friends who were also buffalo-herds to play a game in which they chose a king and generals, cutting flowering reeds to use as flags. The buffalo-herds chose Dinh Tien Hoang as king, and he killed one of his water buffaloes to give them a feast. When the feast was over, he stuck the water buffalo's tail in the ground.

That evening, when he took the water buffaloes home, his uncle noticed that they were one short, and asked him why. Dinh Tien Hoang replied that the buffalo had burrowed its way into the ground in a nearby place on the mountain. His uncle thought this strange, and asked him to take him there to see for himself. When they got there, his uncle saw the water buffalo's tail, which his nephew had stuck in the ground, and supposing him to be telling the truth he grasped the tail and pulled—and fell over backwards. He was very angry and cuffed Dinh Tien Hoang, who ran away. His uncle ran after him as far as the ferry, where the ferryman's name was Dragon: so Dinh Tien Hoang began to shout; "Dragon! Dragon! Hurry up and come to my rescue!" But it was the river dragon that rose up and took Dinh Tien Hoang across the river, and his uncle was terrified and ran back home. Dinh Tien Hoang later became king of Annam.

(Landes, *Contes et légendes annamites*, Text 23).

Premier Scholars *(trang-nguyen)* are favorite characters in folktales, and likewise in narrative poems. They normally achieved their position as a result of the public examinations, but could also be appointed directly by Imperial decree in recognition of their ability, skill or acumen. Sometimes they were very young: we find boys of seven and eight being raised to this rank by the Emperor on account of their sharp wits.[31]

One of them, Trang Hien (Premier Scholar Wise), a man from a village in Nam Dinh province, was appointed by the King for helping him to solve a riddle sent by the Yuan Emperor of China.[32] Sometimes an outstandingly gifted man was promoted a *trang,* as in the case of Trang Ech (Premier Scholar Frog). So called because he was a frog-catcher by trade, he used his magic arts to cure the King of an eye disease by applying to his eye a jade found in a frog's innards. The *trang* were often sent as ambassadors to China, where they distinguished themselves by their erudition and their skill in literary composition. Sometimes the Emperor of China conferred on them the title of Chinese Premier Scholar also; and those who were honored in this way took the title *Luong quoc trang-nguyen,* "Premier Scholar of both kingdoms."[33]

The two most famous Vietnamese Premier Scholars, Trang Quynh and Trang Trinh, were supposedly of supernatural birth: their mother was the goddess Lieu Hanh in two different reincarnations, but in each case as the landlady of a tavern.[34] They were also different anatomically from ordinary mortals: one had too few fingers and the other too many. If they had been physically normal they would have been kings.

There is no space here for a full account of the wealth of Vietnamese fables and folktales. Together they give us a picture of the beliefs and habits, the individual and social customs, and the ethics of early Vietnamese society.

One of the most marked features of the folktales is their tendency to moralize: they set out to edify the reader or listener by showing him that avarice is punished, that human beings are

---

31. Nguyen Dong Chi, *Kho tang,* pp. 222–28.
32. *Ibid.,* pp. 228–31.
33. *Ibid.,* p. 154 and Landes, 1, 10, 7.
34. Landes, 1, 10, 8.

ungrateful—and more so than animals—that envy is to be avoided, and that kindness, humanity, filial piety, and compassion to the poor are rewarded.

SAYINGS, PROVERBS, AND FOLKSONGS

Vietnamese folk literature includes a common stock of folk sayings, proverbs, and folksongs in written form. The *nôm* and *quoc-ngu* compilations of these are relatively recent, dating from the nineteenth and twentieth centuries; but they represent earlier traditions, dating in some cases from the Le or even earlier—though in the latter case considerably altered by the lapse of time and the process of transmission. The École Française d'Extrême-Orient possesses a few books of songs and proverbs, some of which are in *nôm*, some in half Chinese, half *nôm*, and some in half *nôm*, half *quoc-ngu*. Collections in *quoc-ngu* are commoner: the best known is *Tuc-ngu phong-dao* (Popular Songs and Sayings), by Nguyen Van Ngoc.[35]

There are different kinds of folk sayings in Vietnamese: proverbs *(tuc-ngu)*, adages *(ngan ngu)*, and sayings peculiar to a particular area or trade *(phuong ngon)*. Folk sayings may also take the form of aphorisms *(cach ngon)* or precepts *(cham ngon)*. Folk sayings may originate from everyday life (i.e., a chance remark catches on, gets improved, and then is noted down), or else be taken from a book or poem and thence pass into common currency. They may be classified according to their form, i.e., whether long or short and whether rhyming or not. Nonrhyming folk sayings are usually short and show parallelism, e.g., *Ngot mat / chet ruoi* (lit., sweet-honey / die-flies), i.e., "Flies can be caught with honey." In rhyming folk sayings the rhymes are internal (a characteristic of Vietnamese folk sayings), e.g., *Cho cay gan nha, ga cay gan vuon*, "The dog prides itself on being assigned to the house, the hen prides herself on being assigned to the

---

35. 2 vols., published in Hanoi in 1928: *Viet-van thu-xa, Vinh-hung long thu-quan.*

garden"—where *nha* ("house") rhymes with *ga* ("hen"). Folk sayings may also be classified according to their subject matter. They may, for instance, contain a geographical or historical allusion, e.g., *Thanh cay the, Nghe cay than,* "Thanh Hoa prides itself on its might, Nghe An on its spirits" (Thanh Hoa was the birthplace of royal families, while Nghe An was famous for its multifarious temples and local spirits). Alternatively they may consist of salutary moral precepts, animadversions on the social scene, and the like.

Until very recently the Vietnamese still had a propensity for interlarding their speech and writing with sayings. Inserted at appropriate points in the train of thought, they served to help the argument along; they also carried conviction, seeing that they enshrined the age-old truths of accumulated folk wisdom.

Folksongs *(ca-dao)*, like sayings, are of anonymous authorship; but they are not a product of the common people as such. It seems rather that earlier generations of literati, especially those of plebeian origin who retained their contacts among the common people, wrote songs for their own amusement or for the common people to sing on particular occasions (for instance at the spring festivals, or when working in the fields).

Literary contests were prized at all levels of society: the literati exchanged highbrow verses at their banquets and gatherings, and the peasants in the fields exchanged lowbrow ones. Gatherings of young men and girls at the time of the seasonal festivals were the occasion for part-song competitions, and in the course of them romantic play-acting sometimes led to genuine proposals and marriages.

Folksongs take a wide range of forms, from two-syllable to six- and eight-syllable verse *(luc-bat);* but as a rule there is an even number of words in a line. Likewise there is much variation in style, subject matter, and purpose: there are nursery rhymes, songs for workers and peasants, songs for different times of the year, songs for young men and women, and so on. Folksongs may contain historical allusions, references to local customs, moral precepts, romantic declarations, etc.; indeed, there is no subject they cannot cover. In form and content they often come close to folk sayings. *Ca-dao* is so closely attuned to Vietnamese tastes and feelings that it is even used in schools for teaching children their lessons (geography, history, elementary ethics, etc.). Most Vietnamese at some time in their lives have recourse to song for one purpose or another. Here the elder sister sings her little brother to sleep with a lullaby:

Sleep, sleep, little brother, sleep to your heart's content!
Your sister is busy picking mulberry-leaves to feed the silkworms.
You are just five:
Next year you will be six, and will put your mind to your schooling;
You will work at your books, and practice your fencing, so as to gain understanding,
So as not to be outstripped by the civilized world.
Sleep, sleep, little brother, sleep to your heart's content!

Extract from Ha Si Hiep, 60 *bai ca-dao* (Hanoi: Nam-Son, 1952), p. 24.

Lumberjacks keep going and keep together by singing work songs such as this one:

Heave ho!
Come pull together at the timber, heave ho!
Pull it down the hillside into the plain,
Make it into rafts and let it float down the river.
With a fair wind in the sails, it will go bobbing off over the water.
On either hand the trees and grass are verdant green;
We enjoy the procession of changing scenery: what does the length of the journey matter?
Heave ho!
Come pull together at the timber, heave ho!
Pull it up on to the bank to build houses to live in:
Joists, uprights, ceilings,
Lofty walls, wide doors: we shall be utterly at peace,
Husbands and wives, daughters and sons, all of us together;
We shall not care about the lashing wind, we shall not worry about the pouring rain.
Heave ho!
Come pull together at the timber, heave ho!

Pull it into the timber-yard to be sawn into broad planks.
The master craftsmen, working day and night,
Make tables and chairs so that students may study:
And tomorrow, when glory comes their way,
Let them not forget the russet mountains, the green forests and the
flowers of our homeland.
Heave ho!

Folksongs throw light on the public and private life of the Vietnamese down the ages. The next song depicts life in an eighteenth-century household, at the time when the Trinh and the Nguyen were ruling independently of the Emperor. It gives us a picture of the virtues of the Vietnamese wife of bygone days, responsible for the whole running of the household, while her husband devoted himself to study or public service or now and then indulged in the pleasures of idleness:

In the first night-watch, I do the housework;
In the second, I weave; at the third I go to take my rest.
When the fourth watch runs into the fifth
I wake my husband, so that he may study and not lie abed.
Soon the Prince will inaugurate the public examination,
And perhaps my husband's name will shine out on the golden list of
successful candidates.
In order that our parents' labors may be repaid
I prepare the inkstand and the writing brushes, so that he may study.

In contrast to this harmonious household we find another in which, try as she may, the wife is handicapped by an unworthy helpmeet; but nevertheless she continues to carry out all her duties:

My husband is a good-for-nothing;
Cards, dice—he does nothing but waste his time gambling.
To mention it to him would be unseemly on my part and shameful for
him;
Besides, he gets cross and breaks everything in the house.
I talk about it here to you, my women friends;
I still had a few baskets of rice left, and a few pounds of cotton—
I sold them to pay my husband's debts.

I eat if there is anything left over, otherwise I do not eat
So that my husband and children may have their fill.
All the most grievous bitternesses do I undergo.
My husband and children are worth less than other women's;
But in admitting it I fear to bring your ridicule on myself,
For I, the daughter of scholars, am married to a dolt and an ignoramus.
And just as the yellow dragon finds it tedious to bathe in a stagnant pond,
So an intelligent person finds it tedious to live with an ignoramus.

This praiseworthy devotion and resignation on the part of the Vietnamese wife are, as we learn from another folksong, the result of the upbringing given to daughters. Simple, well-tried precepts are handed down from mother to daughter, generation after generation:

Daughter, mind you follow my injunctions.
Learn to sell and trade, so as to be a match for the others,
But do not learn to be the cause of dissension and squabbles,
Or your family and friends will reject you, and people will laugh at you.
Whether you are hungry or replete with food, stay good-tempered,
Curb your appetite, curtail your sleep, and keep yourself busy.
When village taxes are going to fall due—
A silver piece, or a bowl of rice—try to put them by for your spouse.
Above all, be faithful to your husband and do your wifely duty.
Then the neighbors will not laugh at you.
Daughter, mind you remember what I tell you.

Many folksongs are really only sayings, adages, and maxims expressing the satirical wisdom of the Vietnamese—a quality in which they are the equal of the most observant and sophisticated of peoples. On wealth as a substitute for dignity and understanding:

When you are rich, people come to meet you and people see you to your door;

When you are penniless, you may go out early and come home late,
   and nobody cares a hoot.
When you can hardly stagger along for the sack of money you drag
   behind you,
You can talk nonsense and the world will pay heed to the confused
   torrent of your words.

People do not appreciate the blessings within their reach, nor
trust their family and friends: they prefer to put their faith in
strangers:

No one prays to the Buddha he has at home,
But people rush to entreat outside devils and demons.

It is impossible to please everybody:

How should one live, to please people?
Live lavishly and they laugh at you; live frugally and they despise you.
If you are tall, they call you a giant; if you are short, they call you a
   dwarf;
If you are fat, they call you a great barrel;
If you are thin, they say you are hanging your backbone out to dry.

Folksongs may also express the loftiest ethical concepts. Thus
the following stanza epitomizes the foundations of filial piety:

A father's claim on his child is high as the mountain-tops lost in the
   sky;
A mother's right to gratitude is vast as the waters of the Eastern Sea.
The height of the mountains and the vastness of the waters are infinite.
My child, let the nine labors of your parents be for ever engraved on
   your heart!

The nine labors of parenthood are conception *(sinh)*, suckling
by the mother *(cuc)*, caressing and consoling *(phu)*, feeding *(suc)*,
maintenance until the child is full-grown *(truong)*, the food and
schooling needed to bring the child to manhood *(duc)*, the at-
tentions the parents lavish on the child *(co)*, their supervision of
it *(phuc)* and advice and injunctions to it *(phúc)*.

III: VIETNAMESE POETRY BEFORE NGUYEN TRAI (1380–1442)

Very little Vietnamese writing from before the time of Nguyen Trai has survived. It consisted mainly of *nôm* poems, some of whose titles are known; and though a few texts exist which have been ascribed to this period, their authenticity cannot be accepted without reserve.

The period in question covers the Tran (1225–1400) and Ho (1400–1407) dynasties; its two main political features were Vietnam's struggle against the Mongols and her relations with Champa. They provided Vietnamese writers, then and later, with subjects which still recur in modern literature: Vietnamese heroism in the struggle against Mongol hordes, the indomitable courage of Tran Hung Dao, the general who never lost his faith in victory, the Chams' gloom and sadness at the dismemberment of their country, and Vietnamese sympathy for their defeated enemies.

The earliest literary works in *nôm* date from the Tran era. The pioneer in this field was Nguyen Thuyen or Han Thuyen (late thirteenth century), who apparently wrote a *nôm* poem inviting a dangerous crocodile to leave the Red River: but the supposed texts are apocryphal, and certainly do not represent the original. Other names mentioned in the chronicles as fine writers in Chinese and *nôm* include Nguyen Si Co (late thirteenth–early fourteenth century), Chu An (d. 1370) and Ho Quy Ly (emperor from 1400 to 1401); but none of their works have survived.

[51]

The last-named, who briefly usurped the throne, showed considerable daring in his attitude to traditional Chinese culture. According to him the Confucian literati were parrots and plagiarists, entirely out of touch with reality. To bring the Chinese classics within reach of all and so deprive the literati of the advantage conferred by their learning, he set up a translations program from Chinese classics such as *Shih ching, Shu ching*, etc. He also wrote a certain amount of *nôm* poetry himself, and it was collected by Nguyen Trai to present to Le Thai Tong; but none of it has survived.

A long fable in verse entitled *Trinh thu* (The Virtuous She-mouse) is ascribed either to Ho Quy Ly or to an individual of the late Tran era by the name of Ho Huyen Qui. It tells how a pretty little white she-mouse keeps her virtue intact:

One night a white she-mouse who was being chased by dogs took refuge in a hole. The hole was the home of a rat married to a mouse, but at the time the mouse was out hunting and the rat was at home alone. Seeing that the white mouse was pretty, and that she had taken refuge in his hole of her own accord, the rat began to make advances to her, first with flattery and wheedling and then with threats. But the white mouse kept finding counterarguments, and when once the dogs had gone away she was able to take her leave with her virtue unscathed.

At this point the mouse came home, and seeing her husband showing the white mouse out she flew into a rage, bewailing her lot and abusing her husband. Do what he would to explain the true position, she would not believe him. She ran off to the white mouse's to have it out with her; but on the way unfortunately met a cat, and had to flee and take refuge in a pond, where she almost died.

The author, who uses the pseudonym Ho Sinh, had come up to the capital from his home in the country and was lodging near the palace of the Prime Minister, Ho Quy Ly. The rat-hole was at the corner of the Prime Minister's citadel, so that Ho Sinh was an eyewitness to these events. He flushed the mouse out, explained the truth to her, and made her promise not to be jealous any more.

According to Bui Ky[1] the author's name is given in the early editions as Ho Huyen Qui and the work dates from the Tran era. Unfortunately this information is missing from Tu Duc's edition (1875). Furthermore this obviously important *nôm* work is not mentioned either by Le Qui Don or by Phan Huy Chu. The date of composition thus rests on internal evidence. It is true that in the Long Khanh period (1373–1376) Ho Quy Ly had not yet come to the throne; and in the story he is mentioned as Prime Minister. Nevertheless the simplicity of the style and the effortless use of *luc-bat*, taken in conjunction with the similarity of verse and meter to late eighteenth- and early nineteenth-century writing, seem to us to suggest that though something may indeed have been written on the theme in the time of the Tran, the original draft was subsequently revised and improved, and that the version we now possess cannot be earlier than the late eighteenth century.

Trinh Thu is not to be regarded as political satire, nor as a piece of moralizing: it represents simply a scholar's recreation and a warning to women not to be jealous. It has the more point for having been written by a Vietnamese of bygone times by way of self-defence against his principal wife's often well-founded suspicions.

Another piece of *luc-bat* verse for which a very early date, going back to the Tran, has been claimed is a long fable called *Tre coc truyen* (Story of the Catfish and the Toad).[2] Admittedly the versification is sometimes odd by modern standards, and the vocabulary sometimes technical; but these are hardly sufficient grounds by themselves for dating the work to the thirteenth century. Here again the use of the *luc-bat* form and the relatively effortless style suggest that *Tre coc* is not to be classed with the earliest Vietnamese *nôm* literature. The fable has a moral,

1. "Truyen trinh thu," *AFIMA Bulletin* nos. 5 and 6 (January–June 1942), pp. 73–114, and "Trinh thu truyen—Tran trieu xu-si Ho Huyen Qui tien—sinh soan," *AFIMA Bulletin (Khai tri tien duc tap san)* no. 1 (October–December 1940).
2. See *Tre coc tan truyen* transcribed into *quoc-ngu* and published by Xuan Lan, 3d edition (Haiphong-Hanoi: Imprimerie-Librairie Van Minh Nguyen Ngoc Xuan, 1914), 396 lines of *luc-bat* verse.

namely that a friendly settlement is always preferable to the inordinate expense and anxiety of a lawsuit. The point at issue is the custody of the toad's tadpoles; the toad gets them back in the end, because they turn into toads and go after their mother. There are some witty criticisms of legal procedure, and no dearth of satirical comment on the mandarins and officials whose cupidity delays and perverts the course of justice. Some have sought to find in *Tre coc* a reference to the old bureaucratic feudalism, which even under a good king is powerless to prevent abuses by junior mandarins. But in fact the point of the fable is on the human plane, and consequently applicable to any period.

Tre coc is the story of the families of a toad and a catfish, who end up hating each other because of their love for their children. To start with, the female toad gives birth to her young in the catfish's pond. The tadpoles are similar to fish fry, and when the toad and his wife go back home the catfish adopts them and brings them up. Some time later the toad, anxious to see his young ones, comes to the edge of the pond to look for them. During the night he makes such a din that the catfish comes to the surface: the toad asks for his young ones back, but the catfish snubs him sharply, saying that they could not be in the pond because toads are land animals. The toad goes home and discusses the matter with his wife, and they decide to go and lay a charge before the District Magistrate. The toad names as witnesses those who saw his wife giving birth in the pond, namely the carp, the tench, the climbing perch, etc. The District Magistrate instructs his subordinates to institute an enquiry. They start by requiring a retaining fee from the toad, and then issue a writ of attachment against the catfish. The tipstaff arrests the catfish and brings him before the District Magistrate, together with the witnesses designated by the toad. The latter confirm that they know nothing and have been involved in the case against their will. Here the toad intervenes to point out that the witnesses are of the same race as the accused, and hence are incapable of giving evidence against him. Eventually the Magistrate directs that the catfish be kept in custody, and adjourns the hearing. The catfish is then put to the torture. In view of his plight his wife asks the advice of Trieu Dau, who recommends her to a certain Nganh, mayor of a neighboring hamlet: and she goes to see him, taking presents with her. Nganh reassures her, and tells her what she must do: if she is to succeed, she must give presents to the whole staff of the court and to the Magistrate. He then goes himself to the Magistrate's *yamen* to plead the catfish's case. Next the catfish's wife goes before the Magistrate with presents. Eventually the catfish is released and the toad thrown into prison. The toad's wife scours the country in search of help and succor to rescue her husband. The frog advises her to consult a shrewd and experienced lawyer, the tree-frog, and he for his part advises her to give up the whole affair:

Every species reproduces its own kind, so what is the good of arguing?
The catfish is a maniac:
He let himself be carried away by a fit of stupid greed, without stopping to think.
So calm yourself, and stop litigating.
Your children must live in water for the present, and what could you do for them there?
Let the catfish lavish care on them;
They will find their way back to you when their tails fall off, and that will be simpler.

The tadpoles do indeed turn into toads. The toad, followed by his offspring, appears before the mandarin and demonstrates by his evidence that the catfish was lying, and so were the staff of the court and the local officials. The mandarin is incensed: he reprimands his subordinates and gives judgment against the catfish. The toad goes home with his children and lives happily ever after.

There are, however, two works which in their existing form almost certainly date from the fifteenth century: *Truyen Vuong*

Tuong, or the story of Chieu Quan, and the story of Nguyen Bieu.

Of the story of Chieu Quan, the Han princess who in the days of the emperor Yuan (48–33 B.C.) had to leave the Chinese court to marry a Hsiung-nu king, 38 *nôm* octets and 10 quatrains have survived. The use of T'ang metrical rules (e.g., seven-syllable octets), the literary allusions, the affected imagery, and the erudite Sino-Vietnamese turns of phrase all indicate that writers of *nôm* poetry at that time were strongly influenced by Chinese literature. Here is an octet describing the feelings of the Emperor of China at the sight of Chieu Quan, who was being presented to him for the first time:

The longer he gazed upon her, the more his heart was in turmoil.
Heaven never held such fragrance within the prison of its clouds;
Her painted face had the freshness of a thousand flowers blooming in
    spring;
Her brows were arched like the bow of the half-moon hanging in the
    autumn sky.
The fish jumped out of the water and the wild geese came down from
    the sky to do honor to the pink-cheeked beauty;
The peach trees lost their color and the willows their radiance, put out
    of countenance by the grace of the high-born damsel in the pink
    skirt.
Thus she appeared in her sadness;
Had smiling happiness made her blossom like the willow or the plum
    tree, it would have been impossible to describe her!

(From the text given by Hoang Xuan Han and Nghiem Toan in *Viet-
Nam thi van,* p. 23)

The story of Nguyen Bieu occurs in *Nghia si truyen* (Lives of Good Men) by Hoang Trung, who took his Third Degree in 1449. Nguyen Bieu, Hoang Trung's uncle, was sent in 1413 as an envoy to the Chinese general Chang Fu (Truong Phu), who had occupied Nghe An. The Chinese general tested him by making him eat a human head: Nguyen Bieu passed the test and was allowed to leave, but was recaptured by the Chinese, kept prisoner, and later executed. He remained throughout haughtily aloof and steadfastly loyal to his Emperor. *Nghia si truyen* is the earliest of the *nôm* works celebrating the exploits of the great heroes of history; they include poems such as *Chinh khi ca* and many others. Here are Nguyen Bieu's thoughts at the prospect of the gruesome repast he is forced to consume:

Meats precious as jade, eatables costly as pearls—all their flavors we
    already know;
Now comes the latest exquisite delicacy, the feast of the human head;
Minced peacock, even phoenix pie, cannot equal it in succulence.
Bear meat, unicorn's liver, are less of a novelty.
A feast to be compared with the one in the poem "Stags belling,"[3]
Ten times better than the famous banquet of hares' heads;[4]
Yes indeed, it is as tasty as the shoulder of pork
That gave Phan[5] his centuries-old reputation for courage!

3. In *Shih ching, Hsiao ya*, ed. Couvreur, vol. 1, p. 1. The Emperor gives a banquet for his ministers and the envoys of the vassal princes and has this poem sung in their honor, comparing them to a herd of stags belling and browsing together on the steppes.

4. An allusion to one of the poems in *Shih ching, Hsiao ya*, ed. Couvreur, 1, 7, "The Cucumber Leaves" *(Hu yeh)*, which describes a frugal meal with a hare as the centerpiece.

5. Phan Khoai (Chinese Fan K'uai), a dog-meat butcher and one of the retainers of Han Kao-tsu, future founder of the Han dynasty. At the famous banquet at Hong-mon at which Hang Vo (Chinese Hsiang Yü) intended to assassinate his master, Phan Khoai followed him and saved his life by breaking into the antechamber (having first devoured a shoulder of pork and drunk a flask of wine at Hsiang Yü's invitation) and dragging Han Kao-tsu out of the banqueting-hall.

IV: NGUYEN TRAI AND
QUOC-AM THI-TAP

With Nguyen Trai's *Collected Poems in National Language* we come
to an authentic text. It was included as chapter 7 in the anthology of this writer's works compiled by some of Tu Duc's (1829–
1883) scholars and published in 1868 under the title *Uc-Trai di-
tap;* but later É. Gaspardone in his *Bibliographie annamite* (*Bulletin de l'École Française d'Extrême-Orient,* 1934) reported that it
had disappeared. Recently, by a lucky chance, the text of chapter 7 was rediscovered by two North Vietnamese scholars, Tran
Van Giap and Pham Trong Diem, and published at Hanoi in
1956.

This interesting work is important as showing both the state
of poetic Vietnamese in the first half of the fifteenth century
and also the subject matter Nguyen Trai chose. The language
still betrays strong Chinese influence; literary allusions to characters in the Confucian classics and Chinese history abound;
Vietnamese expressions are often obviously modeled on Chinese
ones; and much of the syntax is Chinese. The vocabulary also
contains archaisms, some of which are incomprehensible. The
result is that the style in many passages seems awkward, cumbrous, and lacking in lucidity. Some of Nguyen Trai's subjects
(love of the country and of a quiet life, distaste for the rough-
and-tumble of the court, integrity, rectitude, etc.) are to be found
in the great Chinese poets of the T'ang and Sung, notably Po
Chü-i. But his especial favorite, often most delightfully treated,

[58]

is the pleasures of *otium* or idleness, in the Latin (i.e., the non-pejorative) sense of the word. This is the discriminating idleness of the cultured man, capable of appreciating rustic pleasures but also of devoting his remaining leisure to cultivating his own thoughts and feelings. This discerning delight in *otium*, away from public life and from contact with stupid or unscrupulous men of affairs, was to be celebrated in similar vein by later poets such as Nguyen Binh Khiem.

In Nguyen Trai's case the yearning for *otium* was no mere poetic fancy, but the expression of a genuine and long-felt need. Both during Le Loi's war of national independence and later as a dignitary at the Le court, where he was a target for the vicious intrigues of mediocre and dull-witted courtiers, the life he was obliged to lead was a hard, nerve-racking, and wearing one. After the early death of his master and fellow insurgent, Emperor Le Thai To, the illustrious statesman and orthodox Confucian no longer felt at home at the court of Le Thai Tong (1434–1442); and it is understandable enough that he should have found solace in retirement and solitude.

A tree, a spade—Ah, the joys of the country!
Between the chrysanthemum-clumps and the orchid clusters
I sow beans and millet;
My guest's arrival is joyfully welcomed by the birds and the flowers,
    which all of a sudden start waving.
I boil the tea with water in which the moon still shines.[1]
Like Ba Di,[2] solitude is my delight;
Like Nhan Tu,[3] poverty is my rule.
To be well or ill spoken of is unimportant: I block my ears.
What need is there to court praise or worry about ridicule?

[1]. I.e., water drawn from a spring by moonlight, so that the moon is reflected in the water and seems to be carried away in the bucket.
[2]. Po Yi, son of the king of Ku-chu, fled with his brother Shu-ch'i in order to abdicate the throne to their youngest brother. They took refuge in the land of the Shang; and when the Shang were deposed by the Chou, they preferred to go and live in the woods and eat wild herbs and die there rather than be subservient to the Chou.
[3]. Yen Yuan, Confucius' favorite disciple.

The second major *nôm* work ascribed to Nguyen Trai is a piece of homely didacticism—a genre very fashionable in Vietnam throughout the Sino-Vietnamese period and right up to modern times. Nguyen Trai's book seems to have had the title *Le trieu tuong cong Nguyen Trai gia huan ca* (Book of Homely Instruction by Minister Nguyen Trai of the Le dynasty, Put into Verse). It is a work of some 796 lines, divided up as follows: the instruction of women and children (ll. 1–300), teaching children to lead a good life (301–366), teaching daughters to lead a good life (367–550), a wife's advice to her husband (551–578), and advice to a student to apply himself to his studies (693–796).

This tendency to put rules of conduct, praise for the good deeds of historical figures, and satires on human vices and defects into verse is exemplified by a plethora of *nôm* and *quoc-ngu* works under a variety of titles: Exhortation to Filial Piety *(Khuyen hieu ca)*, Rules for Women *(Nu tac)*, Instructions to Daughters *(Huan nu quoc am ca, Huan nu dien ca, Huan nu ca,* and *Nu huan dien ca)*, and Instructions to Married Women *(Huan phu dien ca* and *Noi huan ca)*.

Other treatises of this kind in *nôm* verse or *quoc-ngu* amount virtually to complete textbooks of manners and conduct for each member of the family, for instance *Bach nhan ngam* (Lament of the Hundred Forbearances), in which the poet sets out in quatrains what the mouth, eyes, and heart, and the parents, husband, and wife etc. must each tolerate for happiness's sake; the various *Giao huan* or Teachings; and *Nhat tinh ngam* (Daily Examination, Put into Verse), which deals with the duties owed to parents, to the Sovereign, between husband and wife, between friends, etc.

The didactic work attributed to Nguyen Trai under the title *Nguyen tuong cong gia huan* or *Nguyen Trai gia huan* is unlikely to date from the fifteenth century. A scrutiny of this writer's Collected Poems in National Language *(Quoc-am thi-tap)* and of *Hong Duc quoc-am thi-tap* (Collected Poems in National Language of the Hong Duc Period) reveals an archaic vocabulary,

Chinese influence in the syntax and phrasing, and no long poems in *luc-bat* (6–8 syllable verse). In view of this it can be stated categorically that works such as Nguyen Trai's *Gia huan,* with their effortless, modernistic style, cannot be the work of fifteenth-century writers. A fortiori, works such as *Truyen tre coc* (Story of the Catfish and the Toad), *Truyen trinh thu* (Story of the Virtuous She-mouse) and *Truyen Vuong Tuong* (Story of Vuong Tuong) could not, at any rate in their extant versions, have been written under the Tran or even under the first of the later Le. To take a parallel in English literature, one has only to glance at a page of Chaucerian or Spenserian verse to see that it is very different from current English. It is harder to understand, both because the vocabulary is full of archaisms and because the syntax still bears the traces of Anglo-Saxon.

Moralizing works of the type of *Gia huan ca* flourished in Vietnam under the Empire and also in the modern period. In a hierarchical society this sort of writing has a part to play in underpinning the social order and maintaining the privileges of the Establishment. Vietnam was, after all, first a Chinese colony, then a monarchy, and then a French colony: and it was naturally in the interests of the ruling power that order should prevail not only in people's public activities but also in their private lives. Moreover in a country with no organized system of social security any private initiative was to be welcomed—whether it took the form of charitable poor relief or of edifying discourses calculated to promote ideas of cooperation and self-help among the common people. Both Confucianism and Buddhism preached humanity as a duty: the former was based on a rational view of the mutability of human affairs and the hope of reward in this life, while the latter offered a delicately mystical approach to human suffering and the hope of reward in the next.

The extract from *Nguyen Trai gia huan* that follows shows how in all periods of history the Vietnamese have been obsessed with natural ills such as famine and drought and man-made ones such as war and civil unrest. Whether these lines were in fact penned

by Nguyen Trai or by some later writer, it was certainly someone who had seen the horror of wars in which whole popula-
tions were reduced to destitution by famine, the destruction of
their villages, and the extortions of the troops. For those in need,
private charity was very often the only hope.

The author's advice to his children is highly moving, especially considering what he must himself have been through. So
far from making him hard, it seems to have brought him added
wisdom and humanity—qualities which are entirely in keeping
with the disillusioned comments on wealth and power found in
many of the poems.

Instructions to Children on How to Behave
(Day con o cho co duc)

Here are my instructions to my children
In case they should come up against a period of strife in the land.
Behave uprightly and humanely,
And then you may look forward to an era of peace in which to enjoy
    Heaven's blessings.

Have pity on those who run in all directions,
Have pity on those who are lost and those who are forsaken,
Have pity on those who hug their babies to them,
Have pity on the aged, and on old folk who are homeless and desti-
    tute,
Have pity on widows and widowers, orphans, and those who are alone.

Have pity on those who lie groaning by the wayside, dying of hunger
    and thirst.
If you see someone starving and parched with thirst, have pity on him;
If he is cold, give him clothing; if he is hungry, give him something to
    eat.
Have pity on people as though they were your own parents,
For they come driven on by unforeseen disaster.

Take them a little money, a bowl of rice,
And say: "This is very little, just a slight help."
Fortunately we live in an area untouched by the troubles;

It is not decent for us to remain unmoved at other people's disasters
and hardships.
As the saying goes: hungry days come in the cold months.

Have pity on people; save a little of your food, soften your hearts and
give them alms.
A mouthful when one is hungry is worth a feast when one is sated!
Though your means be scanty, your kind thought makes your gift worth
a thousand times more.
Wealth is one of the countless possessions that human beings share;
We are born naked and bare, and we die with our hands empty, with
nothing in them.

It behooves you to act according to the rules of humanity and justice
So that the fragrance of your reputation may spread far and wide, and
future generations hand it down one to another as though it were
engraved on a stone.
Kindness enjoys a good name in this world,
And compassionate hearts are our Heaven-sent help.
Disasters and trials will pass.

And to start with a kind deed really stirs up the dust of ages.
Gold was never put into your hands by Heaven,
But peace you should reckon tens of times more precious.
Later, possessing silver and gold galore,
You will live long and enjoy the prosperity vouchsafed by Heaven.

See the people who behave cruelly:
Are they sure they will not later have to face adversity themselves?
When they see poor wretches dying of hunger and cold, they scorn
them;
They take account only of their own interests,
Calculating here, reckoning there,

Hesitating over a trifle, looking twice at a sapek.[4]
These people are hypocrites: they are like papered birdcages, only the
outside of which is visible.
But when they speak they open their mouths like a dragon, like an
immortal.
Their hearts are harder than iron that is wrought,
Their mouths are smiling, as though money were going to drop out
of it.

4. A small coin, equivalent to one thousandth of a tael or liang, issued by the
French for use in Indochina.

Their faces glow with kindness; they are adept at giving their words
the appearance of truth.
To listen to them, you would think they would share their property
and share their homes.
But in fact they have no feelings,
And are like the liar Cuoi, who shows the cloven hoof.
They speak and then start over again;

They promise ten elephants, and you do well to get half a bowl of broth!
When troublous times loom up,
And houses are destroyed, and the populace grievously afflicted,
People are caught up in the whirlwind of an unhappy fate;
Their houses collapse in a moment, reduced to ashes.

Others are forced to become soldiers, pressed men,
And are embroiled in hostilities in the front rank of fighting men.
Others are struck down by an epidemic;
Others again suffer disaster by fire and flood.
When you see these unfortunate people, bear in mind what might
happen to you.

They are there before your eyes, and are truly deserving of pity.
I exhort you, children, not to follow the example of the wicked,
But to keep your hearts full of kind feelings: that way wisdom lies.
The advice your father keeps drumming into you
On what is proper and what is right, is for your guidance.

Follow it, and you will be men;
If you do not, you will be rejected by the world.

(Text AB 406 of the École Française d'Extrême-Orient, ll. 301–366)

V: LE THANH TONG AND
HONG DUC QUOC-AM THI-TAP

The outstanding political event of the early fifteenth century was the liberation of the country from the yoke of Ming China (1368–1628). The years of war waged by Le Loi, who was to become the emperor Le Thai To (1428–1433), were not notable for any great literary flowering. What there is in Chinese consists largely of summonses, decrees, chronicles, and diplomatic exchanges between contemporary Chinese authorities; also writings attributed to the Vietnamese ruler but usually produced by his civil servants or his distinguished minister Nguyen Trai (1380–1442).

With the return of peace in 1428 and the reorganization of the administrative system, writers could once more indulge in the pleasure of writing for its own sake, without bothering about turning out anti-Chinese propaganda or works calculated to stiffen popular resistance. After so many years of turmoil, struggle, and hardship, people looked forward to enjoying some peace and quiet and a respite from stirring times.

As the period of peace with China continued, the country grew in prosperity, reaching a peak under the emperor Le Thanh Tong (1460–1497). His 38-year reign was so prosperous and brilliant that Vietnamese historians call the fifteenth century the Le Thanh Tong century.

This ruler was fond of belles-lettres, and founded a kind of salon or learned society known as Tao Dan, i.e., Mound of Ly-tao, or "altar of belles-lettres." This is from the title of the famous Chinese poem *Li sao* (Vietnamese *Ly-tao*) by Ch'ü Yüan (Khuat Nguyen) of the Chou, in the Warring States period (373–221 B.C.), which is regarded as one of the great models of Chinese poetry. Here the Emperor and the leading literati of his court would vie with one another in writing poems on set subjects; and it is the fruits of this literary activity that have come down to us in *Hong Duc quoc-am thi-tap* (Collected Poetry of the Hong Duc Period), one of the earliest anthologies of Vietnamese *nôm* poetry. In Text AB 292 of the École Française d'Extrême-Orient the pieces are grouped according to subject matter, e.g., heaven and earth *(Thien-dia mon)*, good men *(Nhan dao mon)*, scenery *(Phong-canh)*, and poems about plants, flowers, and trees. The anthology contains over 300 poems, including the Story of Vuong Tuong (269–312); and it presents us with a compendium of the major topics that so frequently recur in the works of pre-nineteenth-century Vietnamese writers, viz., the seasons, the moon, the five night-watches, the twelve months of the year, Han Cao To, Hang Vu, Truong Luong, Han Tin, To Vu, My E, Chieu Quan, the obligations of a righteous man, the scenery of Tieu Tuong, Mount Phat Tich, the river Bach Dang, the four conditions of men (fisherman, woodman, ploughman, and herdsman), the various pagodas, famous Vietnamese temples, and so on. There are many occasional poems by the Emperor and his courtiers, all directly or indirectly laudatory of the Imperial government, the peaceful state of the realm, and the high sense of duty shown by the Sovereign and his mandarins. For instance, in "New Year's Day" (no. 1 in the anthology), a mandarin presents his New Year wishes to the Emperor:

The Creator's mysterious mover turns the cycle of the four seasons.
At the end of winter, the thirtieth of the month is succeeded by the
  first day of spring.
Dazzling, the golden portal of the days of Thuan gleams;

[66]

Radiant, the jade tablet of the calendar of Nghieu[1] comes into view.
The Imperial throne rises to an immeasurable height;
Everywhere, at every point, prosperity spreads among the common
  people.
Allow me, as befits my humble station among the noble mandarins of
  the Court,
To turn toward the Lofty Mountain and respectfully wish our En-
lightened Ruler a happy New Year.

In "In Praise of the Tamarind Tree Growing in the Imperial
Palace" (168), the author sings the praises of the Emperor, whose
bounty extends not only to men (i.e., the granting of the Third
Degree) but over the whole of nature:

This precious tree, by what extraordinary chance has it flourished here?
What ancient predestination accorded it this pride of place?
Its verdant crown, drenched in wholesome sunlight, unfolds new leaf;
Its canopy of thick green foliage retains the warmth of the sun's rays.
It has in some measure enjoyed Royal favor:
Throughout the four seasons it constantly keeps great men's company.
Nobody knows for how many existences already
It has shaded Premier Scholars waiting to enter the Palace.

The Emperor himself liked to write poems about landscapes that
took his fancy while on his travels, such heroes of Chinese antiquity as he particularly admired, and everyday objects treated
in symbolic fashion. But many such poems attributed to him are
probably spurious, especially the later ones. The two verse ep-
itaphs dealing with the story of the lady Thiet Vu (75 and 76)
are probably genuine; but poems with a modern air about them,
like "The Mortar for Husking Rice" (*Coi say,* 235), "The elephant" (*Con voi,* 237) and "The Scarecrow" (*Cao nhan,* 225), could
be simply spurious or else revisions of much earlier texts.

1. Thuan (Chinese Shun) and Nghieu (Chinese Yao) were two of the early Five
Emperors of China. Their reigns (2255–2205 and 2356–2255 B.C. respectively)
were a legendary Golden Age, and their names have remained a byword for
peace and good government.

The theme of the undeserved death of the lady Thiet Vu is known in Europe from the French anthology *Légendes des terres sereines,* by Pham Duy Khiem, in which this very old story appears under the title *La jeune femme de Nam-xuong.* Le Thanh Tong treated it in two octets, and it is obvious that he felt genuinely sorry for the protagonist. The story tells of a young woman who, while her husband was away, used to amuse her small son in the evenings by throwing her own shadow on the wall in the lamplight and telling him it was his father. When the husband, Truong, came home from the wars, the boy refused to believe he was really his father, and told him that his father (i.e., the shadow) had been coming to the house every evening. Truong, thinking that his wife was being unfaithful to him with another man, reproached her bitterly. Desperate and not knowing how to establish her innocence, the young woman committed suicide by throwing herself into the Hoang-giang, as the Red River is called where it passes through the Nam-xuong area. (Nam-xuong is the village where these tragic events took place; a temple was later erected there to the memory of the dead woman.) Here is Le Thanh Tong's second octet, written on the occasion of a visit he paid to the village:

Upstream from the rapids the smoke of incense rises to the sky;
What temple is to be compared with the one to Truong's wife?
Despite the shadow cast by the lamp, had he not heeded the child
The Water Palace would not have gained possession of the young woman.
The two heavenly bodies, Sun and Moon, bear witness to it;
What use are altars and prayers in clearing her of this false indictment?
As I came along, my mind turned to debating her case:
How blameworthy is Truong, whose wickedness is so great!

These examples will be sufficient to show the uninspired and pedestrian nature of the poetry, still trammeled as it is by the recollection of Chinese meters. Despite these defects, however, the poems in *Hong Duc quoc-am thi-tap* are quite easy for the present-day reader to understand. Together with Nguyen Trai's, this represents the earliest anthology of Vietnamese poetry. It constitutes a valuable historical and social document for every aspect of life at an ancient Imperial court; and at the same time it is important for literary history in that it marks the beginning of specifically Vietnamese literature and contains copious examples of themes dear to the hearts of Vietnamese poets.

VI: THE SIXTEENTH CENTURY AND NGUYEN BINH KHIEM

During the whole of the sixteenth century the Le dynasty was in decline, and there was severe unrest which eventually led to its temporary removal from power. Princes of the Imperial family murdered one another, and high officials plotted against one another and against the Emperor. In 1521, in the midst of this chaos, a young general, Mac Dang Dung, seized effective control: he made away with the emperor Le Chieu Tong (1516–1522), took possession of the throne, and founded the Mac dynasty.

Mac Dang Dung was, however, highly unpopular. Starting as a regicide, he discredited himself further in 1540 by going in person to the Chinese border, disrobing, and performing the kotow to the Emperor of China represented by one of his generals. This shameful conduct earned him the contempt of his countrymen, and he had difficulty in retaining the allegiance of those who had been mandarins under the Le. The supporters of the Le included two high officials, Nguyen Kim and his son-in-law Trinh Kiem, and these two joined forces to fight against the Mac. In 1545 Nguyen Kim died of poison, all his powers passing to his son-in-law; and this marked the beginning of the power of the Trinh, who were to overthrow the Mac, restore the legitimate Le dynasty, and make themselves rulers in all but name under the restored dynasty.

Meanwhile Mac Dang Dung's usurpation of the throne led to

nearly a century of unrest and strife between the supporters of the Le and of the Mac. The common people suffered terribly. Officers and mandarins were obliged to opt for one faction or the other, or else to withdraw from politics and administration and remain aloof from the turmoil of the battlefield and the courts. Vietnam was split into two parts, one including Thanh Hoa and the area to the south, the other the whole of North Vietnam.

This state of affairs is reflected in the literature. Few noteworthy works appeared apart from a collection of a hundred *nôm* poems by Nguyen Binh Khiem (1491–1587), *Bach Van quoc-ngu thi-tap* (Poems in National Language by Bach Van)—Bach Van being the author's nom de plume. This writer dominates the sixteenth-century literary scene. He was a typical example of the great Vietnamese literati molded by the influence of Chinese culture. His outlook was basically Confucian, but with traces of Taoism: a gentle, resigned philosophy based on the ephemeral nature of the world and on a return to nature—the latter being practiced first in ordinary everyday life and later leading on a loftier plane to sublimation and eventual oneness with the soul of the Universe. He was a good scholar, and well versed in the books of divination derived from the *I-ching*, so that he also made himself a name as a sort of Vietnamese Nostradamus. Throughout his lifetime, despite having been in the service of the Mac, he managed to remain above factional strife. His wisdom and moderation, his simple way of life, and his gifts as a soothsayer gained him the respect of all, and supporters of both the Mac and the Le beat a path to his retreat, White Clouds *(Bach Van),* to seek his advice about affairs of state and the nation's future.

The *nôm* poems in *Bach Van quoc-ngu thi-tap* take the form of eulogies of quiet country life, rustic pleasures, and the delights of *otium.* Language and style have obviously evolved a stage further than in *Hong Duc quoc-am thi-tap.* Some archaisms survive which are difficult for the present-day reader to understand, usually single-syllable words where nowadays two-sylla-ble words would be used. But in general the language is simple and easy to understand—all the more so because the subject matter calls neither for a wide vocabulary nor for the use of terms denoting abstruse ideas. The "modernity" of the work and its subject matter are strangely suggestive of Nguyen Trai, but there is a stronger element of moralizing and didacticism.

The troubled times in which he lived and the attitude of weary circumspection that he adopted are reflected in Nguyen Binh Khiem's poetry. Poem No. 23, for instance, conveys his convic-tion that wisdom lay in not meddling in affairs of state:

From the realms of glory and renown let us stay aloof, with arms folded.
Already time and again have I escaped from the disaster that strikes
    without warning.
The plum-blossom gleams silver in the moonlight;
The shadows of the bamboos stirring in the wind are like lace.
It is not that I forget the old feelings of patriotism and devotion to the
    Prince,
But in matters of today I shrink from deciding between true and false.
I have traveled over all the mountains and rivers:
How many perilous places there are in the world!

In most of his poems he alludes to the Emperor only to de-pict him as the fountainhead of all happiness for the common people, and to the Empire only to emphasize its entirely peace-ful state. These assertions, the exact opposite of the truth, are of course mere rhetorical devices designed to avoid trouble with the authorities and ensure the continuance of his quiet and tranquil life.

Already old age has taken me beyond fourscore years.
Time passes quickly, like the shadow of a passing horse.
The white plum-trees grow used to the cold after so many months un-
    der snow;
The golden chrysanthemums each time pile up their multitudinous
    blooms.
If wealth is your portion, it is thanks to the Sovereign's favor;

If you are fit to be a man, it is thanks to your parents' virtues.
In my rustic retreat my days slip by in idleness, with never a care.
I live as I please, according to my own sweet will.

(Poem no. 16)

Nguyen Binh Khiem took his Third Degree in 1535, and is commonly referred to in connection with his predictions and oracles as Trang Trinh (Premier Scholar Trinh). We do not possess the original text of these, but various traditions in *nôm* have been published, e.g., *Trinh tien-sinh quoc-ngu* (Doctor Trinh's Predictions in National Language), *Trinh trang-nguyen sam ky dien ca* (The Oracles of Premier Scholar Trinh, Put into Verse), and *Trinh quoc-cong sam* (The Oracles of Duke Trinh). There are many versions of them in *quoc-ngu*. Here, for example, is an excerpt from Pham Van Giao's book *Trang Trinh, than the, su nghiep, thi ca va sam ky* (The life, works, poems, and oracles of Premier Scholar Trinh), Saigon, Éditions P. Van Tuoi:

> The characters *hoa, dao,* and *moc* collapse.
> The characters *thap, bat,* and *tu* flourish.
> The characters *dong* and *a* come out of the sun;
> Another tree will spring up.
> The Eastern Palace will come out of the sun;
> The Western Palace will continue to shine.
> The characters *phu* and *nguyen* will bring forth royal issue.

This text is as cryptic as all prophetic texts, and calls for elucidation. In the old days the literati greatly enjoyed this sort of wordplay on the component parts of Chinese characters, and Vietnamese literature is full of examples of the setting and solving of such riddlemerees by scholars noted for these conceits.

In the first line of the verse above, the oracle conjoins the characters *hoa, dao,* and *moc* to produce the character *le,* "pear tree"—but a homophone of *Le,* the name of two Vietnamese dynasties. Here it is the first Le dynasty (980–1009) that is meant.

[73]

In the second line three other characters, *thap, bat,* and *tu,* are similarly combined to give the character *ly,* "plum tree"—and also the Ly dynasty (1010–1225), which succeeded the early Le. In line 3 the characters *dong* and *a* together give the character *tran,* standing for the Tran dynasty (1225–1400), which succeeded the Ly. In line 4 the reference to another *le* or pear tree means that another Le dynasty (1428–1789) will spring up. In line 5 the Eastern Palace is taken by some to mean the Tay Son (the dynasty that succeeded the later Le) and by others to mean Japan (i.e., a reference to the Japanese occupation of Vietnam in 1940). In line 6 the Western Palace presumably stands for the French, or perhaps again for the Tay Son. In line 7 the characters *phu* and *nguyen* together form the character Nguyen, the name of the last Vietnamese dynasty (1802–1945).

VII: THE SEVENTEENTH AND EIGHTEENTH CENTURIES: Growth and Flowering of *Nôm* Poetry and Narrative Verse

The Le dynasty, which had started so brilliantly with Le Loi (later Emperor Le Thai To, 1428–1433) and his successors, especially Le Thanh Tong (1460–1497), was in decline during the sixteenth, seventeenth, and eighteenth centuries: and this left the way open for attempts on the throne and internecine strife among the princely houses. In the sixteenth century a family of rebel nobles, the Mac (1527–1532), seized the capital, Thang Long (the modern Hanoi), and set up a dynasty there which was to rule the whole of Tonkin until 1532 and subsequently the Cao Bang area until 1592. The Le, having been driven from Thang Long, withdrew with their majordomos, the Trinh, to Thanh Hoa (the central portion of present-day North Vietnam); while further south the Nguyen princes under Nguyen Kim (1468–1545) began the subjugation of central Vietnam.

With the help of the Trinh and the Nguyen the Le managed to get rid of the Mac; but as the price of this they had virtually to surrender their own power to these two princely houses. From the time of Trinh Kiem (1545–1569) omwards, the Trinh took up residence at the court of the Le emperors, and with their willing or unwilling support effectively ruled the kingdom until the end of the sixteenth century. The Nguyen, having carved themselves out an extensive fief in central Vietnam to the north and south of Phu Xuan (Hué), set up a principality which, though nominally subservient to the Le, was in practice independent. Becoming wealthier and more powerful, they eventually clashed with the central authority of the Trinh; and a struggle ensued which lasted throughout the seventeenth and eighteenth centuries. Meanwhile the three Tay Son brothers rebelled against the Nguyen, subdued the whole of their domain, comprising central Vietnam and Cochin-China, and founded the Tay Son dynasty (1788–1802). Despite all their efforts, however, they could not survive against incessant attacks by their enemies, the Nguyen, the Trinh, and the Le. Eventually the Nguyen under Nguyen Anh overcame all their rivals; he succeeded in uniting the country under his rule, and in 1802 proclaimed himself emperor under the name of Gia Long. His dynasty was to last until 1945, ending with the emperor Bao Dai (1926–1945).

Despite the hardship and suffering engendered by the civil wars, particularly in the period 1627–1674, Vietnam extended her frontiers and advanced along the road to economic and social development. Vietnamese influence and settlement spread into Cambodia. In the north the Trinh subjugated the Montagnard peoples as far as Laos, and in the south the Nguyen completely eliminated the Chams and pushed back the frontiers of Vietnam as far as the present-day Cambodian border. Meanwhile from the sixteenth century onwards European crafts and wares, and also Christianity, were being brought into the country by French, Dutch, Spanish, and Portuguese traders. Under Nguyen Anh (Gia Long), French influence secured a firm foothold: and this was further consolidated during the nineteenth century, leading ultimately to the French conquest and occupation.

Developments in literature in the eighteenth and nineteenth

centuries were many and varied. The literati, often themselves well-known statesmen and soldiers, continued to write prolifically in Chinese, producing poetry, chronicles, and specialized (e.g., medical) works. More and more was written in Vietnamese in *nôm* characters, and its standards improved. Literary forms adopted from Chinese, such as seven-syllable verse, *phu* (poems), *kinh nghia* (commentaries on the classics), *van sach* (replies to questionnaires) etc., continued to find favor with the literati, brought up on the literary exercises in the public examinations. Most important of all, however, was the proliferation of poetry in six- and eight-syllable verse *(luc-bat),* which by the end of the eighteenth century formed the bulk of all literary work in Vietnamese. It was also the most original. The late eighteenth century is notable for the narrative poems in *luc-bat,* of which *Hoa-tien* and *Kim Van Kieu* are the outstanding examples.

In these troublous times writers' personalities and emotions came increasingly to the fore. Poetry became more personal, more closely linked both to the writer's inner feelings and to contemporary events. It was also more lyrical. Sentimental love began to play an important part in poetry and narrative verse.

Chinese popular novels and plays seem to have been the fashionable reading matter among the literati, affording them welcome relaxation from the dreariness of the inevitable Chinese classics set for their examinations. A somewhat paradoxical result was that Vietnamese writers had recourse to this light reading, which consisted of love-stories, adventure-stories, and improving tales, for the subjects of their *luc-bat* masterpieces. There also grew up the form known as *dien-ca* ("translation into songs"), or prose texts put into *nôm* verse, which somewhat resembled the verse romances of medieval European chroniclers.

Events in the political arena also left their mark on the literature. The Le had been, after all, the most long-standing dynasty as well as the legitimate one; and in these distressful times poets tended to look back nostalgically at the peace and splendor of the early part of the Le period. There was also a feeling that loyalty was due to a legitimate ruler unseated in a revolt, with its consequent civil unrest and concomitant hardship for the common people. Even when public sympathy was with the rebels, this represented not so much opposition to the Le emperor himself as a reaction to the harsh measures taken by his ministers and associates in his name. In the end the Mac and the Tay Son lost popular support. With the Trinh princes murdering one another in their struggle for power, and the last Le emperors showing themselves ignominious cowards and weaklings, the north of the country was ready by the end of the eighteenth century to welcome the Nguyen.

During this period the romanized system of writing Vietnamese, which had been introduced by European missionaries in Roman Catholic circles, spread hardly at all outside them. The missionaries used it to translate the Catechism, the Lives of the Saints, and other improving works; Vietnamese writers, brought up on Chinese, went on using *nôm* until the end of the nineteenth century.

Nôm Adaptations of Chinese Forms. The most successful of these was *phu*, a form taken from Ancient Chinese poetry. It may be subdivided into archaic *phu*, a lengthy poem with rhymes but without contrasting parallelism, and T'ang *phu*, with rhymes and contrasting parallelism—the latter being the form principally cultivated in Vietnam, either in Chinese or in *nôm*. Next to *phu* the forms most highly developed in *nôm* were *kinh nghia* and *van sach*. Originally *kinh nghia* was properly speaking the explanation *(nghia)* of a quotation from the classics *(kinh);* but later the quotations could be drawn from any source, and in the *nôm* versions they are sometimes folk sayings. *Van sach* is a composition *(van)* consisting of replies to an initial thematic question; the replies must be such as to demonstrate intelligence and cleverness *(sach)* on the part of the person replying.

Unquestionably the best-known writer in these forms was the encyclopedist and historian Le Qui Don (1726–1783). He wrote prolifically in Chinese on serious subjects, but also liked writing

[78]

phu, kinh nghia, and *van sach* on lighter topics treated in a playful and humorous vein. From the number of *nôm* works written by him or attributed to him he must have had a great reputation. His favorite subjects were the young woman who has missed her opportunities and will not now get married, and the mother giving advice to her newlywed daughter. Here, for instance, is part of the *phu* of a young woman who has passed marriageable age *(Gai nho thi phu):*

At night, with nothing to do, propped up on my pillow, I meditate in
    my snow-pure heart, and my tears of sadness flow like dew when I
    reflect pityingly on my sad fate.
By day, all alone, I scrutinize my face in the mirror, with its wrinkles
    under the powder. Frail and slender like the weeping willow or the
    plum tree, I bemoan the wreck of my love life.
I remember that in days gone by
My black teeth shone gleaming bright,
And my heavy tresses fell in luxuriant waves;
My silken turban, with its perfect whiteness against the parting of my
    hair, made me look terribly dainty.
My crêpe-de-Chine breastband produced a splash of scarlet on my
    bosom which was the height of elegance.

Le Qui Don's *kinh nghia,* such as *Me oi con muon lay chong* (Mother, I would take a husband) or *Lay chong cho dang tam chong* (When taking a husband, take one worthy of this name), are widely known and form part of the repertoire of popular verse.

For the most part, however, writers of *phu* chose more serious subjects, such as historical themes, descriptions of famous landscapes, or expressions of individual emotions. Some fine scholars, such as Nguyen Ba Lan (1701–1785), Nguyen Huu Chinh (?–1787), Nguyen Huy Luong (eighteenth century) and Pham Thai (1777–1813), gained distinction as writers of *phu*. For instance in *Nga Ba-Hac phu (Phu of the Meeting of the Three Rivers),* Nguyen Ba Lan took as his subject the confluence of the Red River, the Song Da and the Song Lo at Bach Hac, in Tonkin: and in it he paid tribute not only to the beauty of the landscape but also to the peace and prosperity enjoyed in the reign of Trinh Sam (1742–1782).

This type of *phu,* a combination of the aesthetic and the political, is a common feature in the literature of the period. One of the most typical examples is the *phu* by Nguyen Huy Luong entitled *Tung Tay-ho phu* (In Praise of the Western Lake), in which the poet extols both the scenery of the Grand Lac just outside Hanoi and also the government of the Tay Son emperors. This poem, written in 1801, was challenged by the poet Pham Thai (1777–1813), a supporter of the Le and a fierce opponent of the Tay Son: where Nguyen Huy Luong saw prosperity and bliss resulting from ideal government, Pham Thai found nothing but ruin and misery. Pham Thai's poem bears the significant title *Chien tung Tay-ho phu* (Attack on the *phu* "In Praise of the Western Lake").

THE GREAT NÔM MASTERPIECES

In the seventeenth and eighteenth centuries *nôm* made great strides. For one thing, the struggle between the various political factions compelled their leaders to bid for popular support; but since ordinary people could not read Chinese, the only way for the regional authorities to reach them was by using the vernacular written in *nôm.* Again, the Vietnamese had never been backward in national pride, even in the cultural sphere: and they enjoyed improving the literary quality of their language and its ability to express the finer shades of thought and feeling. The literati, when not engaged in their administrative and literary work in Chinese, took increasing pleasure in writing *nôm;* and the success of these compositions was all the more gratifying for them because it extended well beyond the circle of those with a background of Chinese culture. Thus ordinary people played a major part in the recognition of creative ability.

Writers wrote poetry partly to satisfy their own craving for beauty and partly to try out their talents—which they hoped might win them luster in the eyes of their fellow countrymen. The great *nôm* works were all in poetry, some of them long sentimental pieces and others narrative poems. Their subject matter was still taken from, or suggested by, Chinese literature, but its treatment was thoroughly Vietnamese—rather in the way that Racine and Corneille treated classical Greco-Roman themes in a French idiom.

It is impossible here to list all the many *nôm* works. They share a certain romantic and poetic quality and an enchanting tenderness and melancholy which are characteristically Vietnamese; and the best and most moving examples have triumphantly stood the test of time and popular taste. The varying lilt of Vietnamese six-eight or seven-seven-six-eight verse is deeply moving for a Vietnamese, particularly in passages where a halting rhythm produces the effect of stifled sobs: here both reciter and listener may shiver compulsively with sensuous pleasure.

Chinh-phu ngam (Lament of the Warrior's Bride) and *Cung oan ngam khuc* (A Royal Concubine's Complaint: Stanzas) are similar in style. In one a wife laments her husband's absence at the wars; in the other a member of the royal harem complains of being deserted by her Prince. The form known as *ngam* ("to sing verses in a low voice") consists of rhyming stanzas or strophes made up on a six-eight-seven-seven pattern, and must be recited in a plaintive key. It derives from the Chinese *yüeh-fu (nhac-phu)* forms, and the stanzas or strophes are arranged in sets with contrasting parallelism. Many authors have dealt with *Chinh-phu ngam* in *nôm:* no less than six versions were set out by that sound philologist Hoang Xuan Han in his *Chinh-phu ngam bi-khao* (Research on *Chinh-phu ngam*), but they are all translations or adaptations of the Chinese poem by Dang Tran Con (first half of the eighteenth century). The best-known of the adapters were the woman poet Doan Thi Diem (b. 1705) and Phan Huy Ich (1750–1822); and the most effective and unforced rendering, despite some archaisms, is probably Doan Thi Diem's as given

[81]

by Hoang Xuan Han. It keeps very closely to the Chinese text, yet the idiom is thoroughly Vietnamese. Whether the young wife is sorrowfully recalling the trying moments of parting, or describing the anxieties of her lonely state or her pleasure at the thought of her husband's return, her words are always moving because the feelings they convey are simple and sincere. Here, for instance, she dreams of the day when the war will be over and her husband home again:

I shall invite you, husband, to fling off quickly your warlike attire;
On my knees I shall respectfully offer you a cup of lotus spirit.
For you I shall comb my lustrous hair;
For you, morning and evening, jade-hued paint will adorn my face.
I shall show you my veil, soaked in tears from days gone by;
I shall read you the letters in which I told you of my love;
My declarations of bygone days I shall rehearse in new words.
I shall talk to you of the past and the present, tipsy and sober by turns.
Our glasses I shall empty and replenish to the brim.
In a sweet voice I shall sing you melodies combining slow and lively
   rhythms and high and low notes.

(ll. 475–484 of Hoang Xuan Han's Text B)

The other plaintive ballad regarded as a masterpiece in Vietnam is *Cung oan ngam khuc*, by Nguyen Gia Thieu (b. about 1741, d. 1798), who is better known by his title On-nhu hau (Marquis of On-nhu). As in the case of *Chinh-phu ngam*, its inspiration is not to be sought in any particular Chinese text. The theme of deserted royal concubines is common in early Chinese poetry: we find it in Ssuma Hsiang-ju, in Li Po and in the T'ang poets. Suffice it here to mention the "Hundred Palace Songs" *(Kung tz'u po shou)*, by Wang Kien (ninth century), who wrote:

With round fans, with round fans,
The royal concubines come hiding their faces.
It is three years now since their brows with jade were loaded.
Who cares any more about their music, their music, their music?
The path to the Palace of the Rising Sun is overgrown with spring grass.

[82]

The Vietnamese *Cung oan,* an undoubted masterpiece, requires very careful reading if its poetic quality and the subtlety of its literary allusions are to be appreciated. Every word has been weighed, its position calculated and its resonances studied. Probably only a trained scholar can fully savor all the finer points of this text; and one has only to look at editions such as Le Van Hoe's[1] to see the amount of commentary thought necessary for a proper understanding of even a single line. Nevertheless, Nguyen Gia Thieu's fluent and sensitive descriptions of the deserted concubine's inner feelings must strike even the ordinary reader as well-turned. Here, for instance, forgotten by the King,[2] she proudly reminisces on her beauty as a young girl:

I think in my own mind of the beauteous appearance given me by the
   Creator in my youth.
My radiance shone like a young hibiscus-flower
Whose petals had not yet opened in a full-blown smile.
Consider the lady Ban:[3] her beauty was insipid next to mine.
The bloom of my complexion made all the women jealous;
A glance from my eyes, iridescent as autumn pools, stirred up waves
   of passion that would overthrow fortresses.
The moon strained to catch sight of me through my window-blinds,
Not even trees and plants could stay indifferent to my beauty.

Among narrative poems, which tend to be lengthy affairs of 3,000 lines or more in 6-8 meter, *Kim Van Kieu* is regarded as the great national masterpiece; but two earlier works, *Hoa-tien* (The ornate letter) and Phan Tran (Phan and Tran) have also won great renown. They are both love-stories about a young couple in love and the vicissitudes they go through before they are finally united.

Hoa-tien was first published in *quoc-ngu* in 1916, but the *nôm* text dates from the eighteenth century. It is by Nguyen Huy

1. Saigon: Quoc-hoc va Nhan-dan xuat-ban, 1954.
2. Vietnamese critics take the reference to be to Prince Trinh.
3. Pan tsie-yu (Ban tiep du), abandoned favorite of the Han emperor Ch'eng (32–6 B.C.).

Tu (1743–1790), and is adapted from an extant Chinese tale, *Hua-chien chi*. The author's original *nôm* text is earlier than 1790, and was apparently never printed: the *nôm* text we possess was revised by the author's nephew, Nguyen Thien, probably between 1805 and 1809, and also by Vu Dai Van (1829). The work contains some lines that recur in *Kim Van Kieu;* and though the original version is certainly earlier than *Kieu*, the revised version by Nguyen Thien (i.e., our text) could quite well be later. The difficulty of the text as compared with other narrative poems, however, suggests that basically it is earlier.

Phan Tran is by an unknown author. Its inspiration is to be sought either in a play of the Ming period, *Yü-tsan chi* (The jade-headed pin), or in the story of Ch'en Miao-Ch'ang (Tran Dieu Thuong) from the collection entitled "Women of Olden Days and of Today" *(Ku-chin nü-shih—Co kim nu su)*. But as one of us has written elsewhere,

the *Phan Tran* we possess bears little resemblance to the Chinese *Yü-tsan chi*. The imprint of the author's personality and the quality of the craftsmanship make it an original work of far greater artistic appeal than either the Chinese play or the Chinese story; and the attempt to portray universal human emotions both accurately and effectively in a work of fiction is relatively successful. There is no plot to speak of. A young engaged couple meet again and declare their love. Their vicissitudes are by no means romantic or extraordinary, but movement is provided by the evocation of fleeting changes of mood and the subtle interplay of emotions: the reader is drawn into the workings of the lovers' minds, and sympathetically follows their flirtatious exchanges. This is a far cry from the life-and-death adventures of *Kieu*. Time and place cease to matter: for a brief moment we are given a clear and sensitively observed close-up of the awakening of love between two human beings whose future depends entirely on their own reactions. There are many beautiful lines; and though the language is occasionally precious and the imagery sometimes overlaid by literary allusions, the way in which every little fluctuation in the hero's feelings is conveyed is throughout nothing short of masterly.[4]

4. Maurice Durand, *Phan Tran* (Paris: École Française d'Extrême-Orient, 1962).

Phan Tran is like a play by Racine in the sense that there is no action, only soliloquy or dialogue between the two protagonists, interspersed with short linking passages describing their state of mind. Here, for instance, Phan Sinh, the young man, has just failed in his attempt to persuade Tran Dieu Thuong to give up the religious life and respond to his passion:

With a dazed face and a heart filled with turmoil
Phan Sinh paced hesitantly this way and that; he went in and out, irresolute.
The kindly wind gently wafted with it the scent of incense,
And his paroxysms of grief abated: but straightway he started thinking of her again.
The chirping of crickets sounded faintly in his ears,
And the indistinct cackling of cocks and hens reached his lonely heart.
The drum-beats and the sound of cymbals marking the night watch rang out;
With his books in front of him, he was unable to read. His lute stayed hanging in its place; he was in no mood to play it.

(ll.589–596)

VIII: *KIM VAN KIEU*
AND NARRATIVE VERSE

The best-known Vietnamese narrative poem in *nôm* is *Kim Van Kieu,* by Nguyen Du. There have been various French translations of it, the most recent being that published by Gallimard in 1961 in UNESCO's "Connaissance de l'Orient" series. The title of the work is made up of the names of the three main characters, Kim, Van, and Kieu, the last-named (the central figure) being a young woman called Thuy Kieu. The title is consequently often given simply as *Kieu* or "The Story of Thuy Kieu." Kim Trong is Kieu's first love, and Thuy Van is Kieu's sister, who plays a minor role in the story. The original title of the work was *Doan Truong tan thanh* (A Broken Heart, New Version).[1]

The plot of this long poem has been summarized as follows in the new edition of Nguyen Van Vinh's excellent translation (Éditions Alexandre de Rhodes, Hanoi, 1944):

Thuy Kieu, daughter of a humble family of literati, has a presentiment that to expiate the sins of an earlier life, of which we are told nothing, she is doomed to the miserable existence of a courtesan. Despite this, she becomes secretly betrothed to Kim Trong, son of a neighboring family of literati. During a long absence by her fiancé, however, and in order to save her father from debtors' prison, she

1. Literally "Bowels in torment, new style": in other words, the sad story is a revised version of an old one.

agrees to what she supposes to be a marriage for money, and goes off with her husband, Ma Giam-Sinh—first making her younger sister, Thuy Van, promise to marry Kim instead of her when he comes back.

But Ma Giam-Sinh turns out to be a rogue: after his pretence of marriage he puts her in a house of ill fame kept by an old woman called Tu Ba. When she learns the truth, Kieu tries to commit suicide. Recovering, she falls into the clutches of an impostor, So Khanh, who pretends to want to rescue her, but is really out to ruin her for good. Kieu is obliged to give in, so as not to ruin one of her fellow unfortunates who has stood surety for her, and so she takes up the life of a prostitute.

A young man who is a regular client at Tu-Ba's house falls in love with her, and gets her out of the brothel; and after some trouble with her father, and with the law, he takes her as his No.2 wife. Kieu in her honesty urges him to go to his lawful wife and tell her the position; but the lawful wife, Hoan Thu, is a dominating woman, and once he gets there Thuc (whose courage is not his strong point) dares not say anything, but pretends he has merely come on a courtesy call.

Unfortunately as the result of gossip Hoan Thu has already learnt the truth, and urged on by her mother she decides to have her revenge. When Thuc leaves to go back to Kieu, she sends a gang of ruffians on ahead of him to kidnap Kieu and bring her back to her. They also burn down Thuc's house, and he, thinking his loved one dead, goes back to his wife—to find Kieu there, made into a serving-maid by Hoan Thu. Thuc has not the courage to stick up for the poor girl, but eventually her sweet nature disarms her mistress, and she is given leave to withdraw to a small pagoda belonging to the family. But Hoan Thu is perennially jealous of her, and spies on her; and worried by this she runs away and takes refuge in a Buddhist nunnery run by the priestess Giac Duyen—who for safety's sake (as she supposes) entrusts her to the care of an old nun called Bac Ba.

Alas! Kieu's luck is out, and she is caught up in another cycle of horrors. Bac Ba is an old trickster, and marries Kieu off to her nephew: he turns out to be another Ma Giam-Sinh, and puts the poor girl in a brothel. Once again she takes the eye of a client, a soldier of fortune by the name of Tu Hai, who gets her out of it. Later, returning from a warring campaign triumphant and master of the country, Tu Hai marries Kieu and has his erstwhile enemies ferreted out and put to death.

But Kieu is tormented by the thought that Tu Hai is in rebellion against the Emperor, and begs him to submit. He agrees: the Imperial envoy then has him assassinated, and gives Kieu in marriage to a *tho* mandarin. The poor girl throws herself into the Tsien-tang River and is taken for dead.

In fact, however, the priestess Giac Duyen, warned in the nick of time by a poetess, has once again rescued her and taken her in; and she is finally reunited in a temple with her erstwhile sweetheart Kim, now married to Thuy Van, and all her family. Kim insists that she shall become his lawful wife, to which she agrees, Van remaining his No. 2 wife. From that moment the sins of her earlier lives are expiated, and Kieu and Kim live happily together: but the couple agree to keep their relationship platonic.

As will be seen, the theme is not particularly original: indeed, it is highly reminiscent of a Chinese story called *Chin yün ch'iao chuan* (The Tale of Kim, Van, and Kieu), by an author known only by his pen name, Thanh tam tai nhan.[2] This probably dates from the late sixteenth century; it was commented on in the seventeenth by a noted publicist, Kin Ch'eng t'an (Kim Thanh Than).[3] It is in prose, and is poor stuff compared with Nguyen Du's verse adaptation.

The *nôm* text of the Vietnamese poem runs to more than 3,000 verses; and though the content has given rise to much controversy, there has always been agreement among critics that in beauty of form it has few rivals.

As regards the content there are differing views. One, widely held, is that Kieu represents a pathological case. Based on the heroine of a Chinese adventure story, she appears as a spineless creature with lax morals, ready to be led from one promiscuous relationship to another. Hence it is awkward and embarrassing to regard her as typifying Vietnamese womanhood, or the work itself as the pinnacle of Vietnamese literature. It is

2. *Tai nhan* is a little puzzling. The expression was used in China to denote both an official rank among the Imperial concubines and also "man," person of talent. *Thanh tam* is "tender heart, youthful heart, kind heart." A Vietnamese version of *Kim Van Kieu truyen* has been compiled by Nguyen Duy Ngung and Vu Dinh Long (Hanoi, 1928).

3. Known for his many novels, including *Shui hu (Thuy hu)* and *Hsi-hsiang chi (Tay suong ky)*, and also for a classification of literary masterpieces.

in no sense the life story of a national hero or heroine, and makes no appeal to patriotic tradition or religious feeling. *Kieu* has always been frowned on by the Emperors and by orthodox Confucians—for whom moral respectability is the cornerstone of a stable and well-ordered society and literature a source of moral guidance, not simply of amusement.

Some Marxists interpret the work as nothing but a vestige of feudalism: Kieu is a neurotic creature sinking lower and lower at every step—a victim of the rottenness of the social system of her day. She ends up in a state of confusion and depression in which she passively accepts whatever comes her way. Her behavior is occasionally egotistical and opportunist.

Admirers of the work, on the other hand, base their arguments on a somewhat deeper and more careful analysis of the characterization. Kieu epitomizes the virtues extolled in the ancient Confucian code of morality rooted inter alia in filial piety: though in love with Kim (and destined eventually to become his chaste platonic wife), she sacrifices both love and chastity to save her father, and becomes unwillingly involved in one liaison after another. In her heart she always loves Kim, and hopes one day to be reunited with him. Her character is complex, but kind-heartedness and loyalty are uppermost in it. She is capable of forgiving those who hurt her and of being grateful to those who are kind to her. After marrying the rebel general Tu Hai she has an opportunity to punish Thuc Sinh's wife Hoan Thu, who had tormented and humiliated her, but she forgives her:

The principal culprit brought in was one Hoan Thu.
Upon her arrival Kieu greeted her and said:
"So you too must enter an appearance here today.
Few indeed among women are cruel as you."
Kieu complimented her: "Truly you have deserved the saying
'A good brain and a wise tongue.'
If I spared you, that would be a piece of luck for you.
But if I punished you, that would be mean of me.
So seeing that you have confessed your misdeeds, let it be."

[89]

With these words she ordered her to be released straightway.
Hoan Thu, her heart full of gratitude, prostrated herself before the
  cloud-bedecked court.

(v. 2356 ff.)

At the end of the poem, when Kim and Kieu are reunited, he
realizes how loyal she has been to him:

The limpid mirror of your heart is for me still innocent of all stain.

(v. 3173)

Throughout the poem, the picture of Kieu utterly debauched,
tormented by evil men and women, and debased or self-abas-
ing—all this only serves to emphasize her pureness of heart, as
with a spotless lotus flower growing out of the depths of the
mire.

The divergence of views outlined above led to a controversy
among Vietnamese writers and intellectuals which soon spread
from the literary to the political sphere, becoming increasingly
bitter after World War I. It sprang from the highly favorable
attitude to *Kieu* adopted by the staff of the periodical *Nam Phong*
(1917–1934), led by Pham Quynh—a group of nationalist reformers whose object was the rebirth of Vietnam by peaceful
means under French tutelage. They aimed to use *Kieu* to demonstrate that the Vietnamese language was capable of producing masterpieces to rival those of any other country; that there
was such a thing as Vietnamese, as distinct from purely Chinese,
literature; and that Vietnam had a personality of its own—which
it would display in the cultural field until such time as its progress in Western science won for it the technological and political independence appropriate to its more advanced status. Pham
Quynh wrote in an article, "Études classiques sino-annamites":

When people laugh and say that we Vietnamese have no literature, then
recite Nguyen Du's poetry to them (you all know it by heart), or Nguyen

Cong Tru's, or Ho Xuan Huong's; and ask them how many countries in the world can boast a literature containing such a wealth of splendid expressive verse, in which such diversity and depth of feeling are put into such perfection of poetic form.

Nam Phong's campaign on behalf of *Kieu,* and Pham Quynh's statement "While 'The Story of Kieu' endures, our language will endure, and while our language endures, our country will endure,"[4] started an unprecedented craze for the poem. Newspapers and periodicals were full of praise for the work, arguments in its favor, and adaptations and commentaries on it. School editions, critical essays, and dramatic versions all helped to make it known to a wider public. *Kieu* was to come to be regarded as the embodiment of the national spirit *(quoc hon),* as the sacred book and the gospel of Vietnam.[5]

The main opposition to Pham Quynh and his supporters came from those Confucians, such as Ngo Duc Ke and Huynh Thuc Khang, who took a hard line on the content of the poem. Also, as progressive nationalists, they disliked the spectacle of Pham Quynh and *Nam Phong* successfully influencing the young towards romance and resignation rather than towards innovation and modernism.

All these views, even those diametrically opposed to one another, can be defended on the basis of internal evidence—which goes to show the complexity of the protagonist's character (it is not even clear whether she should be called the heroine or the villain). What is certain is that no Vietnamese can read *Kieu* without experiencing true aesthetic pleasure, and sometimes an absolutely magical thrill. One scholarly emperor, Minh Menh, enjoyed recitations from *Kieu* in the company of a Confucian mandarin, Ha Ton Quyen (1798–1839); and another, Tu Duc,

---

4. *Truyen Kieu con, tieng ta con; tieng ta con, nuoc ta con* (Nguyen Du birthday celebrations at AFIMA, Hanoi, 1924).
5. Nguyen Bach-Khoa, *Van-chuong truyen Kieu, nguyen-tac phe-binh* (Writings on *The Story of Kieu:* Critical Principles): Tap-chi, Van moi, phan khao cuu so 50, January 25, 1945, 202 pp. (Hanoi: Han Thuyen).

declared that he was "mad on the horse Hau Bo and the *nôm* of Thuy Kieu."[6]

Vietnamese critics educated in Europe are unanimous as to the beauty of the poem; they reject the moralistic objections on the principle of "art for art's sake," opining that *Kieu* is a work of manifold and superlative artistic merits. In his book *Khao luan ve Kim Van Kieu* (Essay on *Kim Van Kieu*), Dao Duy-Anh wrote "We love 'The Story of Kieu' not because it points a moral but also because we find Nguyen Du's marvelous style so moving." The nuances of the writing are the essence of Nguyen Du's artistry. It is full of indirect suggestions with touchingly sensitive and gently melancholy associations. Reading his poem, we feel ourselves so closely in tune with the writer that we relive all his characters' shifting moods and trains of thought. They move in a world of his creation, centered around a heroine from a Chinese story with whom he evidently felt such sympathy that the expression of his own feelings enabled him to bring her vividly to life.

According to the biographers Nguyen Du was a shy, gentle person. In his official duties he was obsequious to his superiors, and seemed downcast and unhappy. In the Emperor's presence he was overwhelmed and tongue-tied. The emperor Minh Menh thought very highly of him, and is reported to have said to him:

The Government employs men selected solely for their ability, without discriminating between Northerners and Southerners. You know that I am well-disposed to you: but a man who has reached the rank of Deputy Minister, if he is to do his job properly, should express his views, and not be perpetually hesitant and shy and say nothing but "Quite so."

Nguyen Du's timid exterior hid a proud and fiercely independent spirit. He loved Nature and solitude. He refused to serve the Tay Son, remaining loyal to the Le. His character combined some of the traits of the French romantics: he had Chateaubriand's pride and touchiness, Lamartine's gentleness, and Alfred

---

6. *Me ngua Hau-bo, me nôm Thuy-Kieu.*

de Vigny's tendency to self-denial. In the end when he fell ill he did not look after himself, and died uncomplaining. He had gone through life lost in an imaginary world—a world which he depicted in a masterpiece consisting of a timeless theme conveyed with incomparable artistry.

Scholars, writers, statesmen, intellectuals, women, the common people—*Kieu*'s merits endeared it to everyone. Sentiment, love-interest, adventure, romance, deeds of valor, religion—it has them all. The complexity and contradictions of the human character, with all its nobility and its cowardice, also make it a fascinating study in psychology. But it is the quality of Nguyen Du's writing that remains the key to his preeminence. The scholars of the early nineteenth century praised his skill as a narrator and the perfection of his descriptions of landscapes—which they admired without analyzing them in detail. It seems to us that what distinguishes Nguyen Du's descriptions is above all their poetic quality. He has a feeling for evocative imagery, and a genius for bringing out the essential symbolism of a scene and relating it to a character's state of mind. The following passage, for example, occurs at the end of the day on which Kieu sees the ghost of the singer Dam Tien and meets her with Kim at the festival of Pure Brilliance (Thanh-Minh). Kieu returns to her apartment and goes over in her mind the events of the day:

Kieu was back indoors again within her flowered curtains;
The sun had set behind the mountains, and the sentries' gongs had
　　sounded the ending of the day.
The moon peeped slantwise through the windows,
And strewed specks of gold on the rippling water. The trees covered
　　the courtyard with their shadows.
A crimson camellia drooped its drowsy branches at the eastern end.
A heavy dew was falling, and the boughs of the spring trees hung down
　　to the ground.

　　(from v. 171–176 of Nguyen Van Vinh's translation, new edition).

Here the onset of darkness, the rising of the moon, and the drooping flowers and trees all combine to bring gloomy thoughts into Kieu's mind.

The appealing and reputedly indefinable charm of *Kieu* lies essentially in the musical quality of the poetry. It is really a tone poem, to be chanted now slowly in a choking voice, now sharply with halting gasps. Every word has both a meaning and a tone quality. Nguyen Du most cleverly and lovingly exploits the expressive lilting character of Vietnamese; he enchants the reader with a sequential development of melodic recitatif in which meaning, imagery, symbolism, and music are inextricably interwoven. The difference between *Kieu* and the other narrative poems is that they are more stories while *Kieu* is more a poem. The charm of *Kieu* for a Vietnamese is something like that of Joseph Bédier's adaptation of *Tristan and Iseult* for a European reader.

IX: THE NINETEENTH CENTURY

GROWTH OF NARRATIVE VERSE

Kim Van Kieu, written at the beginning of the nineteenth century, may be regarded as the connecting link between ancient and modern *nôm* poetry. It is the undisputed masterpiece among narrative poems, and marks the beginning of a plethora of such works which make up the bulk of Vietnamese six-eight verse. A mass of them were to appear in this century, the best known (or the most publicized) being *So kinh tan trang, Nhi do mai, Luc Van Tien, Ly-cong truyen, Pham-cong Cuc-hoa, Hoang Tru,* and *Ngoc-Hoa.* A few are readable, even charming: but many are very dull. Bad folk literature is poor stuff indeed: obscure, confused, full of incessant tedious repetition, and written in a deplorable style. Of all the mass of *luc-bat* (six-eight) narrative poems and stories, those listed above, plus perhaps a few others, are of value and have achieved deserved fame in Vietnam. Several have found a place among the set books in school syllabuses.

So kinh tan trang, which slightly antedates *Kim Van Kieu,* is reckoned the first major piece of romantic writing in Vietnamese literature. It is a thinly disguised account of the love affair between the author, Pham Thai (1777–1813) and Truong Quynh-Nhu. Thus it is a personal statement; and it also represents a break with tradition in that it points no moral, but merely portrays Vietnamese life at the time. Its descriptions, again, are of scenes familiar to all: the Hung Vuong and Kim-Son Pagodas, Mount Yen-tu, the Do-son country, etc.

Nhi do mai (Plum-trees in Blossom Again) is an adaptation of the Chinese work of the same name *(Erh tu mei)*. The story centers around a Chinese historical figure, Lü Ch'i, a minister in the time of the T'ang emperor Teh-tsung (780–805) who was renowned for his cruelty, cunning, and turpitude. It traces the rise and fall of one family; and among the subplots we find the murder of a loyal mandarin for attempting to expose tyrannical ministers, the close friendship uniting two families, mutual affection between masters and servants and between friends, an ill-assorted marriage, and the union of a pair of lovers after the young man passes his Third Degree examinations.

Luc Van Tien (named after its hero) is by the great Cochin-Chinese poet Nguyen Dinh Chieu (1822–1888), whose reputation rests as much on his patriotism as on his literary ability. His dignified but unyielding attitude to the French occupation won him the admiration, indeed the veneration, of intellectuals and the common people. The French themselves paid tribute to his high-mindedness, and helped to give currency to his poem; French translations of *Luc Van Tien* appeared from the earliest years of the French presence in Cochin-China. The story has everything: warlike adventures, witchcraft, vivid descriptions, love-interest, human emotion, and melodrama, so that it caters for all tastes. But its most interesting feature is that though much of the incident is based on Chinese models, the author's life and character are clearly to be discerned in it. Nguyen Dinh Chieu, like Luc Van Tien, had to withdraw from the Third Degree examinations and return to his village to nurse his sick mother; like Luc Van Tien, he went blind; and like the innkeeper in the poem he preached noncollaboration with the authorities (the T'ang minister in the poem represents the French occupation):

The innkeeper replied: "In olden days the emperors Nghieu[1] and Thuan[2]

1. Yao (2356–2255 B.C.).
2. Shun (2255–2205 B.C.).

Could not induce either Sao Phu[3] or Hua Do[4] to accept the throne.
Di[5] and Te[6] refused to serve the Chou,
And scorning all preferment were content to live in seclusion in the
hills.
Likewise Y[7] and Pho,[8] men of high distinction,
Calmly engaged in tilling the soil, with never another thought in their
minds.
Thai Cong,[9] with his fishing line as sole companion,
Enjoyed and amused himself from morn to night on the river Vi.
Nghiem-Lang,[10] likewise a man of great gifts,
Wore a simple coat of leaves and was content to live quietly by his fish
hook.
Tran Doan[11] was a man of superhuman intellect;
Yet he spent his life jesting with the wind and the moon, reckoning
pleasures and honors as but dreams.
Men today are no different from those of olden days:
If they wish to be in public life, no one stops them; if they choose to
retire from it, no one prevents them."

In *Ly-cong truyen* (The Story of Ly-cong) the protagonists are
Ly-cong and the princess Bach-Hoa, whose love affair with Ly-
cong is by far the most passionate of any heroine in a *nôm* poem.
It flouts all the conventions. She is a princess, the man she loves
a beggar, yet she bids him visit her regularly in secret at the

3. Ch'ao Fu lived in retirement in the woods during the emperor Yao's reign.
4. Hsü-yü; when offered the throne by the emperor Yao, he refused, and went
and washed out his ears in a running stream. When his friend Ch'ao Fu heard
of this, he drove the cattle he was herding upstream of the point where Hsü-
yü had washed out his ears, so that they might not drink tainted water.
5. I.e., Po Yi (Ba Di).
6. I.e., Shu-ch'i. Yi and Ch'i chose to live in retirement in the hills rather than
serve the Chou emperor Wu-wang.
7. Yi Yin (Y Doan), minister to the first Shang emperor, Sheng T'ang (Thanh
Thang).
8. Fu Yüeh (Pho Duyet), minister to the Yin emperor Wu Ting.
9. Liu Shang (La Thuong) or Chiang Tzu-ya (Khuong Tu-Nha), who was fishing in a tributary of the Wei (Vi) when the Chou emperor Wen-wang found
him and made him his minister.
10. Yen Kuang Tsu-ling (Nghiem Quang Tu-lang), minister to Han Kuang Wu-
ti (A.D. 25–38). In his retirement he used to enjoy fishing in the rapids of the
Che-chiang.
11. Ch'en T'uan retired very young into the Hu-pei mountains, and lived there
for twenty years, devoting himself to poetry and Taoist rites.

Palace; she refuses to give in to her father, and prefers banishment and death to the renunciation of her love—thus infringing the Confucian code of filial obedience; and rather than be unfaithful to Ly-cong she suffers atrocious mutilation at the hands of the Hsiung-nu.

Pham-cong Cuc-hoa (Pham-cong and Cuc-hoa), *Ngoc-Hoa,* and *Hoang Tru* are stories of passionate love between married couples or young people. In content and plot development there is great similarity between them all.

Many of the tales and stories in *luc-bat* verse set out to point morals. In *Nguyen-Dat Nguyen-Sinh,* for instance, the two brothers Nguyen Dat and Nguyen Sinh work hard and well, and in the end pass the state examinations and marry two virtuous and beautiful girls. In *Tuyen phu ngo phoi tan truyen* (Story of a Mistake in the Choice of a Husband) the author portrays the sins of arrogance and pride in a young woman who spurns all her educated, well-born suitors; in the end she is hoodwinked into marrying a rich ignoramus. *Luu-Binh Duong-Le* is a study of an ideal friendship, by Confucian standards, between two men, Luu Binh and Duong Le.

THE POETESS HO XUAN HUONG

This nineteenth-century poetess is a mysterious figure about whom no information is available apart from internal evidence. She was an educated Vietnamese woman, and the features of her work are its skilful composition and its daring crudeness. There are generally two meanings, an unexceptionable literal one and a highly obscene hidden one. The result is that her poems are sometimes used in schools as material for textual analysis—and sometimes banned as pornographic. Of the literati who knew her, only one has been identified: Chieu Ho may be the great scholar of the late Le and early Nguyen period, Pham Dinh Ho (1768–1839); but even this identification is tenuous, resting as it does on nothing but the common factor in the two names. Pham Dinh Ho, author of *Vu trung tuy but* (With a Paintbrush in Wet Weather) seems anyway to have been a person of staid disposition, which is hardly consistent with Chieu Ho's abandoned behavior.

Be that as it may, Ho Xuan Huong's poems are so effortless in construction, so simple and spontaneous, that they rank as the most charming in Vietnamese. At the same time her daring has won her a reputation as an early feminist. She preaches free love, equality of the sexes, and the cause of unmarried mothers; she derides social conventions, ignorant scholars and high officials, and impious monks. Her poems contain virtually no Chinese literary allusions, being essentially Vietnamese in inspiration and form; some are reminiscent of snatches from popular ballads *(ca dao)*, or give the impression of aphorisms or familiar quotations. Most of them are known and recited among all sections of Vietnamese society. Appreciation of her work is partly, of course, a matter of salacious relish—but also of pride in the richness and originality of her genius.

The two examples that follow give an idea of Ho Xuan Huong's work. In the first poem she likens herself to a *banh troi nuoc,* a kind of small Vietnamese sweetmeat consisting of a red sugar center encased in an outer coating of white paste made of glutinous rice. It is round, rather like a small bird's egg; and a number of them are served at a time in a bowl of syrup. The little floating sweet represents the woman who remains pure at heart despite having to endure intercourse with men—as the red sugar center remains independent of the shape imparted to the outer coating:

> My body is white, in shape I am rounded;
> Sometimes I float on the surface, sometimes I am under water.
> Large or small, the hand that molded me matters little:
> I shall always preserve my vermilion heart.

A third interpretation that will occur to the astute reader is that the little sweet symbolizes female sexuality unimpaired by repeated intercourse with men.

In the second poem the obscene double meaning is more obvious. The poetess suggests the sexual act through a description of the working of a loom, in which the shuttle represents the male organ and the web the female:

Night Weaving

When the wick of the lamp is up, everything is all white.
The shuttle flying continually all night penetrates the cloth.
The feet keep pushing down and gently letting up again.
At a stroke the shuttle shoots through, in ecstasy at its own speed.
Broad or narrow, large or small, anything will suit it;
Short or long, the shape is always the same.
The weaver-girl who wants to do a good job leaves in soak a long time;
She waits three autumns before showing its color.

Here there is continual play on words. For example, the explanation of "three autumns" is that *thu,* "autumn," when written with another character, also means "joining together, gathering in, receiving."

OTHER GREAT NÔM POETS OF THE NINETEENTH CENTURY

Many names come to mind, and we shall confine ourselves to the best known. The use of *nôm* reached its peak in the second half of the century: by then Vietnamese was richer and free of Chinese influence—ready to take shape as *quoc-ngu,* spread among all social classes, and receive an influx of Western ideas and terminology. Towards the end of the century *nôm* gradually gave way to *quoc-ngu,* and by the beginning of the twentieth century it was obsolete.

Those writing at the time were principally poets. Let us begin with a poetess, Ba huyen Thanh quan, who was probably a contemporary of Ho Xuan Huong, though an entirely different kind of writer. Her name means "wife of the subprefect of Thanh-quan," from the post her husband held. Little is known about

[100]

her except that she was the daughter of Nguyen Ly (1755–1837), a mandarin in Education in the late Le period, and that she married Luu Nghi, a mandarin from Ha-dong province, North Vietnam, who was subprefect of Thanh-quan in Thai-binh province. Her poetry is earnest, painstaking, and dignified, characterized by lofty sentiments and restrained melancholy; a favorite theme is the familiar landscapes of Vietnam, which evoke in her sorrow at the passing of time and nostalgia for the past and the brilliance of the Le era. One of her most characteristic poems is "Memories of Old Thang Long":

Why has the Creator brought about changes of scene such as take place
    on the stage?
Until now, numberless years have gone swiftly by.
The aura of autumn grass seems to hang over the old lanes, where
    horses and carts once passed;
The glow of the setting sun moves sadly over what were once build-
    ings and palaces.
Though the stones ever impassively endure the test of months and years,
The water still seems to be frowning at the vicissitudes of life.
Like a millennial mirror, the history of bygone centuries reflects pre-
    sent and past events.
At this spectacle I am profoundly grieved.

(from the translation by Duong Quang Ham)

Nguyen Cong Tru (1778–1858) was a high mandarin and a great scholar, and had a brilliant and eventful career. Both by inclination and from loyalty to the monarchy he was opposed to all innovation, and belonged to the Conservatives (*bao-thu*) who set their faces against the reform movement born of contact with the West (the *canh-tan* movement). In the artistic sphere he was known for his fondness for women's songs, and also as an able composer of them: some collections in *nôm* have survived. He is one of a line of statesmen-poets, like Nguyen Trai and Nguyen Binh Khiem before him. Having undergone many vicissitudes, and had experience of human nature and the insecurity of high office, he is particularly appreciative of the pleasure and solace of *otium* and of communion with nature:

I am weary of elbowing my way along the path to glory and profit.
I delight in the company of chrysanthemums and pine trees, of the wind and the moon.
I allowed myself to put a foot inside the circle of the madding crowd
And when I suddenly think of it, I shudder indescribably.

In contrast to Nguyen Cong Tru, Cao Ba-Quat (?–1854) seems to have been an ambitious, turbulent person, highly receptive to new ideas. He came of a poor family, but made a name for himself at an early age by his literary gifts. In 1831 he passed the provincial examinations, but never succeeded in gaining his Third Degree. Despite this, he was regarded as one of the most notable literati of his time. He entered the civil service, was provincial governor in Bac-ninh, and went as a member of a Vietnamese delegation to Singapore: here he came across manifestations of Western material civilization such as electric light, cameras, cars, submarines, etc., and realized that literary examinations were out of date as a basis for education in Southeast Asia and that his countrymen needed to revise their ideas and adopt new aims. Cao Ba-Quat was very conceited and waggish, fond of poking fun at men in high places. He was transferred to a post in Quoc-oai prefecture, Son Tay Province, where he was bored to death. He then allowed himself to be caught up in Le Duy-Cu's revolt against the Hué court, and was captured and executed. He remained scornful and sardonic to the last:

Three rolls of the drum, and the strumpet Destiny will be fulfilled;
One stroke of the sword, and the whore Life will be gone.

From his pen we have many anthologies in Chinese, a few *nôm* poems, some parallel sentences, and one *phu, Tai tu da cung phu* (*Phu* of the Gifted Man Sunk in Abject Poverty) which well illustrates all his traits—intelligence, conceit, ambition, and sardonic humor:

The waves of human passion rise and fall; worldly things are as transitory as passing clouds;

Men greedy for gain are shackled and hamstrung: wearing winged hats, they are at the beck and call of mandarins; encased in armor, they wear out their knees at the ministers' court.

You need the knack of being obsequious to your superiors and ingratiating to everyone else.

Is the smell of the fleshpots so greatly preferable? For to strive for the fragrance of good reputation and merit entails much suffering.

• • •

I am weary of my abasement; glory gladdens my heart; when out of luck a man endures a myriad bitternesses, whereas when well off all is pleasure for him.

So let the world heed this injunction in homely language: when you see a white face, do not laugh and say "A gifted man in desperate straits."

All that is known of Cao Ba-Quat's nephew Cao Ba-Nha is that he was born and lived in the reign of Tu-Duc (1848–1883). He too wrote some fine *nôm* poetry, giving vent to fiery feelings and the bitterness of a man unjustly persecuted by the authorities. For when his uncle was arrested and put to death, together with his two sons, Cao Ba-Nha's father Cao Ba-Dat was also arrested, and committed suicide. Nha managed to escape and go into hiding under an assumed name in Ha-dong, where he married and had two daughters; but some eight years later he also was arrested after being informed upon, and was imprisoned and exiled to the Highlands, where he eventually died. During his captivity he wrote *Tran tinh van* (Statement of My Feelings) in Chinese, appealing to the Hué court for justice and clemency, and *Tu tinh khuc* (Confession) in *nôm*, running to 608 lines of 7-7-6-8 verse, to similar effect. In them he avowed his loyalty to the monarchy, and begged the Emperor for mercy. His protestations had no effect on the Court, and he died in captivity—though nothing is known of the manner of his death. To express one's views in the form of a direct confession, as he did, represents something of a new departure in Vietnamese literature. He attempts to mollify the Court by adducing all manner of grounds for the grant of a free pardon, yet frames a fierce indictment of the tyrannical despotism of the régime for enforcing its arbitrary whims and compelling public approval—which must be intended mainly for the benefit of posterity. His ironical comment on the Hué court, "It will have horse thought stag, as in a game," is an allusion to the Chinese emperor Ch'in-Shih-huang-ti, who made people say a horse was a stag on pain of being beheaded.

A poet soured with life and endowed with a mordant wit was Tran Te Xuong, commonly known as *ong Tu* Xuong ("Xuong of the First Degree"). Having failed the examinations for the Second Degree, he lived a frustrated and miserable life. He was a disapproving observer of the French occupation of North Vietnam, and could not repress his fierce criticism of all those of his countrymen who for one reason or another collaborated with the occupying power. He poked fun at everything and everybody, and especially at himself. His writing is fluent, with unexpected puns and witticisms, and brings to life for us a period in which the Vietnamese way of life was being influenced by French civilization. Many of his poems were extemporized, and have an appealing simplicity and naturalness. Here, for instance, is an autographical thumbnail sketch from the piece entitled "Lamentations on my lot":

Here I am, already over thirty.
I sit and think about my wretched self:
I have sat the Second Degree examinations several times and had no
    success at all;
I had three strips of untilled allotment, and I have sold them all;
I buy rice for my family from one meal to the next, in the usual way;
My wife, as is her wont, has two children in the space of a year;
I should like to climb up a ladder and ask Heaven
Whether it intends to go on tormenting people like this.

(from the translation by Duong Quang Ham)

Nguyen Khuyen (1835–1909) was the last great *nôm* poet of the nineteenth century, and perhaps the greatest. He is commonly known as Yen-do, from the name of his native village in Ha-nam Province, or as Tam-nguyen Yen-do, from the fact that he came in first three times—in the Second Degree, the Third Degree, and the special Palace examinations. He too refused to collaborate with the French authorities of the Tonkin Protectorate; but his poetry is on the whole nonpolitical. It is emotional, and exemplifies the increasing personalization and introspection of Vietnamese poetry. He was a versatile writer, and treated all the poetic themes current in his day. There are many occasional pieces marking events such as a flood, the New Year festival, the topping-out of a new house, or visits from friends; also descriptions of his poverty-stricken existence, messages to friends, and so on. But the main feature of his work is a pervasive melancholy born of meek submissiveness to life and fate, and especially to the increasing depredations of old age. His delicacy of feeling is illustrated in poems such as "Visit from a friend," in which he evinces sober and restrained pleasure at having one of his friends to stay, even though in his penury he has nothing nice to offer him:

After not seeing you for so long, here you are now under my roof.
But my wife and children are away, and the market is far distant.
My pond is deep and the water wide: it is hard to catch fish in it with a cast-net.
My garden is large and the boundary hedges far apart: it is not easy to catch chickens in it.
My cabbages have not yet sprouted from their stalks, and my eggplants still have no buds on them;
My squashes have just lost their "umbilical cords," and my cucumbers are in flower.
Even betel—the first thing one offers to visitors—have I none.
But you have come to see me, and we are together.

(from the translation by Duong Quang Ham)

Yen-do can also employ irony and satire, and be witty at his own and other people's expense. In this poem, for instance, he gently pokes fun at a plain girl who sets out to be seductive:

From what family is this all too lovely girl?
Her neck is slim—with a triple crease in it, like a tortoise's;
Her hair is lustrous—shaped like a moorhen's tail;
Her lips are dazzlingly red—like a chicken's anus.
Her speech is gentle—like the bark of a vicious dog;
Her walk is graceful—like an old elephant's;
When she ogles me, I go all a-tremble with terror.
From what family is this all too lovely girl?

Finally, on the subject of old age, a poem written to mark his seventy-fourth birthday is a good illustration of his meekness and honesty:

This year I am seventy-four:
To be called old, or a mandarin, I do not mind.
In happy moments I take a few cups of wine to boot;
At sad times I recite, after a fashion, some lines of poetry.
Of the old friends of yore, how many are still left?
Of the old stories, nine out of ten were not to my liking.
I should like to live another few years
To see whether the world is still the same.

X: THE TWENTIETH
CENTURY

It is no exaggeration to say that in the period 1900–1975 Vietnamese literature reached heights unequalled in all its history. This flowering was no doubt due to a combination of factors—political, economic and social; but the most important single cause was the introduction of *quoc-ngu* (the system of writing literary and colloquial Vietnamese in the Roman alphabet). It slowly but surely superseded the *nôm* system of transliteration in Chinese characters, which had always been cumbrous to use—indeed, it was not officially recognized by the majority of emperors. But if *quoc-ngu* ushered in a new era in Vietnamese literature, it is because politically the situation was opportune. The French had only recently established themselves in Vietnam (1862, for most historians, marks the end of Vietnamese independence and the beginning of the colonial period); and with the French occupation of the whole of Indochina Western civilization burst with shattering impact into a world long closed to it. The conflict between the two cultures, Chinese and French, was soon to come out into the open and have unforeseen repercussions on literature and politics. Vietnamese literature had acquired respectability in the eighteenth and early nineteenth centuries; the introduction of *quoc-ngu* was to prove a powerful rejuvenating force and trigger off a brilliant revival which has lasted to the present day.

Thus 1862 and the establishment of the French presence in Indochina mark the beginning of the modern period in Vietnamese literature. During the century that followed it made good, if sometimes erratic, progress. Poetry and the novel alternated as the dominant art form, depending on the political situation and various social upheavals; for the period in question covers two world wars, the fall of the Nguyen dynasty, the abdication of the emperor Bao-Dai, the August 1945 revolution, the first and second Indochina wars, and the 1954 Geneva agreements. Under the latter the country was split into two halves, North and South—a repetition of the situation in the eighteenth century, but in far more tragic circumstances—and it was not until 1975 that the two halves were reunited.

The development of Vietnamese literature and the changes in both form and content which it underwent during this hundred-odd years represent salient features in the transformation of Southeast Asia. With *quoc-ngu* as its medium, it made a great leap forward: not only were long-stagnant forms revitalized but new ones came into being under the stimulus of the West, such as journalism, the documentary, the realist novel, and literary criticism.

This hundred-odd years (1862–1975) may be subdivided into ten main periods on the strength of historical landmarks and certain seminal publications—by no means the only possible classification, but a convenient one for practical purposes. The beginning and end of the period are not mere random dates. The year 1862 marks the loss of the country's independence, the discrediting of the absolute rule of the Nguyen, and the retreat of the Vietnamese, as of most other Asian peoples, before Western materialism and mechanization. The year 1975 marks the reunification of the country and the withdrawal of all foreign forces.

SYNOPTIC TABLE OF
MODERN VIETNAMESE LITERATURE

First period (1862–1906): introduction of *quoc-ngu* and decline of *nôm*. Three main trends, one romantic, one patriotic, and one consisting of *quoc-ngu* translations of Chinese and French classics.

Second period (1906–13): the *Dong-kinh nghia-thuc* movement; influence of French and Chinese literature.

Third period (1913–30): rapid development of journalism; spread of French culture through the medium of *quoc-ngu;* decline of traditional poetry; the periodicals *Dong-duong tap-chi* and *Nam Phong;* romanticism.

Fourth period (1930–35): lightning growth of journalism; emergence of the "New Poetry" and the *Tu-luc van doan* group; essays and documentaries; rapid development of the novel.

Fifth period (1935–39): the Popular Front in France; zenith of *Tu-luc van doan;* triumph of the New Poetry; birth of the realist novel, and flowering of various other types of prose fiction.

Sixth period (1939–45): decline of *Tu-luc van doan;* development of the realist novel; birth of Marxist literature; reversion to antiquity; the *Han Thuyen, Xuan thu nha tap, Tri tan,* and *Thanh nghi* groups.

Seventh period (1945–6): development of Marxist literature and emergence of "Socialist realism."

Eighth period (1946–54): two trends, Socialist literature and "marking time" literature.

Ninth period (1954–62): the Geneva agreements and the partition of Vietnam; realism in the North, miscellaneous activity in the South.

Tenth period (1963–75): Second Indochina war: "resistance" literature in the North, various trends in the South.

FIRST PERIOD (1862–1906)

In 1862 the conquest of Indochina began. The French had complete mastery, and foiled all attempts at revolt organized by the Confucian literati. Most sensible intellectuals, both literati of the old school and early French-speakers, realized that the country's future depended on the spread of *quoc-ngu:* the road to independence lay in learning from the West, using French as the key to European technology. Cochin-China (present-day South Vietnam) having been occupied first, it was there that Vietnamese literature in *quoc-ngu* had its first successes. The two

Vietnamese scholars who did most to encourage the spread of *quoc-ngu* were Paulus Cua (1834–1907) and Petrus Truong Vinh Ky (1837–1898).[1] Both were Catholics, equipped with classical Chinese, Vietnamese, and French, and both had the same object in view: the spread of *quoc-ngu* and the gradual phasing-out of Chinese.

Paulus Cua was one of the founders of Vietnamese journalism, and in 1865 started the very first newspaper, *Gia-dinh bao* (Gia-dinh Province News). He wrote books of folklore and fairy tales, and also a large Vietnamese dictionary in two volumes, *Dai-Nam quoc-am tu-vi* (1895–96), with definitions in Vietnamese, which records for us the *nôm* characters of the period. In the fairy tales his style is simple, free-flowing and distinctly colloquial, full of the vivid imagery of the Southern dialect.

Truong Vinh Ky's multifarious works cover all literary fields; he can be called the first real architect of *quoc-ngu* writing. With a command of both French and Vietnamese, he wrote some hundreds of books in a style similar to Paulus Cua's, but on the whole rather more lucid and methodical. Thanks to him *quoc-ngu* attained respectability, and he exerted his influence to have it adopted in primary schools.

Thus the *quoc-ngu* movement, as a result of the efforts of these two writers, was first launched in the South. Meanwhile in the field of poetry, both in the South and the North, three distinct schools were discernible: (a) the Confucian patriots such as Nguyen Dinh Chieu, Bui Huu-Nghia, Nguyen Van-Giai, Nguyen Khuyen, and Tran Te-Xuong, who refused to acknowledge French rule and wrote sorrowful elegiac poems lamenting the loss of independence; (b) the moderate collaborationists such as Ton Tho-Tuong and Hoang Cao-Khai, who accepted French domination as a temporary phenomenon and advocated collaboration, together with reform of the structure of Vietnamese society, in the hope of better days to come; and (c) the blasé romantic defeatists such as Chu Manh-Trinh and Duong Khue,

1. See p. 22 above and note 22 to chapter 1.

who shunned action and sought escape in sybaritic pleasures.

To sum up, the prime feature of this period was the growing strength of *quoc-ngu* and its popularization by every possible means, both in the South and the North (fortunately Vietnamese is fairly standard, apart from a few hundred dialect words peculiar to the South, so that there was no obstacle to its rapid spread). It was a transitional period, and writers still tended to express themselves in verse rather than in prose. Despite the work of pioneers like Petrus Ky and Paulus Cua, the real development of *quoc-ngu* literature was still to come.

SECOND PERIOD (1906–13)

The year 1906 is important in Vietnamese history for the birth of a moderate political movement of reformist Confucians. Under the stimulus of recent events in the Far East, particularly Russia's defeat at the hands of the Japanese, intellectuals were contemplating mass campaigns in favor either of revolt against the French or of reform with French assistance. The moderate party, founded by scholar-patriots such as Luong Van-Can, Phan Boi-Chau, Phan Chu-Trinh, Tang Bat-Ho, and Nguyen Quyen, and known henceforth as the *Dong-kinh nghia-thuc* movement (literally "Dong-kinh unpaid teaching movement," Dong-kinh being another name for the capital, Hanoi), aimed by agreement with the French Government to bring enlightenment and improved education to the common people by means of free classes, given in Vietnamese and reproduced in *quoc-ngu* script. The first classes were held in Hanoi, and the literati concerned, normally so squeamish about the mixing of the sexes, decided to admit women and girls. Nguyen Van-Vinh and Pham Duy-Ton undertook to seek the approval of the French authorities; and the latter, in the person of the Resident, could hardly withhold it, seeing that the Movement was calculated to reinforce their own efforts by organizing talks on cultural topics devoid of anti-French content. Accordingly, in May 1907, the French Government somewhat reluctantly gave its approval.

The classes had by then already been under way for some time at 4 Rue de la Soie, home of the Director, Luong Van-Can, and his young sister (who was running the women's section). In no time the Movement won the enthusiasm of the public, and there were audiences of four or five hundred at each of the evening lectures. All kinds of topics were covered, from the most humdrum, such as hairdressing (the old-style literati still wore their hair in a bun) or the abolition of the practice of blackening the teeth, to the most controversial, such as educational reform and the boycotting of the traditional literary examinations. The leaders of the Movement set up a translation committee to translate Chinese and French books, though the few volumes of translations from Chinese authors were later lost, leaving only some patriotic songs (at which the members of the Movement excelled).

Such a display of public enthusiasm worried the French authorities, and nine months after the start of the meetings, on the pretext that the Movement constituted a potential threat to public order, they stopped the classes and shut the group down.

Though short-lived, *Dong-kinh nghia-thuc* had sown the seeds of social awareness in the minds of the Vietnamese; its leaders' efforts had also stimulated the growing use of *quoc-ngu*, there giving a fillip to literature. The great *Nam Phong* translators such as Nguyen Huu Tien and Nguyen Don Phuc, famous for thus translations from the Chinese (see under third period, below), had worked for *Dong-kinh nghia-thuc;* and it was during their time with it that they used and enriched Vietnamese and created a style. Sons of the group's founders, such as Dao Trinh-Nhat and Hoang Tich Chu, later became well-known journalists. On the political front the group had trained the next generation of reformers and revolutionaries. Though it has been criticized for poor organization and its tendency to put poetry before politics, the fact remains that no other movement in so short a time exerted so great an influence on the Vietnamese people and their literature.

After the closure of *Dong-kinh nghia-thuc,* a series of political events brought the French administration to grips with the Vietnamese nationalists. Then came the Chinese revolution of 1911 led by Sun Yat-sen, a man well known to the founders of the movement. To counter the nationalists' attacks, and also to some extent to satisfy the popular thirst for learning, the French Government was compelled under pressure to open the University of Hanoi; and so, gradually and without much effort, French influence came to outweigh Chinese—not that the latter ceased to be a factor. Indeed, the Western concepts of democracy, revolution, and the proletariat were known to Vietnamese intellectuals through Chinese translations. But once French became widespread it was open to them to do without these and read Rousseau, Montesquieu, Diderot, and Voltaire in the original.

In China also at this time a new mass literature had grown up which included a multitude of translations from Western economists and political theorists. The greatest of the Chinese authors of the "New Culture," and the best known in Vietnam, were K'ang Yu-wei (1858–1927) and Liang Ch'i-ch'ao (1873–1929): their work opened the eyes of many a Vietnamese nationalist intellectual. They decried the monarchy, both in China and Vietnam, regarded Confucianism as the root cause of the country's decadence, and proclaimed the ideals of liberty and equality under a republic. The true dawn of modern Vietnamese literature, as we shall see in the next period, was about to break.

THIRD PERIOD (1913–1930)

The features of this phase were the explosive growth of journalism and the spread of French culture. Following the closure of *Dong-kinh nghia-thuc,* the French Government sought to weaken the grip of traditional Chinese culture by further stimulating the spread of *quoc-ngu.* In this way it hoped to achieve thought-control over the Vietnamese and gradually replace Chinese culture with French. Now the best way of popularizing *quoc-ngu* was by encouraging journalism—French-inspired and French-controlled; and it was this that formed the basis of the new Vietnamese literature. French influence was predominant, and remained so until 1954.

Accordingly in 1913, with the approval of the French Government, the first number of *Dong-duong tap-chi* appeared. Its founder was a Frenchman called Schneider and its editor Nguyen Van-Vinh, who had been a member of the *Dong-kinh nghia-thuc* movement; and it provided a forum for young French-educated writers like Nguyen Van-Vinh himself, Nguyen Van-To, and Pham Quynh, and Chinese-educated ones like Phan Ke Binh and Nguyen Do-Muc. Its officially approved aims were to popularize French culture and support the colonial government against Vietnamese revolutionary intrigues; but the editor, Nguyen Van-Vinh, managed to turn the situation to the advantage of Vietnamese scholarship. Side by side with compulsory articles required under the agreement with the French, he and his assistants published studies on literary, philosophical, and theological subjects, translations of Chinese and French texts on the history of thought, and anthologies of early Vietnamese poetry—all in *quoc-ngu.* From a purely Vietnamese point of view this was valuable work, and established a powerful trend in journalism. *Dong-duong tap-chi* lasted until late 1916, and brought out 187 numbers; but with the outbreak of the 1914–18 war the French administration in Indochina had new problems to face. It needed both to run a recruiting campaign to enlist Vietnamese in the war against Germany and also to woo them with the promise of worthwhile reforms once it was over. At the same time it repeated its prewar step by bringing out a new and higher-level Vietnamese-language journal under the title of *Nam*

Phong (South Wind). Its founder was a Frenchman called Marty and its editor a Vietnamese, Pham Quynh, who had worked under Nguyen Van-Vinh on the "Selections from French literature translated into Vietnamese" feature of the earlier periodical. *Nam Phong* was better staffed than its predecessor, and also set out to be more highbrow. Its staff comprised both old-style liberal literati and young French-trained writers, including Nguyen Ba-Trac, Nguyen Huu Tien, Nguyen Trong-Thuat, Nguyen Don Phuc, Nguyen Ba-Hoc, Le Du, Lam Tan-Phac, Madame Tuong-Pho, Duong Ba-Trac, Duong Quang-Ham, Tran Trong-Kim, Nguyen Trieu-Luat, Nguyen Manh-Bong, Nguyen Tien-Lang, Thieu Son, Le Thang, Hoang Ngoc-Phach, Vu Dinh-Long, and Nguyen Can-Mong.

Nam Phong's stated aims were the same as its predecessor's, namely to uphold French interests and ensure the spread of French culture, but at a higher level. Set up to hymn France's greatness and beneficence, *Nam Phong* did more; and it fulfilled all the secret hopes of its Vietnamese staff. Its articles were of a high intellectual standard, excelling both in style and in content, and dealt with an agreeably wide variety of topics; and the journal gradually became the link between the old Chinese and the new European cultures. In this way each member of Pham Quynh's staff helped to lay the foundations of modern Vietnamese literature and to establish a sort of Vietnamese Academy, which functioned for over seventeen years; thanks to their united efforts Vietnamese attained the status of a literary language.

The only criticism that can be leveled against the group is that consciously or unconsciously it encouraged a romantic, effeminate, sentimental type of writing. Some have seen in this a deliberate attempt by the French authorities to lull the populace into oblivion—the "Mother Country" having her own problems in Europe at the time. To be fair, this was a relatively minor defect compared with the paper's great services to the Vietnamese language. The importance of Pham Quynh's influence has recently been recognized even by the South Vietnamese Government (normally so sensitive over matters of national pride), whose Ministry of Education, with United States help, has brought out a new edition of his works. In any case, as we have seen, there had always been a romantic streak in Vietnamese literature; and even at the time, despite the journalistic explosion and the rapid development of literature, poetry remained highly romantic and emotional—as did the first European-style works of fiction.

Poetry was represented at this time by the poetess Tuong Pho, amongst others, of whom the best known were Nguyen Khac-Hieu, Dong Ho, and Tran Tuan-Khai. Their work was still full of echoes and literary allusions from the Chinese classics, and consisted either of folk ballads or of forms borrowed from T'ang poetry. Thus Tuong Pho stirred a whole generation of readers with the emotional and deeply-felt lines in which she lamented the death of her beloved—the purest "sobbing" to be found in Vietnamese literature so far. But the greatest poet of the period, and perhaps indeed of the first half of the twentieth century, was undoubtedly Nguyen Khac-Hieu, better known as Tan Da. Educated on Confucian lines, he was well versed in Chinese poetry and also in the nuances of Vietnamese; a dilettante and a patriot in his day, a great drinker, open-handed and somewhat eccentric, embittered after being crossed in his first love, sybarite and hedonist—he had, in short, the qualities and defects of the true poet. Despite the success of the New Poetry, he dominated the Vietnamese poetic scene for twenty years (1920–1940); and he may be said to have been both the star performer in classical poetry and also the pioneer of the New Poetry of the succeeding period—thus providing the link between the two schools. His poems, very disparate in form, are always moving because of the beauty of the imagery and the rhythm and harmony of the versification; they have the typically Vietnamese timbre which results from a felicitous choice of assonance and tonality, together with an unusually daring use of words which suggests French influence. He was universally regarded in his day (except perhaps by the stern Pham Quynh, editor of *Nam Phong*) and even afterwards as the greatest and most characteristic of Vietnamese poets.

In addition to Tan Da, mention must be made of Dong Ho, one of South Vietnam's great contemporary poets. He worked for *Nam Phong* from 1923 to 1933, and is known for two of his poems, *Linh Phuong* and *Phu Dong-Ho*. To this day he still maintains the delightful habit of celebrating spring with charming verses each New Year. The poetess Tuong Pho, at present living in retirement on the South Vietnamese coast, is known (as mentioned above) for the depth of feeling in her poem *Giot le thu* (Autumn Tears), published in *Nam Phong* for July 1928 (no. 131).

The Vietnamese novel during this period was still in its infancy. As *quoc-ngu* became more widespread, the staffs of *Dong-duong tap-chi* and *Nam Phong* had started to translate old Chinese works of fiction familiar in the Far East, such as *San kuo che yen yi, Hsi yü chi,* and *Chuei hu.* These translations, thanks largely to the translators' skill, sold well; and consequently devotees of French literature like Nguyen Van-Vinh, editor of *Dong-duong tap-chi,* went on to translate French novels such as *Manon Lescaut* (1932), *Les trois mousquetaires* (1921), and *Gil Blas.* But the first two Vietnamese novels properly so called were *Qua dua do* (The Watermelon) by Nguyen Trong-Thuat and *To Tam* by Hoang Ngoc-Phach, both published in 1925. Neither was much more than a rough draft, particularly the latter, which showed the hybrid influence of contemporary Chinese novels and of *La dame aux camélias.* In the South, a prefect by the name of Ho Bieu-Chanh made himself a great reputation as a novelist, and his books were popular with Southern readers up to 1930. Their realism and moral purpose, and their crisp, vivid style laced with colloquialisms, make them an accurate reflection of the outspoken South Vietnamese character. Though clearly influenced by French writers such as Hector Malot and Victor Hugo, Ho Bieu-

Chanh's individuality shows through in the construction of his books and in his characterization. His work has a unity and originality that distinguish him from the other popular Southern novelists of the time, such as Buu Dinh, author of *Manh trang thu* (Autumn Moon).

French influence was also to be seen in the short story, a literary form hitherto virtually unknown in Vietnam. Novelists such as Pham Duy-Ton, Nhuong Tong, and Nguyen Ba-Hoc wrote short stories with a moral, which greatly appealed to the reading public.

Plays on the Western model first made their appearance in 1915 with Nguyen Van-Vinh's Vietnamese translations of Molière, and on April 25, 1920, the *Khai tri tien duc* cultural association gave a highly successful performance in Hanoi of his *Malade imaginaire* in Vietnamese. The development of the drama took another step forward with Pham Quynh's translations of Corneille's *Le Cid* and *Horace,* which appeared in *Nam Phong.* There followed a plethora of tragedies and comedies by young playwrights, both Northern and Southern: the best known was Vu Dinh-Long, whose *Chen thuoc doc* (The Cup of Poison) was performed in Hanoi on October 22, 1921, in aid of charity. Another playwright was Vi Huyen-Dac, of Haiphong, who first made his name with three- or four-act plays such as *Uyen uong* (The Pair of Mandarin Ducks) (1927) and *Hai toi tan hon* (The Two Wedding Nights) (1929).

FOURTH PERIOD (1930–35)

Present-day literary historians all agree that these five years were politically eventful for Vietnam. Some regard the evolution of the literature from 1930 to the end of World War II as a single sweep; but we prefer to split it into two parts. Thus our fourth period seems to us the critical phase in the explosive growth of journalism and the hegemony of *Tu luc van doan* (Independent

Literary Group). It also marks the triumph of the New Poetry.

The year 1930 was a key year in Vietnamese history, the year in which the nationalist political revolts all fizzled out and in which the Communist Party of Indochina—destined to play a crucial role after World War II—came into being. The year 1935 saw the birth of the Popular Front in France. Between these two dates Vietnamese literature took a great leap forward in almost every sphere. French influence was everywhere paramount; conservative Confucianism was in retreat, and middle-class youth took advantage of the fact to demand the abolition of bureaucratic feudalism and the introduction of a measure of freedom—albeit a freedom limited by the interests of the French administration and the need to solve the economic crisis currently afflicting the business community. During 1930–32 a young French-educated Vietnamese by the name of Hoang Tich Chu, writing in two papers, *Dong Tay* (East-West) and *Ngo Bao* (Midday News), pioneered a grammatical reform involving the adoption of French syntax. But the *Tu luc* group must take the credit for introducing a new concise literary style, modeled on the French classics and as far as possible divested of Chinese locutions and literary allusions. Indeed, this fine group brought new life to every sphere of Vietnamese life—literary, poetic, political, social, and aesthetic (the modern Vietnamese woman's dress is the result of the redesigning of the traditional costume by a member of the group, the artist and designer Nguyen Cat-Tuong). It used satire and cartoons like those in *Le canard enchâîné* to deride the old outdated habits and customs. No reader of the period could ever forget Ly Toet, personification of the ignorant Vietnamese peasant, invented about 1927 by one of the group, the poet Tu Mo, and portrayed in the group's organ *Phong Hoa* (Manners and Morals). So successful was it that the term "Ly Toet" passed into the language as an opprobrious epithet. Stimulated by the group, great debates took place between Phan Khoi, a liberal intellectual, and Hai Trieu, a Marxist journalist, on such subjects as Western versus Confucian logic and materialism versus religious belief (1933). There was also an "Ancient versus Modern" controversy, and many writers espoused the cause of feminism, calling for the abolition of the Confucian moral code and for free marriage. Phan Khoi's realistic and liberal approach won him well-deserved acclaim at this time. In 1935 an interesting debate started between the proponents of "art for art's sake," led by Thieu Son, and the advocates of "art for life," headed by Hai Trieu. It continued until the end of the fifth period (1939), with many writers and thinkers joining one or other of the two camps: Hoai Thanh, Le Trang-Kieu, and Luu Trong-Lu sided with Thieu Son, while Hai Thanh, Son Tra, and Bui Cong-Trung supported Hai Trieu.

In poetry Ho Trong-Hieu (alias Tu Mo) of the *Tu-luc* group achieved deserved success with his satirical folk poems attacking the customs of the time. It was 7- and 8-syllable verse in classical format, and appeared in *Phong-hoa* under the heading *Giong nuoc nguoc* (Cross-currents). But the great advance was made by the New Poetry under the acknowledged leadership of The Lu, also of the *Tu-luc* group; his new-style poems *May van tho* (New Rhymes) were enthusiastically received by the public. In both form and content they showed strong French influence, being emotional and overflowing with love and life; they also extolled the beauties of nature, and the poet's mission. But where they particularly broke new ground was in their use of a limpid style, freed of excessive *chinoiserie,* and of a more elastic and adaptable metrical pattern which gave the poet greater scope for self-expression; they also made use of all the resources of French prosody such as the caesura, enjambment, and alliteration. The Lu was the center of a group of young poets, among them Nguyen Nhuoc-Phap, Xuan Dieu, Huy Can, and Dong Ho.

Realism made its appearance with the birth of documentary feature writing. There was a flood of features on various aspects of society: the life of a rickshawman, the life of a tart, "Hanoi by night," and so on; and three journalists with the same family name, Vu Bang, Vu Dinh-Chi (or Tam Lang), and Vu Trong-Phung, made a name for themselves at this kind of writing. It had the merit of bringing to public notice the worst running sores of society, such as the miserable existence led by rickshaw coolies, prostitution, extortion, usury, and venereal disease. Tam Lang's books included *Toi keo xe* (I Am a Rickshawman) (1932) and *Dem Song Huong* (Nights on the Perfume River); and Vu Trong-Phung published *Cam bay nguoi* (Man-trap) and *Ky nghe lay Tay* (Marrying Frenchmen as a Business) (1934). But despite the growing success of such realist fiction, it could never compete with the works of *Tu-luc* writers such as Khai Hung and Nhat Linh, whose books were a roaring success in both North and South. The group's organ *Phong Hoa* at times achieved a circulation of close to ten thousand.

As for the theater, a play by the realist novelist Vu Trong-Phung, *Khong mot tieng vang* (Not an Echo), was put on in Hanoi in 1931, and was a success. Vi Huyen-Dac, who had already made a name as an author, turned playwright with *Co dau Yen* (The Singer Yen) (1930) and *Co doc Minh* (Miss Minh, Director) (1931); but it was not until the fifth period that this painstaking writer achieved complete mastery of his new medium.

Between 1930 and 1935 Vietnamese society went through growing pains. Spasms of nationalist unrest were quickly quelled by the French authorities, but in sport a measure of freedom was allowed: 1930 was Tennis Year, and 1932 the year of the yo-yo craze. Religious societies also expanded: Buddhist societies were legalized in Cochin-China and Central Vietnam in 1932, and in North Vietnam in 1934. The latter was also the year in which Vietnamese women started to dance in the Western manner and go swimming in the sea in summer. Meanwhile from the sidelines a small group of scholarly writers, including Tran Trong-Kim, Le Du, Nguyen Van Ngoc, Bui Ky, Nguyen Van-To, and Dao Duy-Anh, watched their country's giddy gyrations and strove to safeguard its cultural heritage.

FIFTH PERIOD (1935–39)

In 1935, with the advent of the Popular Front in France, there were slight signs of emancipation in the colonial empire. In Vietnam freedom of the press was proclaimed and censorship abolished, and Socialist and Communist writers used the new freedoms to disseminate the doctrine of democracy and the proletariat. The period marks the zenith of the *Tu-luc van-doan* group and the triumph of the New Poetry. Journalism, freed from the shackles of censorship, made new strides: according to official French Administration statistics, in 1937 there were 110 daily papers and 159 magazines and periodicals; in 1938 there were 128 and 160; and in 1939, 128 and 176.

With the expansion of journalism, branches of the field such as commentating and feature writing, which had started in the fourth period, assumed increased importance. In feature writing the "Big Three" (Vu Bang, Vu Dinh-Chi, and Vu Trong-Phung) were still active. Another extremely gifted and original writer was Nguyen Tuan, whose volume of essays and short stories *Vang bong mot thoi* (Aspects of an Epoch), begun in 1938, was published in 1940. It is individualistic, sophisticated, and outspoken, and also somewhat eccentric. Another good commentator was Phung Tat-Dac, better known as Lang Nhan, who brought a gently waggish cynicism to bear on such perennially thorny questions as the durability of human relationships, virginity in women, promiscuity, and East-West differences. His book *Truoc den* (Under the Lamp) was well received, even at a time when novels had reached a peak in number and variety; there were romantic novels, historical novels, folk tales, realist novels, Socialist novels, spy stories, novels introducing real characters under fictitious names, and so on.

The final triumph of the New Poetry is associated with the *Tu-luc* young poets' salon. It included Xuan Dieu, Huy Can, Luu Trong-Lu, Huy Thong, Che Lan-Vien, Doan Van-Cu, Nguyen

Binh, Bang Ba-Lan, and Anh Tho, all young poets (some not actually members of the *Tu-luc* group) influenced to a greater or lesser extent by French poetry. The best known were Xuan Dieu, Huy Can, and Luu Trong-Lu. Huy Thong was perhaps the first to write verse playlets, such as *Anh Nga* and *Kinh Kha,* two miniature tragedies. The Catholic poet Han Mac-Tu, who suffered from an incurable disease, was the first to hymn the Christian faith, which he did with deep feeling and religious fervor. We must not forget that though this was the golden age of the New Poetry, the last great poet of the classical school, Tan Da, was still proudly struggling in poverty and alcoholism. The leaders of the *Tu-luc* group, who had previously tended to be hostile and unkind to him, now came to his rescue by commissioning him to translate Chinese T'ang poetry for them; and the translations Tan Da has left us are so splendid as sometimes to surpass the beauty of the originals.

Realist novels and documentary feature-writing made great strides following the abolition of censorship. Journalists such as Trong Lang, Nguyen Dinh-Lap, Nguyen Hong, Ngo Tat-To, and Nguyen Cong Hoan made concerted efforts to combat the worst social evils, such as promiscuity, prostitution, the arrogant snobbery of the middle classes, the lickspittle bigotry of the old mandarins, the plight of the penurious peasantry, economically depressed and educationally backward, and pauperism among the working classes. Thanks to their writing, the attention of the town-dwelling public was drawn to the underprivileged—peasants, laborers, and miners. Freedom (or relative freedom) of the press made possible bitter and often well-deserved attacks on outdated colonialist attitudes and the opportunism of a minority of Vietnamese in high places. The realist school also began to intensify its campaign against the *Tu-luc* group; and despite their efforts to remain in the van, *Tu-luc* leaders such as Nhat Linh, Khai Hung, Hoang Dao, and Thach Lam began to realize that the heyday of their group was over.

[123]

When articles in the French press commending André Gide's courageous stand in *Retour de l'URSS* (1939) were translated into Vietnamese in the group's weekly *Ngay nay* (Today), there was an outcry from the Communists. A sharp clash between the two groups ensued, with the staff of *Tuong-lai* ("Future") attacking *Tu-luc* on the unfair grounds that it had corrupted youth and incited Vietnamese womanhood to depravity.

Thus the period 1935–39 was dominated by ideological conflict between the middle-class Fabian intellectuals of the *Tu-luc* group and the realist school of orthodox Communist writers. Vietnamese society was changing unnaturally fast, and in the space of a few years the *Tu-luc* group's grandiose reformist ideas were overtaken by events. By now the works of Western writers such as Balzac, Flaubert, Dickens, Tolstoy, Romain Rolland, Henri Barbusse, André Gide, Pascal, Dostoyevsky, and Goethe were available to Vietnamese readers in translation, and undoubtedly the young writers of the time were greatly influenced by them.

It was the same in the theater. Vi Huyen-Dac, already well known as an author, wrote two new and decidedly realist plays, *Kim tien* (Money) and a comedy called *Ong Ky Cop* (Mr. Secretary Cop), which were staged respectively in February and October 1938. Another playwright, Doan Phu-Tu, wrote successful short plays in a sanguine, emotional vein which were put on in 1937, e.g., *Nhung buc thu tinh* (The Love Letters). He was influenced by French writers such as Alfred de Musset, Henri Duvernois, and Sacha Guitry. We should also mention Phan Khac-Khoan, who wrote historical plays in verse.

The closing year of this period, 1939, was clouded by the death in June of the great poet Tan Da. A few months later came the outbreak of World War II, and in October the death of the young writer Vu Trong-Phung. Vietnam was entering a critical period, from which after six years of war, famine, and hardship it was to emerge in a state of utter chaos.

SIXTH PERIOD (1940–45)

World War II, declared in September 1939, was to change the face of the world. France, defeated in Europe, was in no position to support Indochina, which was consequently cut off from the mother country. Japan was an ally of Germany, and on February 6 the Japanese navy occupied the island of Hainan. With France temporarily *hors de combat,* the Japanese established themselves throughout Indochina under agreements made with General Catroux, the French Governor-General. He was then replaced by Admiral Decoux. Under the agreements of June 20 and September 22, 1940, the Japanese were entitled to land troops and set up bases in the North Vietnamese highlands in order to intensify their attacks on Chang Kai-Chek's China. Admiral Decoux thus found himself faced simultaneously with a Japanese invasion and an upsurge of Vietnamese nationalism, hostile to both French and Japanese—a conjunction of factors which was to lead to the breakup of the old Federation of Indochina.

As long ago as 1933, Vietnamese communists such as Nguyen Van-Tao, Duong Bach-Mai, Nguyen Van-Nguyen, and Nguyen Thi-Luu had formed a united front with Trotskyists such as Ta Thu-Thau, Tran Van-Trach, Phan Van-Hum, and Huynh Van-Phuong and launched a joint French-language periodical, *La lutte,* which first appeared at the end of 1934. This alliance lasted until June 15, 1937, when the two groups split. From then on, the Stalinists and the Trotskyists both went underground, though remaining implacable ideological enemies.

Freedom of the press was abolished and censorship reimposed. The French and Japanese governments used the war as an excuse to control all periodicals and books published in Vietnamese. Thus the literary history of Vietnam was determined by the vagaries of the political situation, which in turn fluctuated according to the course of the war. Youth and the common people were wooed from all sides: the Japanese appealed to the idea of racial and psychological unity implicit in a "Greater Asia," while the French administration sought to counter Japanese influence by tentatively encouraging local patriotism—which it hoped might merge with its own to produce a grand "Empire Youth" movement. A network of rural schools was set up on a provincial basis, and the Faculty of Science was opened. Meanwhile, underground, the political parties were not idle. The Communist party of Vietnam, reorganized by Nguyen Ai-Quoc in May 1941 and thereafter known as the Viet-Minh, was building up its strength in the North Vietnamese highlands. Nationalist parties such as the Dai-Viet, led by Nhat Linh, formerly head of the *Tu-luc van-doan* group, were hounded by the French security services, and Nhat Linh had to flee to China. His flight sounded the knell of the *Tu-luc* group, which had already lost much of its influence in the literary field. The daily spectacle of war and famine was no longer compatible with the Utopian atmosphere of Hoang Dao's or Thach Lam's novels. This was a war in which the Vietnamese themselves had as yet no say, and their frustration was clearly reflected in the literature and poetry of the time. Escapism through sex and opium found an exponent in the poet Vu Hoang-Chuong, whose lament for the ruin of his first love affair through the woman's fault struck a new note of heartfelt grief. His poems are a blend of classical and modern, and he dominated the period. Among columnists Nguyen Tuan remained famous for his pungent, sophisticated writing.

At the same time there were those who tried to combat defeatism, and various ad hoc groups arose in the literary and political fields. They tended, however, to come under pressure either from the French authorities or from the clandestine Communist party. The former hoped to use them as safety valves for incipient nationalism, while the latter, with National Independence as its rallying cry, aimed to win the support of all classes for a "holy war" against both French and Japanese imperialism—meanwhile temporarily soft-pedaling on its doctrine about the class struggle. Political considerations led the French Government to encourage a "back to the Classics" movement— a return to classical antiquity and a revival of the cultural values of former days, on the lines of the Vichy Government's activities in France. It also encouraged the study of Buddhism, Taoism, and Cao Daism, hoping in this way to divert Vietnamese nationalism into relatively innocuous mystical channels. Hence the setting-up of the Tri-tan group, named after its organ, *Tri-tan:* this journal advocated the taking of a fresh look at the classics, and eschewed politics on the grounds that "that is a matter for the authorities." The group set out to publish studies in the classics and ancient history, adopting as its slogan the phrase from Confucius' *Luen yu* "A fresh look at the old to discover the new." The first portion of this program was entirely successful, and the group's work on original sources, its historical essays and its research on folklore remain valid and constitute a mine of useful data. But as regards "discovering the new" the group was a failure. The journal first appeared in mid-1941: it was staffed by scholars with a good grounding in classical Sino-Vietnamese culture, headed by Nguyen Van-To, Lecturer at the École Francaişe d'Extrême-Orient at Hanoi, and his assistants included Hoang Thuc-Tram, Nguyen Tuong-Phuong, Trinh Nhu-Tau, Le Van Hoe, Duong Ba-Trac, Tran Van Giap, the lexicographer Dao Duy-Anh, and many other intellectuals. As might have been expected, the group soon fell into the usual pitfalls that beset scholars: protracted, pointless discussion about the use of a word or a Chinese character in an ancient text, and sterile, tortuous argument about an ill-chosen quotation or a supposedly apocryphal source. Circulation gradually fell away, and public enthusiasm for sinological research declined. Nguyen Van-To, whose old-fashioned bun hairstyle had been ridiculed by the *Tu-luc* group, found himself saddled with the nickname "Old first-and-second folio."

In 1943 the war was raging in Southeast Asia: American and British heavy bombers were raiding Vietnam, the Japanese navy was beginning to suffer its first defeats in the Pacific, and all the signs pointed to a major change in the situation. It was against this background of tension and uncertainty that a group of progressive French-educated intellectuals started the weekly *Thanh-nghi*. They were mostly academics, particularly teachers of law such as Vu Dinh-Hoe, Phan Anh, Dinh Gia-Trinh, Do Duc-Duc, Duong Duc-Hien, and Vu Van-Hien, as well as the agricultural engineer Nghiem Xuan-Yem, the sinologist and *polytechnicien* Hoang Xuan Han, and the humanists Nguyen Van-To, Dang Thai-Mai, Tran Van Giap, Nguyen Thieu-Lau, and Nguyen Trong-Phan; also the doctor Vu Van-Can and the writers Nguyen Tuan and Do Duc-Thu. What this group did was to make available the basic law, sociology, and political theory needed to raise the educational level of the Vietnamese masses. The ordinary people of Vietnam were soon to be asked to decide their own political future, and the group's suggestion to them was a system of democracy on European lines. In addition to political tracts, *Thanh-nghi* published translations of many legal and sociological works and novels by French, English, American, Italian, and Chinese writers (e.g., Somerset Maugham, Pearl Buck, and Ts'ao Yu). But as time went on the leaders of the group became increasingly preoccupied with theory and out of touch with the mass of the people. Moreover in 1945, just before the Japanese takeover, and until the formation of Tran Trong-Kim's first cabinet, the group had already been infiltrated by the Communist Party. The defeat of Japan and the August 1945 revolution finally completed the breakup of the group, although most of its members met again after September 2, 1945, in the various ministries of Ho Chi-Minh's government.

In addition to *Tri-tan* and *Thanh-nghi,* a third group called *Han Thuyen* (from the imprint of its books) gained some influence. Literary historians are too ready to regard it as composed of Trotskyists. In fact, apart from its leader Truong Tuu, a Marxist with slight Trotskyist leanings, and a few militants such as

Ho Huu-Tuong and Luong Duc-Thiep, its members were intellectuals of no particular political complexion, such as the sinologist Dang Thai-Mai, author of *Van-hoc khai-luan* (Debate about Literature), two doctors, Pham Ngoc-Khue and Tran-Huan, the writers and playwrights Nguyen Tuan, Vi Huyen-Dac, Chu Thien, Nguyen Dinh-Lap, Le Van-Sieu, Bui Huy-Phon, Nhu Mai, and Nguyen Duc-Quynh, and artists such as Nguyen Do-Cung.

In 1943 Truong Tuu (alias Nguyen Bach-Khoa) published under the Han Thuyen imprint a book called *Nguyen Du va truyen Kieu* (Research on Nguyen Du and the Story of Kieu), in which he applied dialectical materialism overdogmatically and mechanically; his object was to use the political circumstances of the time to popularize the elements of Marxism. On September 10, 1945, he published another book, *Tuong-lai van-nghe Vietnam* (The Cultural Future of Vietnam), regarded as reactionary by present-day Marxist critics. In addition to these books, and some leaflets on popular Marxism, the house of Han Thuyen published a great many books of all sorts: historical and psychological novels like Chu Thien's and Nguyen Duc-Quynh's, didactic novels like Do Phon's, literary criticism like that of Dang Thai-Mai, and Nguyen Dong-Chi's *Viet-nam co-van hoc-su* (History of Ancient Vietnamese Literature) (1941), Nguyen Dinh-Lap's documentaries, Le Van-Sieu's studies of industry, and so forth. The *Han Thuyen* group also ran two periodicals, *Van moi* (New Writing) and *Van moi tuoi xanh* (New Writing for the Young), which were less successful than was hoped. Dr. Pham Ngoc-Khue's books on popular medicine were well received, as were Le Van-Sieu's on industrial technology.

As for novels, the *Tu-luc* group was on the decline, and young realist novelists were springing up. Documentary features, short stories, and essays were always popular. At the same time the "back to the classics" movement produced a crop of historical novels and recollections of life in olden days—often flavored with a tinge of nostalgia. Such books came from the pens of Nguyen

Trieu-Luat, Chu Thien, Phan Tran-Chuc, Ngo Van-Trien, and Ngo Tat-To. They were mostly published by the Tan-dan publishing house, and their sales were helped by the ever-increasing popularity of the *quoc-ngu* script. Translations of philosophical and medical works also went well.

The literary critics of the day, in addition to Truong Tuu, were Thieu Son and particularly Thuong Sy, whose scholarly reviews appeared regularly for five years running in the daily newspaper *Tin-moi.*

As regards poetry, apart from well-known names such as Vu Hoang-Chuong, Han Mac-Tu, Quach Tan, and Bang Ba-Lan, a number of young men and women formed a group which they called *Xuan thu nha tap;* the best-known members were Nguyen Xuan-Sanh, Bich Khe, Pham Van-Hanh, and Doan Phu-Tu. Their poetry, obscure and incomprehensible, showed the influence of French symbolist poets such as Mallarmé and Paul Valéry. The group's aims were couched in high-flown but meaningless terms, such as "Supreme intellect," "Eternal art," "Continuous music," and "Attempt to discover oneself through the rhythms and harmonies of literature, art, and especially poetry." In addition to this short-lived group there was a clandestine school of revolutionary poets whose best-known member was To Huu.

In the theater, Vi Huyen-Dac wrote *Le chi vien* (The Lychee Garden) in 1943, *Jésus-Christ* in 1942, and *Bach-hac dinh* (The House of the White Cranes) in 1944.

SEVENTH PERIOD (AUGUST 19, 1945– DECEMBER 19, 1946)

This sixteen-month period was among the most eventful in Vietnam's history. The first day saw the Viet-Minh's successful August revolution. Five days later, on August 24, Emperor Bao-Dai abdicated, and on September 2 the Democratic Republic of

Vietnam was proclaimed. But on the 25th the advance party of the French expeditionary force began occupying towns in South Vietnam; and on December 19, 1946, the first Indochina war broke out.

During the relative lull of these sixteen months the provisional government of the Vietnamese Republic set up the Cultural Association for the Defence of the Realm *(Van-hoa cuu quoc),* which in September 1945 organized the first National Cultural Conference. Starting with its second number, the Association's official organ *Tien-phong* (Vanguard) published the text of the basic principles of Vietnamese culture; and a militant called Nguyen Dinh-Thi wrote a leaflet, *Mot nen van-hoa moi* (A New Culture), designed to popularize the theory underlying these principles, which was to serve as the framework for the new "national, democratic, realist" culture of the country. Supporters of the régime continually sought to influence literature in the direction of patriotism and nationalism. There were many translations of Russian and Chinese works on political theory and Marxist economics. With the coming to power of the Communist Party, the party's poet, To Huu, with his revolutionary verve, was regarded as the country's leading poet; and after him came those prewar poets such as Xuan Dieu, Che Lan-Vien, and Te Hanh who had rallied to the Communist government and the new doctrines. Among prose writers men such as Hoai Thanh, Nguyen Tuan, Nguyen Hong, To Hoai, Nam Cao, and Manh Phu-Tu continued to produce documentaries and features with a flavor of Socialist realism. No novels worth mentioning appeared. Only one play was produced, Nguyen Huy-Tuong's *Bac-son:* it was in praise of the Revolution, and went down well. Literary criticism from now on was based on the principles of Marxism-Leninism and dialectical materialism, official doctrine in all Communist countries. The literary critics of the period were Dang Thai-Mai, Nguyen Dinh-Thi, and Hoai Thanh. Socialist realism, the only accepted line in literature and the arts, had hardly time to show its paces before the country was caught up in the long war of resistance which was to last for seven years on end.

EIGHTH PERIOD (1946–54)

Literature inevitably suffered from the effects of the first Indochina war. From this point on, it can be subdivided into two: on the one hand the resistance literature sponsored by the government of the Vietnamese Republic, which had to retire into the highlands of North Vietnam to continue its struggle with France, and on the other a sort of "marking time" literature in the areas initially occupied by the French army and subsequently handed over to various Vietnamese nationalist governments. Some writers and poets followed the Communist government of the Resistance; others, disliking Communist ideology and wartime hardships, returned to Hanoi or Saigon to await the end of the war.

In the nationalist administration's area, writing was virtually in cold storage during these nine years. Translations of Chinese novels were reprinted; there were documentary features, and in particular there were accounts by those returning from the underground Resistance. New publishing houses started up in Hanoi, and some of them, such as Song Nhi and Vo Dat, took up the publication of historical and other learned works. In Saigon the novels of Ho Bieu-Chanh and the *Tu-luc van-doan* group were republished, particularly after Nhat Linh's return to literary life: his new edition of the group's main writings was brought out by the Phuong Giang publishing house in Saigon in 1952. Tan Viet published the works of scholars such as Dao Trinh-Nhat, Tran Trong-Kim, Nguyen Dinh Chieu, and Phan Van-Hum. No poetry of note was produced. Pham Dinh-Tan, Ai Lan, and Huyen Chi were the poets writing in Hanoi, and Ho Van-Hao in the South: their work was mostly influenced by the war.

The literature of the Resistance was taken over by the Lao Dong (the new name adopted by the Vietnamese Communist Party in 1951), and for these nine years (as in other Communist countries) was based on "Socialist realism" and centered around two main themes, the Resistance and agrarian reform. All writers were mobilized and urged to produce poems, plays, novels, or short stories calculated to arouse the fighting spirit of the people. They were urged to live with and among the people and draw strength and creative inspiration from "the tonic of contact with soldiers, workers, and peasants." The fact remains that in the view of literary historians not one notable work was produced. Poetry was represented principally by the work of To Huu, the "Party poet"; and some of his finer poems show genuine feeling and an epic quality. Even today critics in Hanoi disagree as to whether he is to be classed with the school of revolutionary militancy or with that of Socialist realism. Other poets were Xuan Dieu, Tu Mo, Luu Trong-Lu, and Che Lan-Vien: they wrote according to Party directives, and their work is of uneven quality. Among prose writers some familiar names recur, such as Nguyen Dinh-Thi, To Hoai, Nam Cao, and Nguyen Huy-Tuong, and also a young novelist called Tran Dang, who died in 1950. These men wrote short stories in which narrative was more important than description. Another literary genre was war stories and reminiscences, which were well received by the "Vietnam Cultural Association" in 1951–52. In the theater there was Nguyen Huy-Tuong's classic play *Nhung nguoi o lai* (Those That Are Left), and some light plays by The Lu, Tu Mo, and Ngo Tat-To. In 1952 a "back to the roots" movement started, involving the revival of Vietnam's ancient cultural heritage: the folk songs, dances, and operettas of the so-called "feudal" periods were brought out and popularized, and research was done on Vietnamese folklore and that of the Montagnard minorities. Few learned works were produced; Dang Thai-Mai's *Giang van Chinh-phu ngam* (Analysis of the Poem "Lament of the Warrior's Bride") and Hoai Thanh's *Quyen song con nguoi trong truyen Kieu* (The Right to Life in "The Story of Kieu") are about all.

NINTH PERIOD (1954-62)

The 1954 Geneva agreements meant the end of the first Indo-china war and the partition of Vietnam into North and South at the 17th parallel. This deplorable division was simply a reflection of the "cold war" frontier between the Eastern bloc (the USSR and its satellites) and the Western (the USA and Western Europe). Like Germany and Korea, Vietnam was arbitrarily split in two, the northern portion being the Democratic Republic of Vietnam, a member of the Communist bloc, and the southern the Vietnamese Republic, a puppet of the West (the USA and France). From now on Vietnamese literature, like Janus, faced two ways at once. In the early months of the armistice, people were free to opt for North or South; and while some writers left the North and settled in the South, others migrated in the reverse direction. Saigon and Hanoi became the capitals of the two republics.

In the North the first noteworthy cultural event after the armistice and the reestablishment of the people's government in Hanoi was the National Assembly of Artists and Men of Letters, held on December 16, 1954, with the object of reviving and popularizing the country's artistic and literary heritage. In 1956 a literary prize was awarded for works originating with the Resistance; and that year also saw the beginning of a new era in literature, coinciding with a drive towards speedier socialization of the country—a drive which came as something of a blow to the middle and lower-middle classes. In China this was the so-called "Hundred Flowers" period: its effects made themselves felt in North Vietnam in the *Nhan van, giai pham* affair, a revolt by writers and poets opposed to the régime, which the government in the North condemned as reactionary. After this Lao Dong took a firm hold on the situation, and called on writers to make a greater effort to raise the cultural level of their works and learn from the masses. A message from the Central Executive of the party to the 2nd Cultural Congress stated that "The people calls on all artists to adopt the role of 'spiritual engi-

[134]

neer.' " Poets like To Huu had to hymn the return of peace, the new happy life under Socialism, the greatness of the So-cialist brother-countries, and Socialist realism. These require-ments obviously left little room for maneuver; and so we find Xuan Dieu's book of poems *Rieng chung* (Private and Public) (1960) being criticized by a young militant on the grounds that it contained two I's, an essentially collective "I," which was ac-ceptable, and an "I" with no collective or communal connota-tion, which smacked of outworn individualism.

The poets of the day, apart from To Huu, were Huy Can, Xuan Dieu, Che Lan-Vien, Xuan Xanh, Luu Trong-Lu, Ma-dame Van Dai, and Madame Anh Tho. Fiction was exemplified by Nguyen Huy-Tuong's *Truyen anh Luc,* on agrarian reform, and Nguyen Ngoc's *Dat nuoc dung len,* on the Resistance. Nov-elists such as Nguyen Cong Hoan and To Hoai were getting old by now, but there were also young writers like Dao Vu, Vo Tung-Linh, Nguyen Khai, and Vo Huy Tam; all sought to portray the new life in the mines and cooperative farms. There were also innumerable war stories and ex-soldiers' reminiscences, in which great feats of arms were recounted in terms of Socialist realism. But even the official critics still had much fault to find with all these writers, young as well as old: they were lacking in political and cultural maturity, depth of thinking, and skill in presenta-tion.

The theater took on a new lease of life, and the stock of plays adopted from European drama was revived and refurbished, the big names in Western-style theater being Hoc Phi, Buu Tien, and Nguyen Hung. But in comparison with other art forms the theater made relatively little progress. On the other hand much excellent work was done by sinologists and Vietnamese scholars (e.g., the Le Qui Don group) in the field of learning and the translation of early Vietnamese classics from the Chinese. In-deed, it is thanks to them that we possess translations of *Cuong muc* (Annals) and works by Nguyen Trai, Le Qui Don, and Phan Huy Chu whose importance is recognized by everyone con-cerned with Vietnamese studies.

In South Vietnam, where French influence still predominated despite the impact of American culture, writers did not have to work to a prescribed plan—apart from the anti-Communist line which was a feature of Government policy. Let us be quite clear: neither in North nor South Vietnam was there true freedom of the press in the sense in which the phrase is normally used in the West, and both governments recognized this—though the arguments they used were diametrically opposite. The government in the South urged on artists and men of letters the official doctrine of "social individualism," based on the ideals of progress and respect for the human personality. There was also a government party of the same persuasion.

In the last year or two of the period, literature in the South showed signs of change, e.g., a revival in poetry and the novel. There was evidence of headway in historical, philosophical, and literary research; and here the names of Nghiem Toan, Nguyen Duy-Can, Nguyen Hien Le, Thanh Lang, Buu Cam, Bui Khanh-Dan, Nguyen Van-Trung, Nguyen Manh-Bao, and Vuong Hong-Sen come to mind. Work on Vietnamese linguistics was done by research workers already known in the South, such as Le Ngoc-Tru and Nguyen Bat-Tuy, and by an American-trained academic, Nguyen Dinh-Hoa. A major translation programme from early historical and literary texts in Chinese was undertaken, with U.S. financial help, by the Ministry of Education's Translation Bureau. Thus scholars concerned with Vietnamese studies now have two sources of supply for *quoc-ngu* translations, one in the North and one in the South.

Journalism and feature writing had their ups and downs. The senior men such as Vu Bang and Tam Lang were joined by keen young writers like Ngu I. Book reviews in the newspapers and the Vietnam Pen Club's Review of Books appeared over new names—apart from those of Thieu Son and Thuong Sy. The only new columnists to compete with Lang Nhan and Trong Lang were Hieu Chan and Vu Khac-Khoan—the last-named being better known for his work in the theater. In this latter field there were some new plays by Vi Huyen-Dac; and a new playwright, Anh Tuyen, began to make his mark.

For some time now there had been signs of a quickening in poetry. There were still the same three schools, romantic, symbolist, and realist; and many young men and women had taken up poetry as a career, bringing with them new ideas and techniques. Vu Hoang-Chuong, Nguyen Vy, Dong Ho, Bang Ba-Lan, Dinh Hung, Quach Tan, and Madame Tuong Pho were already well known as poets before the war; they were now joined by a new crop from a mixture of schools, such as Bui Giang, Doan Them, Pham Dinh-Tan, Anh Tuyen, and Madame Minh Duc. In the opinion of Mr. Minh Huy, the new existentialist school of poetry was represented by a small group of young men such as Nguyen Sa, Bui Giang, Cung Tram Tuong, and Quach Thoai; most of them studied in France, and were probably influenced by Sartre, Heidegger, and Saint-John Perse.

The novel, like poetry, showed signs of a revival. Apart from the late lamented Nhat Linh, formerly head of *Tu-luc van-doan,* who died on July 7, 1963, and "old guard" novelists like Vu Bang, Tchya, and Tam Lang, they were mostly young writers like Doan Quoc-Sy, the overprolific Binh Nguyen Loc, Vo Phien, Ngoc Linh, Son Nam, Ngu I, Nhat Tien, Madame Nguyen Thi-Vinh, and Madame Linh Bao. The Government of South Vietnam sought to stimulate writing by offering prizes. The National Literary Prize was instituted in 1956 by the Cultural Section of the Information Office, and was first awarded in the following year in four separate divisions for fiction, poetry, plays, and learned works. Prizes were subsequently awarded for 1958–59 and 1960–61.

TENTH PERIOD (1963–75)

Literature continued to develop in both the North and the South. This was a crucial period, and two important events in it were to have a great bearing on Vietnamese literary history. The first was the coup d'état in Saigon on November 1, 1963, which overthrew the government of the Catholic president Ngo Dinh Diem. It came as a bombshell not only to Vietnamese politicians but also to writers and poets in the South, who saw in it the promise of greater intellectual freedom and of the lifting of the censorship imposed by Ngo Dinh Nhu (President Diem's brother). The official doctrine of the Diem government and the government party, the Can Lao (somewhat akin to a Labor Party), was "community personalism" combined with anti-Communism: but it commanded only lukewarm support among most writers. As for community personalism, a makeshift adaptation from the ideas of the French philosopher Emmanuel Mounier, it remained a dead letter. In objective terms writers had greater freedom in the South than in the North, especially after the overthrow of the Diem government on November 1, 1963. The abolition of censorship freed them overnight from all trammels and constraints: and they reacted with enthusiastic but uncoordinated activity, like fracture patients who have been confined in plaster for over eight years and have just had it removed.

The second notable date, which was of worldwide importance, was August 5, 1964. From then on, and particularly from February 7, 1965, the US Seventh Fleet shelled the coast and a number of built-up areas of North Vietnam. The intensive pounding of North Vietnamese cities by the Americans which started in February 1965 marked the beginning of the second Indochina war. Hence 1964 is to be seen as a key date: it saw the birth of a whole literature of anti-American resistance in the North, which continued to grow in intensity until the fateful date of April 30, 1975, when the US Army finally withdrew from the whole of Vietnam.

This twelve-year period (1963–1975) was highly eventful for prose and poetry both in the North and the South; and we propose to give a brief account of developments in both halves of the country.

In the South, after a series of coups d'état, the reins of power eventually ended up in the hands of the Catholic general Nguyen Van Thieu. Like the Diem government before him, he kept the anti-Communist war going with the heavily armed support of the Americans. Be it noted also that on December 20, 1960, during the Diem period, the FLN (National Liberation Front) was established in South Vietnam with help from the government in the North. The FLN took as its aim the overthrow of the nationalist Thieu government and the freeing of South Vietnam from the American yoke. Thus a resistance literature grew up in the South: it was the work of nationalist and Communist freedom fighters in the South itself. In the government camp the emphasis was placed on the war with the North and on goodwill towards the Americans, who had come as friends to save the Vietnamese from the clutches of Communism. The US Army took up positions everywhere to fight alongside the South Vietnamese army against northern troops who had infiltrated into the South, and also against the FLN guerrillas.

The US Army, with its 700,000 white and negro troops, severely disrupted the everyday lives of ordinary Vietnamese. People were already torn between two conflicting ideologies: and the bombings, the destruction of crops, the defoliation campaign, and the impact of death and bereavement on all classes of the population eventually reduced the mass of the people, uncertain of their future and caught between two fires as they were, to a state of acute mental distress. Though officially the US Army had come as a friend to help the South Vietnamese government, which was not strong enough to stand up alone against the threat from the North, in practice it behaved as though it were in conquered territory. There were continual clashes between it and the South Vietnamese, arising out of racial and sexual friction, cultural differences, the contrast between standards of living, mutual lack of understanding, and political ineptness on the part of the Americans. A whole new literature sprang up: it reflected the lives of ordinary Vietnamese in the cities, where US Army units were stationed, and in the countryside, where the fighting was fierce and the wretched inhabitants found themselves obliged to range themselves with one side or the other according to the vicissitudes of the battle.

Two distinct trends can be discerned among the new generation of novelists and poets. On the one hand there were those who recorded the physical and moral ruination of Vietnam, the depraving and damaging effect on the social order of forced cohabitation with a blindly destructive foreign army, the unemployment, the poverty, the high cost of living, the prostitution of respectable girls and women, and the evil influence of the dollar, and at the same time the appeal of the comparatively "pure" and more wholesome ideology of Communism. Most of these writers were torn between their hatred of Communism and their distress at finding themselves powerless to stop the US Army ravaging and battering their country. They also felt guilty and embarrassed to be describing the horrors of a war in which they themselves were taking no part. This trend is exemplified by Le Tat Dieu, Ta Ty, Madame Nguyen Thi Thuy Vu, and Madame Tran Thi Nha Ca.

Another group eschewed realism and objective writing and relapsed into anarchic romanticism or narrow individualism, publishing novels with an undue admixture of eroticism and pornography. The best-known novelists in this group were Chu Tu, Tuy Hong, Hoang Dong Phuong, and The Uyen: their books often became best-sellers among a blasé and demoralized public. Right-minded journalists and writers sounded the alarm in several government newspapers and magazines to warn the public against this dubious, debased type of writing. Some of these progressive writers, such as Vu Hanh (real name Nguyen Duc Dung), Le Vinh Hoa, Son Nam, and Vien Phuong, even earned the approval of the government in the North. But there was another group of writers who had the courage of their political convictions and remained resolutely anti-Communist: they included Ky Van Nguyen, Do Thuc Vinh, and in particular Doan Quoc Si, Vo Phien, Nguyen Manh Con, and Ho Huu Tuong.

[140]

We must also note the influence of existentialist philosophy in South Vietnam: it was popularized as a result of a number of articles and translations that appeared in various books and newspapers between 1955 and 1963. In 1955 a serious journalist wrote an article on the kind of fascination that existentialism seemed to exert on the South Vietnamese intelligentsia: it was called *Critique de l'existentialisme de J-P. Sartre par un intellectuel petit-bourgeois,* was by Nghiem Xuan Hong, and appeared in the journal *Quan Diem* (no. 3, June 27, 1955). The best-known existentialist poet of this period was undoubtedly Thanh Tam Tuyen; there were others more lyrical or more romantic, such as Vu Hoang Chuong, Dinh Hung, To Thuy Yen, Nguyen Sa, and Nha Ca.

Fortunately there was still a minority of research workers and writers who, despite the hardships and sufferings of a fratricidal war, still continued to do research and publish at their own expense serious work on literature, poetry, linguistics, and Vietnamese history. They included Le Ngoc Tru, Phung Tat Dac, Toan Anh, Gian Chi, Vuong Hong Xen, Dong Ho, and Do Trong Hue.

In the theater nothing startlingly new appeared. Apart from the works of Vi Huyen Dac, there were some plays by Tran Le Nguyen and Vu Khac Khoan. The latter's play *Nhung nguoi khong chiu chet* (Those Who Do Not Wish To Die) was given an impromptu performance on a stage at Dalat, and was published in Saigon in 1971 (184 pp.). The veteran playwright Vi Huyen Dac (who died in 1977) had already in 1962 brought out a play in four acts and a prologue called *Gengis Khan,* written in French. This is not to be confused with the play written in Vietnamese by Vu Khac Khoan under the title *Thanh Cat Tu Han* (the Sino-Vietnamese pronunciation of Genghis Khan) (Saigon, 1962). In 1963 Nghiem Xuan Hong wrote a three-act play called *Nguoi Vien Khach Thu Muoi* (The Tenth Traveler), which was published in Saigon by Éditions Quan Diem (277 pp.). In 1968 the great scholar and artist Vuong Hong Sen published a volume of reminiscences about the Revived Theater under the title *Nam muoi nam cai luong* (Fifty Years of the Revived Theater), which was published by Éditions Pham Quang Khai (254 pp.). In 1966, with financial help from the Asia Foundation, Vu Khac Khoan brought out a new edition of the old folk play so familiar to Vietnamese audiences *Quan Am Thi Kinh* (Saigon: Éditions Dao Tan, 1966, 98 pp.). The new edition was naturally accompanied by a commentary by Mr. Vu himself. This was the first in a series aimed at producing new editions of the best-known pieces of Vietnamese folk theater. At the same time as Vu Khac Khoan and his coworkers, who included Vu Huy Chan and Tran Trong San, were so engaged, the lexicographer Le Ngoc Tru, with the help of a number of research workers including Tran Van Huong and Pham Van Luat, brought out new editions of some folk plays once fashionable in the South, such as *Sai Vai, Kim Thach Ky Duyen, Kim Van Kieu,* and *Ngu Ho Binh Tay.* In 1962 Than Van, of the École Supérieure de Pédagogie at Saigon, brought out a new edition, based on research by Professor Nghiem Toan, of a play very popular with South Vietnamese audiences, *San Hau.* The publication of these period plays was undertaken by Éditions Khai Tri of Saigon, under the direction of Le Ngoc Tru.

To help literature to emerge from the doldrums it was in, President Nguyen Van Thieu's office instituted literary prizes. The idea was not new: the earliest known literary prize was that set up in 1924 under the auspices of the Khai Tri Cultural Society of Hanoi. In 1936 the Tu Luc literary group (which included Nhat Linh and Khai Hung among its members) set up its own literary prize, which was very popular with readers. During World War II two other literary prizes came into being, one established in Saigon in 1941 by the *Hoi Khuyen Hoc Nam Viet* (South Vietnamese Society for the Advancement of Education), and the other, the Alexandre de Rhodes Prize, instituted in Hanoi in 1943 under the aegis of the French colonial government.

After the 1954 Geneva Agreements, which ratified the temporary division of Vietnam into two halves, the first known literary prize in South Vietnam was that instituted in 1957 under the Ngo Dinh Diem government. Some 206 entries were received of works published between 1954 and 1957. The jury was chosen from among the most eminent figures in the world of literature and poetry; the first chairman was Doan Quan Tan, and he was assisted by a great many well-known writers and poets including Dong Ho, Ho Bieu Chanh, Vi Huyen Dac, Vu Hoang Chuong, Vu Khac Khoan, Tran Tuan Khai, and Nghiem Toan. Further literary prizes were offered in 1958/59, 1960/61, 1966 and so on. By this means many poets became known to the public, including Anh Tuyen, Mai Trung Tinh, Nha Ca, and Tue Mai. Writers such as Nguyen Manh Con, Binh Nguyen Loc, and Vo Phien received awards. Senior research workers received prizes for their work in the fields of literature and philosophy: e.g., Thanh Lang for his work on folk literature, Nguyen Manh Bao for his research on the I-Ching, Le Ngoc Tru for his Vietnamese Dictionary, and Nguyen Hien Le and Gian Chi for their "Concise History of Chinese Philosophy."

In addition to these governmental literary prizes, there were also literary prizes set up by private bodies such as the Tinh Viet group and the journal *Tieng Chuong;* but they did not arouse as much interest as the state awards. The Pen Club of Vietnam also gave a literary prize for the period 1964–65. The Buddhist Party of South Vietnam gave a short story prize in 1966. The 1966 Pen Club novel prize was awarded to Le Tat Dieu for his novel *Dem dai mot doi* (One Night That Lasts a Lifetime).

On the other side of the barricades, among the FLN, the freedom fighters in the cause of Communism and anti-Americanism also set up literary prizes to foster the spirit of resistance. Thus the Nguyen Dinh Chieu literary prize (1960–65) came into being, and aroused a certain amount of interest among the South Vietnamese resistance. Its jury of 12, set up on December 31, 1965, with Tran Bach Dang, Delegate for Information, Culture, and Education of the South Vietnamese FLN, as its chairman, selected 54 works and awarded three categories of prize:

—*special prizes*, awarded to two books, *Tu tuyen dau to quoc* (In the Front Line for the Motherland), a collection of resistance fighters' letters, and *Song nhu anh* (To Live Like You), the life story of the activist Nguyen Van Troi, told by Phan Thi Quyen and set down by Tran Dinh Van;

—*official prizes (proxime accessits)*, awarded to 8 collections of memoirs, reminiscences and short stories; 1 novel, *Hon dat* (The Clod of Earth), by Anh Duc; 3 volumes of collected poems by Giang Nam, Thu Bon, Thanh Hai and other less well-known poets; 2 plays by Nguyen Vu; and revolutionary songs and short films;

—*consolation prizes*, awarded to two "Revived Theater" plays by Tran Ngoc, and other original works.

Following the setting up of this Nguyen Dinh Chieu literary prize, a new wave of writers and poets began to make their names in the period 1965 to 1975. They included men and women such as Vien Phuong, Le Vinh Hoa, Hoai Vu, Cuu Long, Nguyen Khoa Diem, Dinh Quang Nha, and Duong Thi Minh Huong. According to some Marxist literary critics, this flowering of writers and poets among the South Vietnamese resistance was merely a continuation of the literary trend that started during the first Indochina war, i.e., among the anti-French resistance. Among playwrights the historian of contemporary literature Hoang Nhu Mai singles out in particular Nguyen Vu, a playwright from the South with some ten plays already to his credit: they were short, but of great revolutionary and patriotic merit. He invariably represented the conflict as being between South Vietnamese youth and American imperialism: and his works were recognized as a useful instrument of popular education for the glorification of the revolutionary fighter. Nguyen Vu's two best-known plays are *Mua xuan* (Spring) (1967) and *Duong pho day lua* (Blazing Streets) (1969).

In North Vietnam, from the first bombings right up to April 1975, government and people mobilized for all-out defensive war and resistance to the American aggressor. All resources and energies were placed at the disposal of the state and the Party. As Dang Thai Mai, Chairman of the Union of Vietnamese Writers and Artists, put it in his report to the Fourth National Congress of Vietnamese Writers and Artists held in Hanoi at the end of January 1968, "the transition from peace to war is by no means an easy one." But the writers and artists achieved it quickly and smoothly. The central problem was to defeat the aggressor. To this end Vietnamese writers "did their utmost to train and lead the literary and artistic intelligentsia, to increase the prestige of the nation's cultural heritage, and to safeguard in their writing the purity and clarity of the national language." All writing was devoted to the glorification of revolutionary heroism. Poetry, both lyrical and satirical, took on a new lease of life; and various prose genres such as news reports, essays, diaries, and memoirs flourished. The life stories and reminiscences of servicemen and revolutionary activists were in great demand among a public eager for information. Dispatches from front-line areas, such as Quang Binh province and the island outpost of Con Co, had an enormous readership. Novels and short stories also dealt with the life of the peasants on the cooperative farms, coping with the practical side of the war against the Americans.

It is customary among literary critics and historians to classify North Vietnamese writers under three heads: (a) those who had already achieved fame long before the August 1945 revolution, such as Nguyen Cong Hoan, Nguyen Tuan, To Hoai, Nam Cao, Nguyen Huy Tuong, and Nguyen Hong; (b) those who made their name during the period of anti-French resistance (1945–54), such as Nguyen Dinh Thi, Tran Dang, Nguyen Van Bong, and Vo Huy Tam; and (c) the third generation of writers who began to come to notice during the second Indochina war against the Americans, led by the Party along the road to Socialism and the unification of the country. They included *inter alia* Nguyen Ngoc, Nguyen Khai, Ho Phuong, Vu Thi Thuong, and Nguyen Minh Chau.

In the first category a special place must be reserved for the novelist Nguyen Cong Hoan, who died in 1977. Born in 1903 at Xuan Cau, Bac Ninh province, he was best known as a writer of short stories. Between 1930 and 1945 he produced about thirty novels and two hundred short stories. In them he castigated the misdeeds of French colonial rule, the penury of the Vietnamese peasantry and the extortionate activities of the Vietnamese mandarins in the pay of the French administrations. After the Ho Chi Minh government came to power he held high office in the state Cultural Service, and in 1957–58 was appointed chairman of the Society of Vietnamese Authors. After the August revolution he seems to have produced far fewer short stories, devoting himself rather to writing a few novels, the best known being *Tranh toi tranh sang* (Light and Dark) (1956, over 300 pp.), *Hon canh hon cu* (Muddle) (1961) and *Dong rac cu* (The Heap of Old Rubbish) (over 500 pp.). In "Light and Dark" the author describes Vietnamese society as it was before the August 1945 revolution, vegetating whilst awaiting the cataclysm that was to bring this transitional period to an end. The second novel, "Muddle," deals with the same situation but from a different viewpoint. The third ("The Heap of Old Rubbish"), on the other hand, describes the varied activities of Albert Thua and his wife, enriching themselves at the expense of the poor during the period of French colonial rule. In addition to these three novels, Nguyen Cong Hoan wrote some occasional short stories about the underground and the Resistance. He has also left us two interesting books about his own experiences as a writer: firstly *Viet tieu thuyet* (Writing Novels), written in collaboration with Vo Huy Tam, and secondly *Doi viet van cua toi* (My Life as a Writer), published in 1971 by Éditions Van Hoc. Despite the fact that he moved some way along the path of So-

[146]

cialist realism, the two novels he brought out during World War II, at a time when he was in a state of ideological turmoil, namely *Thanh dam* (Sobriety) and *Danh tiet* (Virtue), published in 1943 and 1944 respectively, earned him the disapproval of Marxist critics.

The famous essayist Nguyen Tuan, author of the remarkable book *Vang bong mot thoi* (Echoes and Reflections from the Past), published in Hanoi in 1940 by Éditions Tan Dan, was a writer of a very different stamp. Born in Hanoi on July 10, 1910, he liked an easy life, good living, and the pleasures of a middle-class existence, and seems to have found it hard to adapt to the way of life expected of a revolutionary Communist militant. Now a member of the Executive Committee of the Vietnamese Society of Arts and Letters, he is one of the very few romantic or individualist writers to have been more or less accepted by the new literary movement that grew out of the August 1945 Communist revolution. His output from 1945 to 1975 consisted predominantly of essays written in the revolutionary army, with which he served in the northwest Highlands: they include *Tuy but khang chien* (Essays Written During the Resistance) (1955–56), *Song Da* (The River Da) (1960), and *Ha noi ta danh my gioi* (Our City of Hanoi Well and Truly Beat the Americans) (1972).

One writer who certainly adapted well to the Communist revolution was the young novelist To Hoai (real name Nguyen Sen), born on August 10, 1920, in a village on the outskirts of Hanoi. He started writing early, and his novels became known well before the end of World War II. His most popular works since the advent of the Socialist Republic are feature articles and short stories dealing with the Highland areas, e.g. *Truyen tay bac* (Tales from the Northwest) (1953), and a novel, *Mien tay* (The West), published in 1967.

Another novelist in the same age group as To Hoai who took part as a Communist militant in the August revolution was Nam Cao (real name Tran Huu Tri). Born on October 29, 1917, in a province south of Hanoi, Nam Cao was killed in action in 1951. He has left us some collections of short stories, including *Doi mat* (Two eyes) (1948) and *Chuyen bien gioi* (Frontier Stories) (1951).

Of the writers in the second category, i.e. those who grew up and made their name during the anti-French resistance, the most noteworthy are probably Nguyen Dinh Thi, Nguyen Van Bong, and Vo Huy Tam.

Nguyen Dinh Thi, born in 1924 at Luang-Prabang in Laos, returned to Vietnam in 1941 and took part in the various political movements. After the August 1945 revolution he was a Delegate, and he is now both Vice-Chairman and Secretary-General of the Vietnamese Society of Arts and Letters. Nguyen Dinh Thi is not only a novelist but also a poet, literary critic, and playwright. His novels and short stories are exceedingly popular, the best known being *Xung kich* (Attack) (1951), *Ben bo song Lo* (On the Banks of the River Lo) (1957), and *Mat tran tren cao* (The Upland Front) (1967). The latter has already been brought out in a French translation.

Nguyen Van Bong, born on January 1, 1921, at Quang Nam, Central Vietnam, started his career as a journalist in the central provinces. From 1954 to 1956 he was on the editorial staff of the daily *Nhan Dan* (The People), and from 1962 to 1969 he was posted to the South, where he adopted the nom de plume of Tran Hieu Minh. He is the author of some short stories and novels, the best being *Con trau* (The Buffalo) (1953), which tells of the life of Vietnamese peasants in the enemy-occupied area. After the first Indochina war he brought out collections of short stories such as *Ve thanh pho* (Back to the City) and *Nguoi chi* (The Big Sister).

Vo Huy Tam, born on December 28, 1926, in Nam Ha province, wrote about the life of Vietnamese coal miners in the mining areas of North Vietnam under the French administration. His most important work, a novel called *Vung mo* (The Mining Area), originally appeared in 1951 under the title *Dinh cong*

[148]

(Strike Action). In 1961 he brought out his second novel, *Nhung nguoi tho mo* (The Miners), which tells of the miners' happier lot under the Socialist government.

The third category of writers comprises those who grew up under the August revolution and became the new creative impetus behind the Socialist Republic and the unification of the country. They include Nguyen Ngoc, who like To Hoai excelled at descriptions of the Highland areas, Nguyen Khai, Nguyen Kien, Chu Van, Dao Vu, and Nguyen Thi Cam Thanh, all of whom wrote a good deal about country life. Huy Phuong, Xuan Cung, and Le Phuong, on the other hand, chose to describe the lives of working men and the jobs they did. Others again, such as Bui Duc Ai, Doan Gioi, Le Kham, and Ho Phuong, found their inspiration in the lives of the South Vietnamese freedom fighters. Young writers from the ethnic minorities began to make a name for themselves: they included Hoang Hac and Nong Minh Chau.

In the theatrical field, there is no denying that much has been done to popularize the old-style folk theater. A number of actor-research worker teams have between them written dozens of books on the old-style Cheo and Tuong plays. On Tuong, for instance, we have excellent books such as *Cheo va Tuong* (The Cheo and Tuong Theaters), by Hoang Ngoc Phach and Huynh Ly (1958), *Tim hieu nghe thuat Tuong* (All About the Tuong Theater), by Mich Quang (1963), and *So thao lich su nghe thuat Tuong* (Outline Study of the History of Tuong), by Hoang Chau Ky (1973). In his book *Hoa trang* (Makeup) (1970), Nhu Dinh Nguyen explains the main principles underlying makeup in the old-style Vietnamese theater, and the ideas of Vietnamese actors on the subject.

The traditional Vietnamese theater or *Tuong* is certainly the oldest type of theatre in Vietnam, and bears no relation to modern Western-type theater.

Vietnamese theater today may be thought of as comprising four branches: the two classical genres, *Tuong* and *Cheo*, the

[149]

"Revived Theater" or *Cai Luong*, and the spoken theater which is written and performed on Western lines.

Tuong, Hat Tuong, or *Hat Boi* is the classical theater, probably Chinese in origin. Following the Vietnamese victory over the Sino-Mongolian army in the reign of the Emperor Tran Nhan Tong (1258–1308), a Chinese prisoner-of-war in the hands of the Vietnamese army by the name of Li Yuan Ki taught the Vietnamese the techniques of the Chinese theater. In this theater the main object is to inculcate love of one's country, loyalty to the Emperor, and filial piety. The language is highly stylized and full of Chinese literary allusions; the gestures betray a very highly developed symbolism; and the music, performed by an orchestra comprising strings, wind, and percussion, is lofty and magnificent. The action moves at a majestic pace; the costumes are impressive and glittering; and the highly colored makeup also conveys a precise symbolism from which even the most inexperienced spectators at once recognize traditional characters such as the Emperor and Empress, the irascible general, the treacherous mandarin, the servile courtesan, the Demon, the Fairy, and so forth. Initially this theater was the preserve of the Emperor, the nobles, the literati and the intelligentsia: but the Vietnamese soon made changes in it and turned it into a specifically Vietnamese type of theater. Thus the female parts were played by actual women, not by men dressed as women as in China; and the costumes and makeup were different. Next, two kinds of *Tuong* emerged, *Tuong Truyen*, i.e., the theater based on Chinese and Vietnamese history, and *Tuong Do*, the fictional theater, in which all the characters are fictitious and quite unhistorical. A demand for this type gradually grew up also among the ordinary people, who liked to go and hear the singing, watch the action, and enjoy the flowery language and the epic or lyric poetry. But *Tuong* could not compete with *Cheo*, which was genuine folk theater. It was essentially comedy, the theater of the people created by the common people and often handed down orally from one generation to another. This folk theater of jokes and songs probably goes back a very long way to the early days of the Vietnamese nation, and probably grew out of the religious rites and songs exchanged between young men and women at harvest festivals and during work in the fields. According to the experts *Cheo* was widely known as early as the tenth century, and already included impromptu poetry, mime, singing, and dancing. *Cheo* plays are often about love of the land and of work, hatred of social injustice, resistance to tyranny, and steadfastness and loyalty to friends. The basic rules of this theater were laid down in 1501 by Luong The Vinh (b. 1441), the theoretician of *Cheo*. It was in the past and still is one of the forms of entertainment most prized by the ordinary people, who find in it relaxation from their everyday worries and wide-ranging moral sustenance. It is common knowledge that in *Cheo* the poor, unfortunate, and weak are the embodiment of all the virtues and always triumph over the cupidity and wickedness of mandarins and emperors.

In South Vietnam a new genre of theater, *Cai Luong,* grew up well before 1918 out of the choral and orchestral concerts organized by Tong Huu Dinh, and it took shape in 1921 with writers from Nam Tu to My Tho. The operas were divided up into acts, and the epic style gave way to free dialogue, psychological interplay, and recitatif interspersed with tuneful arias. This "Revived Theater" was of course Western in conception and influence.

It leads us on to the fourth and last type, the present-day "spoken theater" or modern theater, conceived and produced on European lines. This theater came into being during the French colonial occupation thanks to the efforts of Nguyen Van Vinh in 1915 and Pham Quynh in 1920; these two writers started by translating the plays of Molière and Corneille into Vietnamese. The first purely Vietnamese play in this tradition was *Chen Thuoc Doc* (The Cup of Poison), by Vu Dinh Long in 1921. It goes almost without saying that the modern theater still remains the most fashionable genre today, and is regarded as a highly effective instrument of political and ideological propaganda. There are now over sixty professional companies, and they are sustained by the École des Arts Théâtraux, set up in 1959. Among the best-known plays are such pieces as *Doan tan di vo phuong Nam* (The Train Leaving for the South), *Doi mat* (Eyes), *Tien tuyen goi* (Call from the Front), and *Tinh rung* (Love of the Forest). This movement did not prevent the revival of traditional *Tuong* folk plays such as *Quan Am thi kinh, Luu Binh Duong Le* (The Two Friends), *Kim Van Kieu, Thach Sanh,* and *Son Hau.* Modern writers are sometimes able to abridge very long traditional plays to bring them into line with today's tastes: thus for instance the play *Tam nu do vuong,* which in the old days required four consecutive nights for a single performance, has been rewritten as *Ngon lua hong son,* which only takes one evening. Modern authors also excel at historical plays, the best known examples being *Tieng goi non song* (The Call of the Motherland), *Trung vuong khoi nghia* (The Revolt of the Two Trung Sisters) and *Tran quoc toan.* Modern playwrights in North Vietnam include Nguyen Huy Tuong (1912–1960), author of three plays and several novels. Most plays today are inspired by patriotism and revolutionary militancy, these being also easier to work in than duller topics such as the building of Socialism or everyday life after the unification of the country.

POETRY IN NORTH VIETNAM

From 1963 to 1975 poetry in North Vietnam was essentially political, centering in particular on the war against the American "invaders." The best-known and also the most popular poet was still To Huu (b. 1920), whose real name was Nguyen Kim Thanh. Poets established before 1945 admittedly remained in the majority in North Vietnam, and continued to deploy their poetry as a weapon against the South and the Americans. They included, among others, Xuan Dieu, Luu Trong Lu, Huy Can,

Te Hanh, and Huyen Kieu. The latter brought out two collections of poems in 1964, *Dao nhi vang* (Yellow Deer Island) and *Mua cay* (Ploughing Time), and a further collection, *Bau troi* (The Sky) in 1976. Another poet previously known only as a literary critic, Hoang Trung Thong, has brought out some collections of poems, the most popular being *Dau song* (The Crest of the Waves) (1968) and *Trong gio lua* (In the Scorching Wind). His latest collection of poems came out in 1977 under the title *Nhu di trong mo* (As Though I Were Walking in a Dream).

Of the new generation of poets who rose to fame in the period 1963–75, i.e., those of the "Second Resistance," let us begin with two woman poets. Phan Thi Thanh Nhan, born in Hanoi in 1943 of a modest family, started as a journalist in 1961. In 1973 she brought out a volume of poems under the title *Huong tham* (Secret Perfume), and their tenderness and quiet lyricism were well received. The other woman poet, Xuan Quynh (b. 1942), already has three collections of poems to her credit, including *Choi biec* (Emerald Buds) and *Gio Lao cat trang* (Wind from Laos and White Sand) (1974). She started out as an artiste with the Popular National Song and Dance Ensemble, and began to write in 1960; since 1964 she has been an editor on the weekly *Van Nghe* (Art and Letters). Turning to the men poets, first there is Le Anh Xuan, who was born in the South in 1940 and died in 1968. He left some posthumous poetry which has been collected together and published in 1971 under the title *Hoa dua* (Coconut Palm Flowers). Bang Viet, a native of Hué (b. 1941), has brought out two collections of poems, including *Bep lua* (The Hearth) (1968). Pham Tien Duat (b. 1942) is known for his two volumes of collected poems, *Vang trang quang lua* (The Moon with a Halo of Fire) (1970) and *Tho mot chang duong* (Poems Marking a Stage) (1972). Lastly there is a young poet, also born at Hué, called Nguyen Khoa Diem, the author of two volumes of poems, *Dat ngoai O* (Suburban Area) (1972) and *Mat duong khat vong* (The Road of Hope).

Apart from these poets who have already made something of

a name for themselves, there are other younger poets who brought their first poems out in collective editions such as the two-volume anthology *Hoa tram mien* (Flowers from Everywhere); this contains a selection of poems written in 1974–75, and was published in 1976 by Éditions Van Hoc of Hanoi. The young poets represented include, among others, Hoang Vu Thuat, Le Duy Phuong, Nguyen Bui Voi, Tran Nguyen, Tuan Lan, and Vo Thanh An.

To end this chapter, it is only right to mention that Marxist historians of contemporary Vietnamese literature like to regard President Ho Chi Minh as one of the greatest poets of modern times. In fact his collection of poems in Chinese, describing his impressions and state of mind as a prisoner in a Chinese jail, deserves to be well-known. Entitled *Nguc Trung Nhat Ky*, it has been translated into French by Phan Nhuan under the title *Carnet de prison* (Prison Notebook). In the preface to the French translation Phan Nhuan writes: "In men like Ho Chi Minh, intelligence and sensitivity are but one. There is no hidden door between the private person and the man of affairs. The same enlightenment born of suffering informs both reason and feelings, both the man of action and the poet."

From this "Prison Notebook" we extract two poems (from the French translation by Phan Nhuan):

On Reading "Anthology of the Thousand Poets"

The ancients liked to hymn the glories of nature:
Rivers, mountains, smoke, snow and flowers, moon and wind.
Today's verses need to be armed with steel;
Poets too must be able to fight!

Evening Air

The rose opens and the rose
Fades without knowing what it

[154]

Does. It only needs the scent of roses
Straying through a prison house
To bring all the world's injustices
Howling at the prisoner's heart.

XI: JOURNALISM
IN VIETNAM

Journalism was unknown in Vietnam until the arrival of the
French. A brief note on the new genre which contributed so
much to modern literature may therefore be useful. An ex-
haustive account would require a volume to itself: we shall confine ourselves to the broad outlines, with the emphasis on the
three major periodicals of the first half of the twentieth century, *Dong-duong tap-chi, Nam-phong tap-chi,* and *Phong-hoa Ngay-
nay.*

The history of Vietnamese journalism falls into five main periods: 1865–1907, 1907–35, 1935–40, 1940–45, and 1945 to the
present day. In a brief account such as this we shall merely pick
out the most interesting phases in the growth of the genre.

With the arrival of the French in South Vietnam, the public
began to be aware of the news from the first newspaper to be
published in Vietnamese, *Gia-dinh bao,* produced in Saigon in
1865. By order of the French government of Cochin-China, it
was printed in *quoc-ngu.* In North Vietnam the first newspaper
came out in 1892, entitled *Dai-Nam dong-van nhat bao;* it was
published under the aegis of the Viceroy *(Kinh-luoc),* in Chinese
characters. Subsequently other periodicals were launched by
private individuals, particularly in the South, where the *quoc-
ngu* script quickly caught on. In 1900 *Nong co min dam* came out
in the South in *quoc-ngu,* in 1905 *Dai-Viet tan-bao* in the North
in Chinese and *quoc-ngu.* The latter was managed by a French-

man called Babut and edited by Dao Nguyen-Pho. In 1907 *Dai-Nam dong-van* changed its name to *Dang-co tung-bao;* its editor was Nguyen Van-Vinh, its staff included men such as Phan Ke Binh, and it was printed in Chinese and *quoc-ngu.* These periodicals were still written in very archaic, academic language reminiscent of classical Chinese, and their style was often stilted, repetitive, and tedious, full of parallelisms and Chinese literary allusions. Their contents were mainly official statements and communiqués from the French authorities and the Vietnamese Imperial Government.

With the appearance of *Dang-co tung-bao* under Nguyen Van-Vinh's editorship a new phase began. Weekly and monthly magazines sprang up, with a literary and poetic flavor. Some had clearly defined aims, and side by side with romanticism and sentiment the first signs of rational journalism on the Paris model began to appear. The following are the most important newspapers and periodicals started between 1907 and 1935:

Dang-co tung-bao	1907
Luc-tin tan-van (daily)	1913
Dong-duong tap-chi (weekly)	1913
Trung-Bac tan-van (daily)	1915
Nam-phong tap-chi (monthly)	1917
Dai-Viet tap-chi	1918
Hoc-Bao	1919
Thuc-nghiep dan-bao (daily)	1920
Huu-thanh tap-chi	1921
An-nam tap-chi (editor Tan Da)	1926
Tieng dan (first daily paper in Central Vietnam)	1927
Phu-nu tan-van (first women's magazine)	1929
Phu-nu thoi-dam	1930
Van-hoc tap-chi	1931
Chop bong (first film magazine)	1932
Phong-hoa tuan-bao	1932
Khoa-hoc pho-thong (popular science magazine)	1934
Ngay nay (weekly)	1935

The existence of all these newspapers and magazines favored mass education and the spread of *quoc-ngu*. Editorial staffs, when put to it, gradually developed a more lucid style, freer of Chinese locutions; but at the same time, in translating philosophical and scientific terminology, they enriched Vietnamese with a new vocabulary borrowed either direct from French or from Chinese and Japanese, their Far Eastern predecessors in journalism. Newspapers helped enormously to unify Vietnamese culture: they kept the South Vietnamese informed of what was going on in the North, and vice versa. The language became more standardized. The South Vietnamese, being the wealthier, were the best customers for the literary productions of the North. Thus the press helped the Vietnamese to get to know each other and to appreciate their ethnic and cultural unity.

Of the three periodicals which had a significant influence on literature, the first was *Dong-duong tap-chi,* a weekly which appeared on Thursdays. Its first number, dated May 15, 1913, was headed "Special edition of *Luc-tinh tan-van*" (a daily published in the South since 1910), which seems to indicate that *Dong-duong tap-chi,* printed in Vietnamese, was started to cater for North and Central Vietnam. Its founder was a Frenchman called Schneider and its editor Nguyen Van-Vinh. It comprised two series: an original one of 85 issues (May 15, 1913–December 31, 1914) in large format, taken up mainly with news, and a new series of 102 issues (January 10, 1915–December 31, 1916) in a smaller format, which carried much more in the way of popular educational features, leaving the news to a new daily, *Trung-Bac tan-van.* From the start of the new series the periodical came out on Sundays instead of Thursdays. It had a total life of three years and seven months, and published 187 issues in all. Nguyen Van-Vinh's colleagues were Nguyen Do-Muc and Phan Ke Binh. Each issue of about 32 pages included (particularly in the second series) a dozen or so major features: official communiqués, discussions on or translations from Oriental and Western philosophical works, school texts, articles on Vietnamese history, Vietnamese translations of French stories, selected French, Chinese, and *nôm* texts with translations and notes, a Vietnamese course for Frenchmen and Vietnamese, discourses on Vietnamese linguistics, and so on.

On the literary and educational side Nguyen Van-Vinh and his colleagues did a good job. As regards politics, despite mistakes in emphasis and some exaggerated attacks on the old-style patriotic literati, he at least made his aims clear: overt collaboration with the French, the establishment of clubs where Frenchmen and Vietnamese could meet and make friends, and a reconciliation with the old classical tradition in order to preserve the cultural heritage and moral values of the past. In this way he successfully popularized the essentials of Vietnamese culture—mounting for the purpose an all-out campaign for the use of *quoc-ngu*. *Dong-duong tap-chi* thus contributed much to the molding of contemporary *quoc-ngu* literature, and its articles on literature, philosophy, theology, and poetry paved the way for *Nam Phong*—which was to do still better by aiming to raise the educational level of ordinary people.

Nam Phong tap-chi, the second of our trio of periodicals, started during World War I. Actually *Dong-duong tap-chi* had gone downhill since 1914, and the French Government wanted another journal of higher intellectual caliber to support its colonial policy. Accordingly in 1917, with the help of Louis Marty, Pham Quynh founded *Nam Phong*, whose avowed main object was the preservation of French interests and culture. Pham Quynh, like Nguyen Van-Vinh before him, drew his staff from writers with a classical Chinese education, plus a certain number of French-educated men (see above, chapter 10, under third period). As stated in the second issue of the journal, Pham Quynh and his colleagues aimed to replace the old Chinese culture with a new Vietnamese one, produced by grafting Western, and particularly French, thought on to the original rootstock of the national heritage. Pham Quynh, the editor, wrote on almost every subject, and it is largely due to him that the vocabulary of Vietnamese was enriched with a new philosophical and scientific terminology. *Nam Phong* was a monthly, its first number being that for July 1917. Each number ran to some hundred quarto pages, printed in two columns. The last issue was no. 210, for December 1934. In addition to the portion printed in *quoc-ngu* the journal also included a Chinese section, which continued up to no. 192. Starting with no. 60 it also had a supplement in French. From May 1934 until the end of the year it came out only quarterly. One innovation to Pham Quynh's credit was the production in February 1918 of a special number to mark the Vietnamese New Year: it had a pink cover, and contained a selection of poems celebrating the New Year. This innovation was later copied by other newspapers and periodicals.

Nam Phong carried many more articles than *Dong-duong tap-chi;* though its primary interest was in literature, it concerned itself also with philosophy, theology, history, travel, linguistics, education, the arts, science, politics, economics, and sociology. A bird's-eye view of the paper's development may be obtained by reading three articles: "Preface," by Pham Quynh in no. 1, *"Nam Phong* Yesterday and Today," by Nguyen Tien-Lang in no. 199, at the time of the change of management, and *"Nam Phong's* Achievements—General Conclusions," by Nguyen Huu Tien in the closing issue, no. 210. Some literary historians consider that though Pham Quynh and his staff did an excellent job for Vietnamese literature, they played into France's hands by introducing an element of sloppily effeminate sentimentalism, which gave Vietnamese youth a taste for "soporific" poetry and novels and tended to lull them into passivity. But in Pham Quynh's defence it must be said that the magazine was used by a number of Vietnamese patriots to provide ammunition in the cause of Vietnamese and Asian culture; and that his tactful endeavors to run with the hare and hunt with the hounds were on balance (despite the necessity for concessions to the French) to Vietnam's advantage. It would be less than honest to regard Nguyen Van-Vinh and Pham Quynh as mere servile collaborators or the tools of French cultural diplomacy; though this is the view adopted by critics whose judgment is warped by ideological bias, and young chauvinists holding outdated existentialist views long since rejected in Europe. Pham Quynh and his colleagues put Vietnamese literature on a firm footing, and the only reason the journal ceased publication at the end of 1934 was that times had changed and a new trend in literature had begun. It sprang from French-educated and French-oriented members of *Tu-luc van-doan.*

This third grouping grew up around two magazines, *Phonghoa* and *Ngay nay.* In 1932 Nguyen Tuong-Tam, alias Nhat Linh, a young French-trained science graduate, brought together a number of keen young writers and poets and founded the *Tuluc van-doan* (literally, "Own Strength") literary group. At the same time, by way of backing for his literary and community work, he started a progressive humorous weekly, *Phong-hoa* (Manners and Morals), and a publishing house, *Doi nay* (Life Today) to publish books by members of his group and others. In 1935 Nhat Linh brought out another quarto weekly, *Ngay nay,* which was more artistic and more lavishly produced. *Phonghoa*'s cartoons did more to destroy the old out-of-date habits of Vietnamese society than all Pham Quynh's earnest articles in the preceding period. Indeed, *Tu-luc* was successful on almost every front it fought on between 1932 and 1940, thanks partly to its members' novels and partly to the two magazines. Thus the latter can really only be considered in the context of the whole *Tu-luc* group.

As already mentioned (chapter 10 above), the leading members of this group were Nhat Linh, Khai Hung, The Lu, Hoang Dao, Thach Lam, Tu Mo, Nguyen Cat-Tuong, Nguyen Gia-Tri, To Ngoc-Van, and Tran Binh-Loc. It attacked on three main fronts, literary, social, and political. On the literary front (where it had most success) it campaigned for the use of a concise, lucid style modeled on French, without irrelevant vestiges of Chinese influence such as parallelisms and literary allusions (often incomprehensible to the young). In the social field it adopted a progressive line, advocating the abolition of superstitious and anachronistic practices such as divination, resort to mediums, and village rivalry and canvassing for the position of headman or of mayor. It also campaigned for slum clearance, and supported the rights of the individual against both the dictatorial patriarchal family and the rigidity of old-style Confucianism. On the political front, at a time when French authority was still extremely strong, it directed its attacks against the mandarinate, whose obsequiousness to the French Resident contrasted with its extreme arrogance to ordinary people. It was also critical of the poor implementation of the 1884 treaty, and of the French Government's artifical division of Vietnam into three separate protectorates.

The *Tu-luc* writers borrowed the modern techniques of European journalism to compel and keep their readers' attention. Phong-hoa was somewhat on the lines of *Le canard enchâiné,* and used the same methods. Each number included one or two essays or short stories, and an installment of a serial which was later printed as a whole. Novels that stirred Vietnamese public opinion, such as *Nua chung xuan* (Unfinished Spring), *Hon buom mo tien* (Butterfly Heart Dreaming of a Fairy), *Doan tuyet* (The Break), and *Tieu-son trang-si* (The Knights of Mount Tieu), were all first serialized in the magazine, one installment a week, so that its readers waited impatiently for the next number to come out. There were also numerous cartoons featuring a typical Vietnamese peasant as the victim of modern society and embroiled in some comical situation or other. Thus everybody got to know the cartoon characters Ly Toet (the poor simple-minded peasant), Xa Xe (the fat village yokel, nonchalant and credulous), and Bang Banh (the nouveau-riche braggart); and their names passed into common parlance. The magazine also included a short humorous piece, "For a laugh," and a brief commentary on events in Vietnam and abroad. But the feature which some feared and many more reveled in was the section given over to lampoons on personalities of the day; it fearlessly ridiculed them for their political or personal conduct, for their vices or shortcomings, or even for some quite harmless idiosyncrasy. The reader was treated to a long series of caricatures of political and literary figures: e.g., Nguyen Van-Vinh portrayed as a caster of horoscopes, Nguyen Van-To, the scholar, with his outmoded flea-ridden bun (he eventually became so weary of such cartoons that he had it cut off—which only goes to show the influence *Phong-hoa* had on the customs of the time), and the great poet Tan Da depicted as an inveterate drunkard, with a red nose and a bottle in his hand. There were certainly some who deliberately provoked the magazine's staff in the hope of being pilloried in this way, and then being able to use the fact as a public testimonial. To be lampooned in *Phong-hoa* became a matter of pride, a sacrifice on the altar of fame.

A double page in each issue was devoted to women's fashions; the tangible result of the group's influence was the reform of women's dress and the enhancement of feminine beauty under the lead of the painter Cat-Tuong. One page was of course reserved for the New Poetry, and featured the leader of the school, The Lu, and young disciples of his like Xuan Dieu, Huy Can, and Huy Thong. Two columns were often devoted to attacking other papers or drawing attention to howlers by professional colleagues.

Taking the paper all in all, its staff was obviously genuinely keen to change things; to improve the lot of women and young people, to destroy the old basis of Vietnamese society and replace it with a more rational and democratic one, and to free Vietnamese women from the shackles of Confucian morality and give them a glimpse of the satisfactions of a new and normal life. There was no lack of social work for them to do: the improvement of the living standards of the peasantry, for example, and slum clearance in the suburbs of Hanoi and the villages. Hence novels by *Tu-luc* writers are all to some extent polemical works, often imbued with burning zeal. Moreover the courage, self-sacrifice, altruism, and sometimes idealism of the

[163]

characters in these novels (e.g., *Nua chung xuan, Doan tuyet,* and *Con duong sang*) served as an inspiration to the readers of 1932–40. Nhat Linh and Khai Hung were, of course, often unduly severe and sometimes unreasonable in their attacks on every aspect of the established order. Though they succeeded in turning public opinion against the more grossly outdated features of society, they never actually put forward a realistic program of social reconstruction. They were no doubt hampered by the political circumstances of the time. Be that as it may, no other group of writers since the start of journalism in Vietnam had such resounding and lasting success in so many fields—literature, poetry, the arts, sociology, and feminism. What is more, the work of the *Tu-luc* group enabled the language to weather a difficult period and achieve the standing of a modern literary medium.

XII: THE NEW POETRY

The New Poetry *(Tho Moi)* properly dates from 1932, with the launching of the *Tu-luc* group's periodical *Phong-hoa*. In essence it represented a reaction against the classical school, whose most highly prized forms were modeled on Chinese T'ang poetry. This classical poetry was governed by strict rules prescribing both the number of lines and the rhyming pattern, so that poets commonly had to execute verbal acrobatics in order to conform to them. What is more, the classical poet was utterly impersonal and did not allow his feelings to show: any expression of emotion or subjective reaction was taboo. Language and imagery were largely formalized, consisting of stereotyped or symbolic phrases hallowed by centuries of usage in Vietnam, China, and Japan.

The founders of the *Tu-luc* group aimed to break out of this straitjacket: and to this end, helped by the growing influence of French romanticism, they supported The Lu's New Poetry movement in their crusading magazine *Phong-hoa*. They opened their campaign by publishing Phan Khoi's poem *Tinh gia* (Old Love) in the special New Year number for January 24, 1933. The writer was an outspokenly progressive Confucian, and the poem had previously appeared in the woman's magazine *Phu-nu tan-van* (no. 122 of March 10, 1932). The following is an attempt at a translation.

Old Love

Twenty-four years ago,
On a wet and windy night,
By the pale light of a candle
Beneath a narrow roof
Two young heads of hair, close together, softly lamented:
"Alas for us! Deep is our love, but impossible our union;
Affection will quickly be followed by unfaithfulness;
Better we should part now."
"What ingratitude is this?
How could we bear to leave one another?
Let us make love as much as we can;
God has so decided it, and the die is cast.
We are not husband and wife, but lovers:
Why therefore talk of faithfulness and eternity?"
Twenty-four years later
A chance meeting in a strange place,
Two heads, one as silver as the other.
"Had we not known each other before
How would we recognize one another?"
Just to recall their love of yesteryear
Furtive glances out of the corners
Of almond eyes . . .

This poem is regarded today as having started the New Poetry; yet to be absolutely objective it is not the first of the genre.
Indeed, if New Poetry is taken to mean complete freedom from
limitation on rhyming pattern and line length, together with the
uninhibited release of emotion, then the great classical poet Tan
Da was the father of the New Poetry, without knowing it, long
before Phan Khoi. His well-known poem *Tong biet* (Farewell) is
justly famous for its gentle melancholy and melodious, haunt-
ing rhythm. An attempt at a translation follows.

Farewell

Peach-tree leaves strew the paths of Paradise,
The brook's farewells and the accompaniment of the oriole's song,

What sorrow and bitterness!
Six months in Paradise,
One step: earth.
Of the dream of yesteryear and this remnant of love, no more than
  that!
The weathered stone and the faded moss
And the flower drifting on the sliding water,
And the crane's flashing flight in the heights of the Empyrean!
Heaven and Earth, farewell! Farewell for ever!
Over the entrance of the cave,
The summit of the mountains
And the bowers of bygone days
The heedless moonlight, ever playful.

Others of Tan Da's poems are at least as beautiful and moving as the finest of the New Poetry. In an article on Tan Da in
the journal *Indochine* for October 13 and 30, 1940, his brother-
in-law, Nguyen Tien-Lang, gave French versions of some of his
poems, from which the following are taken.

To be drunk is, when you think about it, very wrong.
Wrong I am quite willing to be; drunk I wish to stay.
Is not the earth drunk, or why else does it spin?
Is not the sky drunk, or why else is its face red?
And who laughs at them?

The First Lotus-flower in Bloom on the Pond

On the pond what is lovelier than the lotus-flower?
Here is one in bloom before any of the others,
On the surface of the water, at the foot of the clouds, this feminine
  beauty, like a stranger . . .
Green calyx, white corolla, and at its heart the yellow stamens . . .
Humming, a cloud of butterflies swarms about it,
While in the distance a solitary boat rows slowly.
It is done: your beauty, O flower, has opened now, and you can never
  close again!
And you seem, maidenly modest, still afraid lest your sisters envy you.

In a sense the New Poetry can be said to have always existed, both in Vietnam and in China. Long before the Han era, there was a great vogue for poems set to the music of the Imperial court *(yüeh-fu)* or to Chinese folk melodies; and the foremost T'ang poets such as Li T'ai-po and Po Chü-i were not above writing for this medium. In Vietnam, where the language with its five tones has a sing-song quality in any case, proverbs, adages, and rhythmical prose passages have always constituted an anthology of poems with an infinite variety of rhymes. Hence what is known as the New Poetry is perhaps no more than a reversion to type, caused by the impact of French romantic poetry.

For the poets of this *nouvelle vague,* the poetry of 1932 differed from classical poetry in both form and content. As for content, it had to express all the emotions and hymn all the beauties of nature (such as mankind). It had to be "a lute with a thousand tunes," "a brush with a thousand colors." The poet needed to let his love or hate, his desire or resentment, show through; he also needed the gift of portraying the myriad beauties of everyday life and the changing facets of the material world. He was no longer content to rely on imagery and symbolism worn threadbare by centuries of use.

As for form, the founders of the New Poetry preached complete freedom both in line length and in rhyme. The rules of prosody were liberalized to conform with those current in French poetry. From now on a poem could consist of any number of lines, and a line could have anything from one to twelve syllables, arranged in no prescribed order. The rhyming pattern became flexible: rhymes could henceforth be continuous, alternating, or in any other pattern. The even tone *(bàng)* and the uneven *(tràc)* could be mixed. After World War II, especially in South Vietnam, the trend was towards the *vers libre* of Gustave Kahn and Jacques Prévert and the rhythmic stanzas of Paul Fort; and a perusal of the work of some of the existentialist poets of the South leads to the conclusion that they even tended to re-

[168]

ject rhyme altogether and write long lines using only assonance, after the manner of Paul Claudel. All these changes re-
flect the overwhelming influence of French poetry, which likewise
impelled Vietnamese poets to adopt all the devices of French
prosody such as enjambment, alliteration, and the caesura.

Vietnamese New Poetry can be roughly divided into three
phases: the period of birth and rapid development (1932–45),
a period of confusion (1945–54), and a period of internal change
(1954–62). The most exciting was the first, when it was in a really
fiery, aggressive phase. From 1932 to 1940 the dominant influ-
ences were the school of The Lu and his circle of young poets
such as Luu Trong-Lu, Xuan Dieu, and Huy Can, and "independent" poets like Han Mac-Tu, Nguyen Binh, Nguyen Nhuoc-
Phap, Bang Ba-Lan, and Anh Tho. We must also in fairness
not forget *Bach-nga* (The Swan), a group started in Hanoi in
1936 by Nguyen Vy (now running the Saigon paper *Pho-thong*).
Nguyen Vy opined that Vietnamese New Poetry represented a
harmonious blending of traditional Vietnamese poetic forms with
French classical poetry (see *Pho-thong*, no. 106, p. 77). According to him, his own volume *Tap tho dau* ("Early poems"), published in 1934, showed such originality of rhyme and freedom
of form that it marked the zenith of the New Poetry—a statement for which he must himself bear the responsibility. Nguyen
Vy has also given us his résumé of the main landmarks in the
lightning growth of the New Poetry, which is perhaps worth re-
producing:

1932:   poems by Phan Khoi and Tan Da written according to the old
        rules of prosody *(co phong)*.
1933:   *Nguoi son nhan* (The Montagnard), by Luu Trong-Lu; poems
        by The Lu; Pham Huy-Thong's volume of poetry *Yeu duong*.
1934:   *Tap tho dau* (Early Poems), by Nguyen Vy; Pham Huy-Thong's
        volume of poetry *Anh Nga*.
1935:   *May van tho* (Some Poetic Rhymes), by The Lu; *Tieng dich song
        O* (The Sound of the Flute by the River O), by Pham Huy-
        Thong; *Ngay xua* (In Days of Yore), by Nguyen Nhuoc-Phap.

1936: *Gai que* (The Peasant Girl), by Han Mac-Tu; formation of
Nguyen Vy's group *Bach-nga* (The Swan); Phan Khoi's poems
Chuong dan thi thoai.

1937: *Tan ngoc,* by Pham Huy-Thong; *Dieu Tan,* by Che Lan-Vien.

1938: *Tho tho,* by Xuan Dieu.

1939: *Tieng thu* (Voices of Autumn) by Luu Trong-Lu.

1940: *Lo buoc sang ngang,* by Nguyen Binh; *Lua thieng,* by Huy Can.

We give below translations of some extracts from poems by
leading poets of the first phase.

I am but passionately in love
With beauty, in its myriad shapes and guises.
I take up the pen of poetry to portray
And the thousand-fretted lute to hymn
Beauty—silent, raging or innocent,
Like the sublime and mighty beauty
Of mountains and rivers, and poetry, and thought.

—The Lu, *Cay dan muon dieu* (The Lute with a Thousand Tunes)

The Fairy Queen's hair streaming beside the wellspring,
Soft whispering of the pine trees on the lonely dune,
Pink clouds halted behind the pass,
Trees gilded by the sun in the gathering dusk.

—The Lu, *Tieng sao thien-thai* (The Heavenly Flute)

Love, do you not hear the sobbing of Autumn
Beneath the pallid moon?
Do you not hear the likeness of her absent husband
Rise up all a-tremble
In the mind's eye of his lonely wife?
Love, do you not hear the forest in autumn,
And the whispering autumn leaves,
And the tawny fawn, startled,
Stamping underfoot the withered yellow leaves?

—Luu Trong-Lu, *Tieng thu* (Voices of Autumn)

[170]

To be a poet is to shiver with the wind,
To dream by moonlight and to frolic with the clouds;
To have one's soul pinned to a thousand heartstrings,
Or torn apart by a hundred different loves.

—Xuan Dieu, *Cam Suc* (Poetic Feeling)

How is love to be explained,
And what does it mean? One evening
It captivates us with its gentle sunlight,
Its fluffy clouds, and its plaintive breeze.

—Xuan Dieu, *Vi sao* (Why?)

January is as alluring as two lips very close to.

—Xuan Dieu, *Voi vang* (Haste)

Impossible Love

The dead leaves
Fall,
Covering the whole surface of the lake;
Imperceptible
Ripples . . .
The boat glides along, parting the leaves,
And suddenly the pale star rises
From the depths of the watery mirror . . .

—Vu Hoang-Chuong, *Tinh si* (from Simone Kuhnen de la Coeuillerie's French translation *Poésie grise,* 1940).

Beyond the curtain of lianas, the rain falls ceaselessly.
Nostalgic atmosphere, endless night.
I seem to hear the faint sound of footsteps;
I am alone . . . unspeakable misery . . .

—Vu Hoang-Chuong (from Simone Kuhnen de la Coeullerie's French translation *Nuages,* 1943)

Night-time Depression

Like a child in its cradle
I would that very gentle arms
Might rock my grieving spirit
And be as it were a kindly shelter
For my heart—a traveler lost
On a remote deserted road.

—Nguyen Vy, *Dem sau ve* (from the French translation by Huynh
Khac-Dung)

Unsullied Night

Tonight I shall not lie spreadeagled beside the incense-burner
Listening to the liquor chuckling in the glass,
The music swirling in the smoke,
And Time brushing past my eyelids . . .

—Nguyen Vy, *Dem trinh* (from the French translation by Nguyen
Van-Con)

From 1963 to 1975 the most active and prolific poets in South
Vietnam were Vu Hoang Chuong and Nguyen Vy. Dong Ho
continued to write classical poetry on the lines of Tan Da's.
Alongside the two major figures (i.e., Vu Hoang Chuong and
Nguyen Vy) a new generation of poets arose, including Dinh
Hung, Nguyen Sa, Cung Tram Tuong, Bui Giang, Tue Mai,
and Hoang Huong Trang.

In North Vietnam the chief proponents of the New Poetry,
such as The Lu, Xuan Dieu, Huy Can, Che Lan Vien, and To
Huu, were still writing. But poetry in general took a new direction, being entirely given over to the glorification of Socialism
and the Vietnamese Communist Party. Poets were expected to
hymn the benefits of the Socialist régime and proclaim their
hatred of the American invaders and their "lackeys." Many young
poets from the Southern Resistance, such as Giang Nam, Thu
Bon, and Thanh Hai, were held in high esteem. We give below

translations of some of the most representative works by North Vietnamese poets of this period:

Evening

The old man sits by the window
In the sinking sun, this autumn evening,
His back bent, weaving a basket.
Tomorrow he will sell it for a handful of rice.

His skinny trembling hands
Tug at a strip of golden bamboo
To the accompaniment of a lament
From his parched lips.

Until the moment when the evening light fades,
And the dead leaves drop off and fall
And float inertly past in front of him;
Then the old man puts down the strips and looks at the sky.

—To Huu.

The Cuckoo

When the cuckoo calls its flock
The spring rice is beginning to ripen,
And the fruit on the trees is already filling out with sugar;
In the shady garden there rises
The gentle leaven of the crickets' song.
Corncobs with their golden ears fill
The courtyard, all ruddy with sunlight;
So blue it is, the sky seems wider and higher:
Kites sing as they slide through the air.

I feel summer waking close to my heart,
And my feet itch to shiver this cell to smithereens.
Oh, summer!
It is smothering me, choking me to death!
Outside in the firmament
The cuckoo goes on calling.

—To Huu

Winter

Last night it came back, the wind from the eastern sea;
Autumn seems to numb earth and sky,
And the mountains round about are perhaps already cold.
The forest shivers, and the rustling sound echoes away into the distance.

In the prison courtyard, some Malabar almond trees:
Leaves and branches sigh under the weight of winter sadness.
With my back to the lonely night, I listen:
The icy wind creeps into the cracks of the cell.

With neither blanket nor mat,
Nakedness of solitude stretched out in the middle of the dungeon,
I hear my voice talking to myself.
Great craving for friends—I strew my affection to the four winds.

—To Huu.

Pham Hong Thai[1]

Oh, to live and die like you,
Hating the enemy, loving one's motherland:
In life a bomb-blast,
In death as pure as limpid water.

—To Huu

(The four poems above are from the French translations in *Sang et Fleurs* [Paris: Les Éditeurs Français Réunis, 1975].)

Spring Flowers in the South

In sunny springtime I traveled through the South:
Never will I forget its young soldiers.

1. In 1924, while Governor-General Merlin was on a visit to the town of Sa Zien, Pham Hong Thai attempted to kill him with a bomb. He failed, and threw himself into the river Chau Giang.

They are the tender buds of spring bursting on the trees;
Flowers bloom on their lips, rivers smile in their eyes.
Nineteen, the age when uniform becomes too tight even before it shows
   signs of wear.
Their step is still unsure, but resolute and keen.
They are unaccustomed to battle—all they know is working in the fields;
But they go to their baptism of fire, volunteers to drive out the enemy.
They have no sweethearts to write to
Of their hates, angers, griefs, or joys.
In the chilly forest night they share the same blankets,
And squabble laughingly over a brief warm at the campfire.
They dream dreams full of sunlight and roses—
The loveliest and most naive of dreams;
They are birds that have never yet crossed the ocean;
They yearn for the open sea; the horizon seems paltry to them.

—Giang Nam

You Have Got Into University

Tomorrow, when the motherland is unified,
Tomorrow, you will come back and give me lessons,
And we shall not have to write on the wall with coal any more
Or dread the horror of the police searches.
You will say to me "Come on, big brother, courage!"
And I shall smile, remembering the moonlight,
And our motherland, that gave you wings
And the honor of marching with those up at the front.
I shall need to keep a long sleepless night
To tell you about the South, and its struggle and agony:
"In those days, little sister, I had
But one school on earth—the Revolution!"

—Giang Nam

My Workshop

My workshop
   is protected by the clouds
   and hidden by the mountains;

[175]

Its bamboo roof
   interwoven with forest leaves
   disguises it.

These leaves that camouflage it
   are sometimes fresh,
   sometimes withered;
The rocks round about it
   are sometimes blue,
   sometimes white:
But my workshop
   keeps its ardent heart
That neither hunger nor opulence,
   ugliness nor beauty
   manages to upset.

The night is late,
   the sky faintly starry:
Our love for humanity
   will never be extinguished.
Today, we are building tomorrow:
With our clothes soaked in sweat,
   we sing of Freedom.

—May Trong, a worker-poet (from the French translation in *L'ouvrier vietnamien à travers ses poèmes* [Hanoi: Éditions Lao Dong, 1957]).

XIII: THE CONTEMPORARY
VIETNAMESE NOVEL

By novel we mean the art form in the forefront of Western literature during the nineteenth century. It has of course always existed, in every civilization and period.

Fiction in Vietnam before the French occupation was still at the stage of the "courtly romances" in verse that flourished in France between about 1130 and 1250. (In France at that time the word "romance" meant the vernacular, as distinct from Latin, the learned language; and so it was applied to everything written in Old French.) The French "romance" of the twelfth and thirteenth centuries was not a prose narrative but a long piece of octosyllabic verse, and this was the standard pattern in Vietnam before the advent of the French (see chapters 8 and 9). Most were in six- and eight-syllable verse (6-8), or in six-eight couplets alternating with seven-syllable couplets (6-8-7-7).

Contemporary Vietnamese fiction on the European model dates only from World War I, with the publication in *Dong-duong tap-chi* and *Nam Phong* (see chapter 11) of short stories by Pham Duy-Ton, Nguyen Ba-Hoc, and Phan Ke Binh. In the South, translations were produced of old Chinese tales like *Feng shen, San kuo,* and *Tung Chou lieh-kuo;* and from 1912 the scene was dominated by the popular novelist Ho Bieu-Chanh. Thus the contemporary novel started life in South Vietnam. Ho Bieu-Chanh's works were known only in Cochin-China, not at all in the North. It was not until 1925 and the publication of Nguyen

Trong-Thuat's *Qua dua do* (The Watermelon) and Hoang Ngoc-Phach's *To Tam* that the novel made an impact on a national scale. *Qua dua do* was an attempt at a historical novel by a Confucian scholar still steeped in Chinese influence; though ill-constructed and written with complete disregard for historical accuracy, it was nevertheless hailed by most intellectuals of the day as a praiseworthy advance in the literary field. *To Tam*, a love story strongly influenced by *La dame aux camélias*, was a typical sentimental melodrama, and brought tears to the eyes of a whole generation of middle-class readers; indeed, it acquired remarkable celebrity. It is true that at that time (1925–30) French romanticism was all the rage in Vietnam, and the public were so eager for French culture that they welcomed with fanatical enthusiasm anything from the West, whether good or bad. Following in the wake of this wave of romanticism, which was given added impetus by novels such as *To Tam, Van lan nhat ky,* and *Tuyet hong le su,* there was an epidemic of suicides among young people, rejected or disillusioned lovers, and abandoned mistresses, who threw themselves into either the Grand Lac or the Petit Lac at Hanoi. Fortunately this morbid trend was short-lived.

Between 1930 and 1935, and especially after the advent of the *Tu-luc* group in 1932, the Vietnamese novel developed rapidly. Here, as in poetry and journalism, the *Tu-luc* writers were in the van. From 1932, and again in the years following the establishment of the Popular Front in France (1936–37), when the Movement for the Propagation of *quoc-ngu* was led by the socialist Phan Thanh, the Vietnamese novel made tremendous strides. It reached its zenith in the years before World War II (1935–39), as evidenced by the multiplicity of differing styles.

Historians of modern Vietnamese literature disagree about the classification to be adopted: Duong Quang Ham, Vu Ngoc Phan, Kieu Thanh-Que, Le Thanh, and in more recent times Thanh Lang all had their own ideas of how writers of the various schools should be grouped. Any scheme of classification is of course a hazardous affair, especially when the same writer can quite well, to judge from his works, be both a romantic and a realist (or a Socialist and a Conservative). At this distance in time, however, we feel able to suggest a broad classification. Contemporary Vietnamese fiction takes three forms: (a) short stories, an initial stage through which all well-known novelists seem to have passed; (b) essays and reminiscences *(Tuy but)*, a form likewise borrowed from the West, in which the writer lets his pen roam freely where it will: the best-known exponents of this form are Nguyen Tuan (now in Hanoi) and Lang Nhan (now in Saigon); and (c) novels proper, which exhibit a multifarious variety of styles. The main types of novel are:

(i) the romantic, comprising the vast bulk of the fiction written during this period. It ranges from mythological-historical works, through picaresque Montagnard tales (in which the action takes place in the Central Highlands, supposedly infested with brigands, ghosts, and Shamanist sorcerers), to "black novels" after the manner of Walpole and Anne Radcliffe;

(ii) the Socialist-realist type, including the polemical works of the *Tu-luc* group (Nhat Linh, Khai Hung, Hoang Dao, and Thach Lam), didactic novels (Tran Tieu, Bui Hien, Nguyen Cong Hoan, Vu Bang, and To Hoai), documentaries (Vu Dinh-Chi, Vu Trong-Phung, Trong Lang, and Ngo Tat-To), realist novels (Nguyen Hong and Truong Tuu), and satirical or humorous novels (Do Phon); and

(iii) the scholarly type, aimed at preserving Vietnam's ancient cultural heritage; these came from the pen of Nguyen Van Ngoc, Tran Trong-Kim, Le Du, Bui Ky, Nguyen Van-To, and Tran Van Giap.

With the 1954 armistice and the splitting of the country into two, writing did not escape the influence of politics. As already mentioned, in the communist North the novel was centered around Socialist realism, and concerned itself mainly with the achievements of the Party and the anti-Imperialist struggle. In the South it was relatively uncommitted, confining itself to portraying the ravages of war and the blessings of liberty, and to preaching the renewal of society by the path of individual freedom. At all events, despite the war and the seven years of independence, during which an uneasy alliance between Communists and Nationalists made possible the emergence of a sort of "committed" writing, no author of world class to compare with Céline, Bernanos, Pasternak, Hemingway, or Graham Greene appeared in either North or South. Obviously contemporary Vietnamese writing was still far from reaching the stage of the "symphonic" novels of Proust or Dostoyevsky. Nhat Linh's attempt, after his return to civilian life, to produce a novel sequence in the manner of Roger Martin du Gard was frustrated by his untimely death. The time has not yet come for the Vietnamese novel to race ahead, as in Europe and especially France, to the level of the *nouvelle vague*. Nevertheless the current revival in the fields of poetry and fiction shows that Vietnamese literature is striving to chart a course for itself; where this will take it, only time will tell.

ANALYSIS OF SOME NOVELS BY
TU-LUC WRITERS

Doan-tuyet (The Break), by Nhat Linh (Hanoi: *Doi nay*, 1935; new edition, Saigon, 1958).

Loan, a modern young woman of good family, is in love with Dung, son of a provincial governor during the French occupation. Dung is a militant with revolutionary leanings; and his father, fearing victimization by the French Government, refuses to acknowledge him publicly as his son. Loan for her part is forced by her family to marry Than, a man she does not know. The final interview between Loan and Dung is terrible. Loan comes away in despair and marries Than, a dreary, spineless young man who lives with his cantankerous mother, his naughty little sister, and his insolent concubine. Thus placed against her will in an antiquated, feudalistic atmosphere, she rebels against her weak, apathetic husband and his family. She is misunderstood by her mother-in-law, who taxes her with being too modern, and is jeered at and insulted by her sister-in-law and the concubine. One night, during a violent family row, Than loses his temper and picks up a copper vase to hit Loan; she in self-defence arms herself with a metal paper-knife, and her husband accidentally falls on it and is killed. Loan is charged with manslaughter and arraigned before the court, but is acquitted thanks to the skill of her advocate, who makes an eloquent and moving plea in her defence. Loan leaves her husband's family and goes to work on a newspaper. Dung, the militant, hearing of Than's death and Loan's break with her earlier life, writes to a couple he knows begging them to do all they can to help him get in touch with Loan again and renew their earlier love. Loan, told of this by the couple, is transported with joy at the thought of her future happiness.

Doi ban (The Two Friends), by Nhat Linh (Hanoi: *Doi nay*, 1936).

This novel can be regarded as a sequel to the previous one. In "The Break" the main character was Loan, the modern woman, struggling in a backward, feudalistic society. In "The Two Friends" the author plays on his readers' enthusiasm for the mysterious Dung, the militant revolutionary: everything is left blurred and nebulous, but he is the main character, and Loan plays only a minor role.

The scene is set at an historic moment for Vietnam: the death of the great patriot Phan Chu-Trinh. Obeying the call for a strike to mark the great man's death, Dung takes the opportunity to go and stay awhile in the country with his father, the erstwhile provincial governor. He cannot bear the stifling, antiquated atmosphere of his home, where everything is mannered and artificial. He is in love with Loan and she with him, but the two young people have not yet had a chance to avow their mutual love. Meanwhile Dung and his great friend Truc have kept in touch with other militant revolutionaries. In order to damp Dung's revolutionary ardor, his father, the old mandarin, tries to marry him off to a well-born young woman called Khanh. Dung agrees, but on the day before the wedding he and Truc flee to China.

In *Doi ban*, as in *Doan tuyet*, the author tries to make the character of Dung, the militant lover, mysterious and appealing. He does this by describing the stagnant, claustrophobic world of the old mandarins and the tragedies of jealousy and pride that go on beneath its placid, middle-class surface. In these two books Nhat Linh has managed to convey a grim picture of life under the old order. His realistic descriptions are often full of destructive humor directed against bourgeois society. Though he occasionally goes too far, his writing is imbued with sincerity, fierce opposition to the misdeeds of an outdated mandarinate, and deep solicitude for the peasantry in their material and intellectual penury. Nhat Linh's work, like Khai Hung's, shows marked French influence both in thought and style; the latter ranges from brisk and straightforward to airy and fanciful, and (especially in *Doi ban*) achieves an unprecedented subtlety and polish. Here are two short extracts from *Doan tuyet:*

On her wedding night, Loan smiled ruefully at the thought that when all was said and done she was little better than a whore. A whore prostituted herself for a living; she, with her eyes shut, was giving herself to Than, whom she did not love, simply to gratify her parents. . . .

All the year long Dung was on the move. Now he stopped for a few days on the estate of a friend of his, and as the Old Year was dying, sipped a glass of wine in the fine spacious house. Yet he still felt himself one of the common people. He took tremendous pleasure in being absorbed and lost in this mass of nameless, ageless beings, in living their life and experiencing their desires, like a blade of grass among myriads of others in a broad meadow. . . .

Hon buom mo tien (Butterfly Heart Dreaming of a Fairy), by Khai Hung, with foreword by Nhat Linh (Hanoi: *Doi nay,* 1933; new edition by Nhat Linh, Saigon: *Phuong-Giang,* 1954).

This was Khai Hung's first novel. The following is a synopsis of the plot.

Ngoc, a young student at the Agricultural College, is spending his holidays at Long-giang Pagoda, where his uncle is the Superior. There he makes the acquaintance of a young monk, Lan, whose innocent beauty greatly intrigues him: he suspects him of being really a woman, and several days of observation strengthen this conviction. One day the opportunity comes for him to satisfy his curiosity: Lan is sent to Long-van Pagoda with presents for the Superior, and Ngoc obtains permission to go with him. As they are about to start back the rains come on, so that the two young people have to stay overnight at Long-van Pagoda; and the young student, seizing his chance, presses Lan to share his bed. An argument follows, during which Ngoc pulls Lan to him: Lan's habit suddenly tears, exposing a woman's breasts, tightly strapped up. Ngoc gives a gasp of surprise and releases Lan, who runs away. From then on she (for Lan is in fact a young woman) tries to avoid Ngoc. The latter apologizes, and tells her he is in love with her; he swears to sacrifice everything for his desperate love, at which Lan is deeply touched. After this talk Ngoc leaves the pagoda and returns to Hanoi. One Sunday evening, Ngoc returns to the pagoda and swears to Lan to love her platonically always; in return he asks her permission to come and see her as often as possible, whenever his college holidays permit.

I swear that I will always keep this oath. As Buddha is my witness, I will dedicate my whole life to the devoted worship of your sweet pure self . . . I have no family any more. My "large family" is now humanity and the universe, and my small family our two selves, seeking refuge in the charity of Buddha. We love each other in our hearts and minds, and even Buddha cannot prevent our doing so. . . .

Lan agrees; and the two lovers part in a gloomy twilight landscape. The closing scene is somewhat reminiscent of Alphonse Karr:

At that moment, in the subdued light and with the strokes of the bell dropping slowly one by one, everything seemed to be swallowed up in the vast silence. Lan, standing with her hands folded in an attitude of prayer, gazed with dreamy eyes at the path of trodden earth winding along at the foot of the hill. The evening breeze soughed softly. The leaves were falling.

This novel (or love song) has impressed most modern critics with its enchantingly light touch and its dreamlike atmosphere, faintly tinged with an aura of Buddhism.

Nua chung xuan (Unfinished Spring), by Khai Hung (Hanoi: *Doi nay,* 1934; reprinted Saigon: *Phuong-Giang,* 1957).

This is one of this talented writer's best-known novels, and also certainly one of his best. It is a polemical piece, and the author is unsparing in his attacks on polygamy, the shocking extortion of village headmen, and all the forms of social injustice prevalent in Vietnam in those days. The following is a synopsis of the plot.

Mai, a young woman of gentle birth, lives with her younger brother, Huy. They are orphans. Their father was one of the old literati. The two young people are completely poverty-stricken, and Mai can no longer find the money for her brother's school fees. Just at this moment she happens to meet Loc, an old pupil of her father's, who readily agrees to help her financially. Loc is a senior official in Hanoi; his father, a high mandarin, has long been dead, and only his mother, willful and cantankerous, is left. Loc and Mai are deeply in love, and soon Mai becomes pregnant; but Loc's mother does not wish him to marry a poor girl, and by a mean trick separates the two lovers. Mai manages to overcome her difficulties and bring up her child. Courageous and cynical, she refuses all proposals of marriage (from a doctor and a painter, both moved by her sad beauty). Five years pass, and Mai's brother Huy becomes a school-teacher in a town in central Tonkin. Mai and her child live with

Huy in an oasis of peace and contentment far from the capital, Hanoi. As luck would have it, her erstwhile lover Loc meets the painter, Bach Hai, at a private viewing; and the latter, unaware that Loc was and is Mai's only love, tells him of his own devotion to her, adding that Mai will have none of his offer of marriage and is proudly struggling on in her poverty and isolation. The artist is loud in his praises of Mai's virtue and courage. With a flash of enlightenment Loc sees through his mother's trickery: he realizes that it was she who engineered the whole thing in order to part him from his beloved. He knows now that Mai is still pure and virtuous and loyal to their early love; but the damage is done. Loc is anxious to make amends. He appreciates the greatness of Mai's sacrifice in giving up everything, in her youthful prime, for the sake of his own selfish happiness, searches for her high and low, and manages to find her retreat. She forgives him, but refuses to go back to living with him again, and furthermore reminds him of his obligations as a husband—he having meanwhile obeyed his mother and married the daughter of a high mandarin. She agrees to stay celibate for the rest of her life out of loyalty to her first love and to keep intact the chaste memory of her "unfinished spring." Loc, happy and with his mind at rest, promises her to devote himself henceforth to good works in order to be worthy of her love.

As we have said, this book is a scathing indictment of polygamy and arranged marriages, and a plea for freedom of choice and enduring love—and hence for love matches founded on mutual affection and congeniality. It is well written, and the characterization is excellent: Loc's mother, for instance, typifies the proud, shrewish woman of the old middle class, repository of the outdated traditions of a decaying society. The character of Loc is also well drawn: he represents *petit-bourgeois* intellectual youth, which has absorbed French culture but still lives in an underdeveloped society—with the result that his life is a perpetual conflict between ancient traditions and the modern world. The character of Mai, on the other hand, is overidealized: she is represented as beautiful, advanced, upright and virtuous, courageous to the point of foolhardiness, and both realistic and idealistic (which may help to explain the book's popularity with women readers of the time). But the work has many merits: as a psychological study it is excellent, the characters' states of mind being skilfully dissected; and it is an accurate reflection of Vietnamese society around 1930–35, well portraying the conflict between new and old. Khai Hung's style is in general clear and readable, occasionally pungent and incisive, and free from excessively Chinese locutions. Readers find his simple yet melodious prose—colorful, evocative, and passionate—highly appealing.

Tieu-son trang-si (The Knights of Mount Tieu), by Khai Hung (Hanoi: *Doi nay,* 1940; third impression, Hanoi, 1952, 2 vols.).

This historical novel is an account of the heroic struggles of a small band of knights loyal to the Le kings after the latter were dethroned by Nguyen Hue, leader of the popular uprising known as the Tay Son revolt, at the end of the eighteenth century. Vietnam was at that time in a state of utter chaos; Nguyen Hue, the Tay Son king, had to contend both with the Chinese invasion and with the machinations of those who supported the legitimate Le dynasty. The main characters are Quang Ngoc, the leader of the knights, Nhi Nuong, his mistress, Pham Thai, Le Bao, and Quynh Nhu; and the love story of Pham Thai, the cavalier poet, and the beautiful Quynh Nhu, both actual historical figures (see chapter 9) is grafted on to the civil war theme. Khai Hung's achievement is to have woven this true story into the fabric of his picaresque novel in such a way as to produce a synthesis of fact and fiction which has both grandeur and charm. He has all the skills of the true novelist: he compels his readers' interest by the use of suspense, through the doughty deeds of the little band of heroes, ready to sacrifice everything to bring down the hated régime, and through the enchanting love story of Pham Thai and Quynh Nhu. Historical facts are respected, and the painstaking descriptions of certain episodes bring vividly before us the exciting life of these brave and idealistic fighters. The novel ends on a note of poignant sadness with the suicide of Quynh Nhu and the defeat of the conspirator-heroes.

GENERAL COMMENTS ON KHAI HUNG'S WORKS

Of all the *Tu-luc* writers, Khai Hung was the most prolific and the most popular with the youth of his day. French-educated, and considerably influenced by French romanticism, he was essentially a bourgeois liberal intellectual. His aim was to use literature and the press to reform society: and consequently most of his writing was polemical. This applies even to his historical novel "The Knights of Mount Tieu," adjudged one of Vietnam's best books in the nationwide poll organized in 1943 by the Saigon bookseller Khanh-Dam. Khai Hung was the mouthpiece of intellectual youth; together with Nhat Linh, he campaigned against large families, the mandarin class, polygamy, and arranged marriages. He shows acute insight into the spirit of self-sacrifice that animated young people (particularly in Hanoi), and his meticulously detailed descriptions of their states of mind are admirable. Like the narrative poems of the eighteenth and nineteenth centuries, most of his novels have happy endings; but whether this is due to the influence of tradition or to deliberate optimism is hard to say. In his campaign against the vestiges of feudalism, he extolled the virtues of individualism and freedom of choice. Khai Hung was of one mind with his colleague Nhat Linh in putting forward to the young a plan of action and a program of reform: he favored a return to the land and the raising of the peasants' standard of living, and was keen to give young intellectuals a purpose in life. The 1935 Popular Front in France also helped Khai Hung by influencing him away from romanticism and towards realism. An extremely perceptive observer, he has left us a fascinating and detailed picture of the life of the great provincial mandarins and their treatment of the poor folk of the paddy fields. It amounts to a bitter indictment of the former for extortion, defalcation, abuse of trust, and all manner of corrupt practices. He also has a felicitous pen for the lives of the peasants, their hopes and aspirations. His descriptions of the scenery of the delta, the pagodas and the calm beauty of the Vietnamese countryside by moonlight are hymns to the beauty of nature—as witness this passage from *Hon buom mo tien:*

In the West, behind the verdant green of the hills, the reddening sun glinted through the interstices of the dark green leaves. The moss-grown roof of the pagoda melted into the fields, the trees, and the grass. In a moment the walls and the whitewashed brick colonnades grew blurred against the deep purple of the landscape. In this calm and peaceful atmosphere the strokes of the bell fell in slow sequence, as though to enhance the beauties of nature with a tinge of Buddhism. The whispering leaves, the gracefully curling smoke, and the rustling rice-sheaves all seemed to be answering Shākya-Muni's call to follow him into eternal nothingness.

Buddhism is seldom absent from Khai Hung's works, as witness this further passage from the same book:

Outside, the flower-decked wall, bathed in pale moonlight, cast its shadow over the flagged courtyard. A few leafless frangipani trees, with their graceful bearing, hung down amidst a riot of manioc. Both living and lifeless things seemed to have a meekness suggestive of the calm and gentle aura of Buddhism.

Some critics have found fault with Khai Hung for overidealizing Buddhism, indeed for sedating Vietnamese youth with the twin opiates of romance and religion; and there may be some substance in this criticism. Nevertheless it must be appreciated that for Khai Hung two young people's love for each other, even

[188]

if blighted, is bound to lead on to a love of humanity in general. Thus in *Nua chung xuan* (Unfinished Spring), Loc says to his beloved:

And why should I not think about a family, a much bigger, extended family—society, humanity? I shall devote all my will and all my abilities to serving it; and from time to time, in my moments of leisure, I shall think of you and cherish your sweet and lovely memory. Oh, God! I feel so happy; I have a clear view of my brilliant future. From now on my life will be utterly changed.

To sum up, Khai Hung fully achieved his aims and exerted a crucial influence on both literature and society. He was one of the greatest novelists of the first half of the twentieth century. In addition to his novels he wrote a large number (six collected volumes) of short stories of high literary merit, two plays (*Dong benh* and *Tuc luy,* the latter in verse), and some children's stories. Between 1933 and 1942 he produced nine novels, not counting two (*Ganh hang hoa* and *Doi mua gio)* written jointly with Nhat Linh. His last novel, *Ban Khoan* (or *Thanh duc*), appeared in 1945. He was unable to finish his novel *Xieng xich,* which came out in the new series of *Ngay nay.* His main achievement was that he helped to shape a true national literature and to raise Vietnamese to the status of an international literary language.

GENERAL COMMENTS ON NHAT LINH'S WORKS

As we have seen, Nhat Linh was the moving spirit of the *Tu-luc* group. He and Khai Hung had similar ideas about social reform, and seem to have complemented one another. Nevertheless, looking at their works there are obvious differences. Whereas Khai Hung's characters, by and large, are sanguine and idealistic, Nhat Linh's seem to suffer from frustration, and to be more committed and cerebral. They are always hard at it campaigning or working for some cause or other. The typical characters in Nhat Linh's novels, such as Dung in *Doan tuyet* (The Break) and *Doi ban,* and Doan in *Toi tam* (Darkness), are probably reflections of the author's own personality. Reading his novels makes one realize his great sincerity—as, for instance, when he makes Dung say, in the introduction to *Doi ban:*

You and our friends, I am sure, share my pain and anxiety. We who live in a rapidly developing society have unhappinesses in common which, strange as it may seem, have been for some time our only pleasures.

Elsewhere Dung says of himself:

I suffered an injustice the moment I was born. I lived in wealthy surroundings to which I am not entitled, and which I have neither the right nor the wish to enjoy. It grieves me.

Obviously it is Nhat Linh himself who is pained and despairing. He meant to reform society. His plans for reform, as we have seen, were worked out in concert with Khai Hung; and up to a point they succeeded. We must not forget that the reforms were proposed at the time of the Popular Front in France, yet they required the approval of the French Government. On some points Nhat Linh won complete victory: the emancipation of Vietnamese womanhood, the weakening of the "extended family" tradition, the right of young widows to remarry, and an amelioration in the educational and living standards of the peasantry. Here is what Dung has to say about country folk in *Doan tuyet* ("The break"):

I believe in progress. We can improve their lot. They may be so inured to poverty that they are no longer aware of it—or if they are, they have no way of expressing it. It is for us to tell them our wishes and aspirations for them, and to see to it that they come to have the same ambitions as ourselves. I have long hoped that our peasants might be less oppressed and persecuted. We must firmly believe that our hopes can be fulfilled, and that our peasants will hope as keenly as we do.

His love for the ordinary people, for the mass of poor un-educated peasants, was most sincere. The only pity is that the political circumstances of the time did not allow him to carry his reforms through within the law. This is why in his books the revolutionary militant tends to be a romantic and often a de-featist militant, seeking an outlet for his frustrated idealism in the anticolonialist revolt.

As leader of the *Tu-luc* group Nhat Linh influenced all its members, especially Khai Hung. In literary technique Nhat Linh is a step ahead of Khai Hung: he is more observant, more ra-tional, and more methodical. He has the gift of making social problems meaningful by illustrating them in real-life situations. His characters generally have an aim, albeit occasionally vague, and hence appear less contemplative and more dashing than Khai Hung's. Nhat Linh's style, which is frequently adapted to fit his train of thought, is a model of lucidity, conciseness, and balance: it is less appealing than Khai Hung's, but more suc-cinct and incisive. Thanks to these stylistic qualities, Nhat Linh could describe in minute detail the most complex and subtle of moods, or accurately portray the beauty of work as seen by poor laborers.

Together with Khai Hung, Nhat Linh remains the outstand-ing figure in contemporary fiction. It is thanks to these two writers that Vietnamese prose has attained its present richness. It is possible to find fault with their political activities; but even the most doctrinaire critics are forced to admit that they made an unrivaled contribution to the corpus of contemporary Viet-namese literature, and enabled it to attain a higher position on the global scale.

BIBLIOGRAPHY

Most of the research on Vietnamese literature, including the most substantial and careful pieces of work, has naturally been done by Vietnamese; though some French scholars also have worked in the field.

Many articles in *quoc-ngu* on general and specific topics are to be found in periodicals such as *Nam-Phong* (South Wind), *Dong-duong tap-chi* (Indochina Review), *Bac-ky tri-tri tap-san* (Tonkin Journal of Public Education), *Khai-tri tien-duc tap-san* (The AFIMA Bulletin), *Giao-duc tap-chi* (Educational Review), *Van-hoa nguyet-san* (Cultural Monthly) and *Tri-tan tap-chi* (Modern Review). These are all prewar periodicals; but there are many present-day ones in both North and South, and learned work on Vietnamese literature has enjoyed a marked revival—as may be seen from a perusal of periodicals such as the North Vietnamese *Van Su Dia* (Literature, History, and Geography) and the South Vietnamese Ministry of Education's *Van-hoa nguyet-san* (Cultural Monthly).

There is no French-language journal specializing in the subject. Worthwhile contributions are occasionally to be found in the Saigon journals *Excursions et Reconnaissances* and *Bulletin de la Société des Etudes Indochinoises;* and bibliographical notes appear in the *Bulletin de l'École Française d'Extrême-Orient.* The latter has carried the two major scholarly bibliographies of Sino-Vietnamese literature, "Première étude sur les sources de l'histoire d'Annam," by Pelliot and Cadière (vol. 4, pp.617–71), and Émile Gaspardone's "Bibliographie annamite" (vol. 34); and these are supplemented by Tran Van-Giap's article in French on "Les chapitres bibliographiques de Le Qui-Don et de Phan Huy-Chu" (*Bulletin de la Société des Études Indochinoises* 13, Saigon, 1938). There are also interesting articles in the old French Governorate-General of Indochina's *Bulletin de l'Instruction Publique,* and in the more readily accessible *France-Asie.* For the sake of completeness we should also mention Henri Cordier's *Bibliotheca Indosinica* (Publications de l'École Française d'Extrême-Orient, 2 vols., 1914–15), though it deals only very sketchily with Vietnamese literature.

BIBLIOGRAPHY

There is a plethora of textbooks in *quoc-ngu*, but they are of uneven quality. Many are elementary, being designed for use in primary and secondary schools. The first serious scholarly work was Duong Quang-Ham's *Viet-nam van-hoc su-yeu* (Short History of Vietnamese Literature), published in 1944 by the Indochina Education Service; a second edition was brought out in Hanoi in 1951. The best recent book seems to us to be Pham Van-Dieu's *Van-hoc Viet-nam* (Vietnamese Literature), published by Tan Viet in Saigon in 1960. All this literary criticism is distinguished by being admirably informative, clear and objective. The two books mentioned give detailed bibliographies either chapter by chapter or consolidated at the end. A group of critics in North Vietnam have made an interesting attempt at a compendious account of the subject—*So thao lich su van-hoc Viet-nam* (Draft History of Vietnamese Literature) (Hanoi: Van Su Dia, 1957), 5 vols.

Relatively few general accounts of Vietnamese literature exist in French. All Georges Cordier's books, though out of date and poorly documented, are readable and worth consulting, particularly his *Études de littérature annamite* (Saigon, 1933). One of us (MD) has published some essays on the the subject in *Connaissance du Vietnam* (Hanoi-Paris: Publications de l'École Française d'Extrême-Orient, 1954) and in *Encyclopédie de la Pléiade: Histoire des littératures*, vol. 1 (Paris: Gallimard, 1955). In 1962 the magazine *Europe* devoted a special number to Vietnam: it contained articles on all literary genres, and translations from writers and poets living in North Vietnam. The first volume (début–1913) of *Les chefs d'oeuvre de la littérature vietnamienne*, by Duong Dinh Khue (assisted by Nguyen Qui Hung), was published by Kim Lai An-Quan in Saigon in 1966. Then we may mention *Anthologie de la poésie vietnamienne* (Paris: Éditeurs français réunis, 1969) and *Anthologie de la littérature vietnamienne*, 3 vols. (Hanoi: Éditions en langues étrangères, 1972, 1973, 1975). One of us (NTH) has published a general article in a French encyclopedia, "Viet-Nam, littérature", *Encyclopaedia Universalis* (Paris, 1973).

There is a plethora of articles in Vietnamese on specific authors and books. On Sino-Vietnamese literature, in addition to the books mentioned three paragraphs earlier, Phan Ke-Binh's *Viet-han van-khao* (Sino-Vietnamese Literature), published by Trung Bac Tan-Van (Hanoi, 1930), is useful if not very readable. Many of the Chinese classics, such as the I Ching, Ch'uen-tsiu and the T'ang poets, have been transliterated and translated into Vietnamese with notes. Well-known scholars such as Tran Trong-Kim have written on Buddhism and Confucianism. Vietnamese translations or adaptations of much Chinese material

[193]

have been produced by Vietnamese authors. North Vietnamese scholars have translated the whole of the *Cuong muc* annals (see p. 12 above); and *Linh-nam trich quai* (Anthology of the Strange Beings of Linh nam), *Viet-dien u linh tap* (Anthology of the Unseen Powers of the Land of Viet), *Truyen-ky man-luc* (Giant Anthology of Wondrous Legends) and *Tang-thuong ngau-luc* (Random Jottings on the Vicissitudes of This World) are among works to have been translated into Vietnamese either in the North or the South or in both simultaneously.

Much *nôm* has been transliterated into *quoc-ngu;* and a stream of learned work on it has appeared and continues to appear. All the major *nôm* poems mentioned in the text have been transliterated; and critical articles on all the narrative poems have been published either separately or as introductions to actual editions.

French translators and adapters have concentrated on the *nôm* narrative poems—especially, of course, on *Kim Van Kieu:*

Crayssac, René. *Kim Van Kiéou, le célèbre poème annamite de Nguyen Du.* Hanoi: Le Van Tan, 1927.

des Michels, Abel. *Kim Van Kieu tan truyen* (Publications de l'École des Langues Orientales Vivantes, 11th Series), vols. 14 and 15. Paris, 1884–85.

Nguyen Van-Vinh. *Kim Van Kieu.* Hanoi: Éditions Alexandre de Rhodes, 1942.

Xuan Phuc and Xuan Viet. *Kim Van Kieu* (UNESCO "Connaissance de l'Orient" Series, no. 12). Paris: Gallimard, 1961.

Other verse romances and poems have also been translated into French:

Bajot, Eugène. *Histoire du grand lettré Louc Vian Té-ien.* Paris: Challamel aîné, 1887.

Cordier, Georges. *"Bich-cau ky ngo* ou *La rencontre merveilleuse du Canal de Jade,* poèmes tonkinois," in *Revue Indochinoise* 21, no. 1 (1919).

——*Cung-oan ngam khuc,* poème annamite (French translation with notes), in *Études Asiatiques* 1, pp. 175ff. Paris: Publications de l'École Française d'Extrême-Orient, 1925.

des Michels, Abel. *Les Poèmes de l'Annam: Luc Van-Tien ca dien,* texte en caractères figuratifs, transcription en caractères latins et traduction. Paris: Leroux, 1883.

Duong Quang-Ham. *Nguyen Dinh-Chieu: Luc Van Tien* (French translation). Hanoi: Éditions Alexandre de Rhodes, 1944.

Durand, Maurice. "La complainte de l'épouse du guerrier de Dang Tran Con," in *Bulletin de la Société des Études Indochinoises*, new series, 28, no. 2 (1953).

——*Phan Tran*, text, translation and commentary. Paris: Publications de l'École Française d'Extrême-Orient, 1962.

Landes, Antony. *Nhi do mai* (French translation), in *Excursions et Reconnaissances*, vols. 4 and 8.

Nghiem Lien. "Nguyen Dinh Chieu: Luc Van-Tien" (French translation). *Bulletin de la Société d'Enseignement Mutuel du Tonkin* 7 (1926).

Collections of legends have also been translated into French, and all Gustave Dumoutier's books are worth reading, though they are more anthropological than literary in character.

Various collections of Annamese stories and legends were published in French during the colonial period; but they are not taken from actual texts, being rather arrangements of material furnished to the authors by Vietnamese literati or storytellers. We have used:

Landes, Antony. *Contes et légendes annamites*. Saigon: Imprimerie coloniale, 1886.

Landes ms. B.1 (Annamese folktales). Paris, Société Asiatique.

More recent translations of literary texts are our own: by MD of *Viet-dien u linh tap* (Anthology of the Unseen Powers of the Land of Viet), in *Dan Viet-Nam*, no. 3, Publications de l'École Française d'Extrême-Orient, and by NTH of *Truyen ky man luc* (Giant Anthology of Wondrous Legends), UNESCO "Connaissance de l'Orient" Series, no. 15 (Paris: Gallimard, 1962). Still more recent is *Le Trésor de l'homme: contes et poèmes anciens et modernes du Vietnam* (Paris: Éditions de la Farandole, 1971).

Literary data is also to be gleaned from the following books in French on miscellaneous subjects:

Durand, Maurice. *Technique et panthéon des médiums vietnamiens (dong)*. Paris: Publications de l'École Française d'Extrême-Orient, 1959.

——*Imagerie populaire vietnamienne*. Paris: Publications de l'École Française d'Extrême-Orient, 1960.

Gaspardone, Émile. *La vie et les oeuvres de Nguyen Trai*. Lectures delivered at the Collège de France, 1952–54.

Nguyen Van-Huyen. *Chants alternés des garçons et des filles en Annam*. Paris: Geuthner, 1934.

Pham Quynh. *Le paysan tonkinois à travers le parler populaire*. Hanoi: Éditions Alexandre de Rhodes, 1943.

In the field of modern literature there is practically nothing except in Vietnamese, plus some articles in French periodicals. The following are the works we have consulted, together with some manuscripts kindly sent us by the authors themselves or by Vietnamese literary critics—in particular Messrs Ngu I and Thuong Sy (to whom our warm thanks are due):

Bach Nang-Thi and Phan Cu-De. *Van-hoc Viet-nam* (Vietnamese literature, 1930–45), 2 vols. Hanoi, 1961.

Bang Ba-Lan. *Ky-niem van thi si hien-dai* (Reminiscences about Poets and Writers of Today), vol. 1. Saigon: Éditions Xay Dung, 1962.

Bui Xuan Bao. *Le roman vietnamien contemporain* (1925–45). Saigon, 1972.

Giao trinh lich-su van-hoc Viet-nam (Lectures on Vietnamese Literary History), vols. 4 and 5. Hanoi, 1962.

Hoai Thanh and Hoai Chan. *Thi-nhan Viet-nam* (Vietnamese Poets). Hué, 1942.

Hoang Nhu-Mai. *Van-hoc Viet-nam hien-dai* (Contemporary Vietnamese Literature, 1945–60). Hanoi, 1961.

Hop tuyen tho van Viet-nam (Selected Vietnamese Literary and Poetic Texts), vol. 4. Hanoi, 1963.

Minh Huy. *Nhung khuynh huong trong thi ca Viet-nam* (Trends in Vietnamese Poetry). Saigon: Éditions Khai-tri, 1962.

Nguyen Tien Lang. "Panorama de la poésie vietnamienne contemporaine," in *Littératures contemporaines de l'Asie du Sud-Est*. Paris: Éditions l'Asiathèque, 1974.

Nguyen Tran Huan. "Panorama du roman vietnamien contemporain," *ibid.*

Pham Thanh. *Thi-nhan Viet-nam hien-dai* (Contemporary Vietnamese Poets). Saigon: Éditions Khai-tri, 1959.

The Phong. *Luoc-su van-nghe Viet-nam* (Brief History of Vietnamese Literature and Art: Postwar Writers, 1950–56). Saigon: Éditions Dai-Nam Van-hien, 1961.

"Vietnam et l'enseignement supérieur en Vietnam, Le," in *République Démocratique du Viet-Nam*. Hanoi, 1968.

Vu Ngoc-Phan. *Nha van hien-dai* (Contemporary Writers), 5 vols., new edition. Hanoi: Éditions Vinh Thinh, 1951.

Turning now to work on Vietnamese literature published in English, the list is less exiguous than might be expected. Most of it has come out during the past twenty years.

"Afro-Asian Writings: Literature and the National Liberation Movement in Vietnam." Report of the D.R.V. Delegation to the Third Afro-Asian Writers' Conference. Cairo, 1968.

Boi Lan. "Letters and Arts in American Times," in *Vietnamese Studies,* no. 14 (1967), pp. 45–46.

Boudarel, Georges. "Nguyen Du and 'Lamentation of a tormented soul,' " with illustrations, in *New Orient* 5 (April 1966).

Burton, Eva. "Communication in Vietnamese Poetry," in *Van-hoa nguyet-san* 13, no. 9 (September 1964) pp. 1265–73.

Ca van Thinh. "Patriotic Literature in Nam Bo in the 1860s," in *Vietnamese Studies,* no. 14 (1967), pp. 31–44.

Dang Thai Mai. *Van tho cach mang Viet-Nam dau the ky XX* (Vietnam's Revolutionary Prose and Poetry of the Early 20th Century). Hanoi: Nha Xuat Ban Van Hoc, 1964.

Esthetic Psychology of Kim-Van-Kieu, or Kieu's Real and Dream World. Saigon, Éditions Dat to, 1966.

Glimpses of Vietnamese Classical Literature. Hanoi: Foreign Languages Publishing House, 1972.

Le Huy Hap. *Vietnamese Legends,* revised edition with annotations. Saigon: Éditions Khai Tri, 1963.

Le Xuan Thuy. *Kim Van Kieu, by Nguyen Du,* English translation with footnotes and commentary. Saigon: Éditions Khai Tri, 1963.

"Marvelous Encounter at the Farm of the West, The," in *Viet my* 9, no. 3/4 (December 1964), pp. 2–12.

Monigold, Glenn W. (comp.). *Folk tales from Vietnam,* with illustrations by Jeanyee Wong. Mount Vernon, N.Y.: Peter Pauper Press, 1964.

Nguyen Dinh Hoa. *The Book of One Thousand Characters,* in *Van-hoa nguyet-san* 12, no. 10 (1963), pp. 1665–78.

Nguyen Dang Liem. "Vietnamese Folk Songs," in *Hemisphere* 12 (July 1968), pp. 32–33.

Nguyen Dinh Thi. "Vietnamese Literature," in *Soviet Literature,* no. 9 (September 1955). Hanoi, 1956.

Nguyen Du. *The Tale of Kieu.* English translation and annotation by Huynh Sanh Thong, historical background by Alexander Woodside. New York: Random House, 1973.

Nguyen Khac Hoach. "Compassion in Nguyen Du's Life and Work," in *Viet My* 11, no. 3 (September 1966), pp. 37–40.

Nguyen Khac Kham. *An Introduction to Vietnamese Culture* (East Asian cultural studies series, no. 10). Tokyo: Center for East Asian Cultural Studies, 1967.

——"Chinese Classical Studies in Old Vietnam: Their Past Impact upon Vietnamese Thought and Literature," in Tokyo University of Foreign Studies, *Area and Culture Studies* 20 (1970), pp. 169–87.

Nguyen Ngoc Bich (ed.). "The Poetry of Viet Nam," in *Asia*, no. 14 (Spring 1969), pp. 69–91.

O'Harrow, Stephen. "Some Background Notes on Nhat Linh (Nguyen Tuong-Tam, 1906–1963)," in *France-Asie/Asia* 22, no. 193 (1968), pp. 205–20.

Raffel, Burton. *From the Vietnamese: Ten Centuries of Poetry.* New York: October House, 1968.

Robertson, Dorothy Lewis. *Fairy Tales from Viet Nam, illustrated by W.T. Mars. New York: Dodd, Mead, 1968.*

Schultz, George F. *Vietnamese Legends Adapted from the Vietnamese.* Rutland, Vermont, and Tokyo, Japan: Tuttle, 1965.

——"Four Vietnamese Folk Stories Adapted from the Vietnamese," in *Viet-my* 10, no. 1 (March 1965), pp. 2–9.

——"Tu Thuc's Marriage to a Fairy," in *Vietnam Bulletin* 6, no. 12 (November 24, 1971), pp. 12–15.

"Some Achievements in the Development of Culture, Literature and Art," in *Vietnam* 152. Hanoi, 1970.

Sun, Ruth Q. *Land of Seagull and Fox: Folk Tales of Vietnam,* collected and retold, with illustrations by Ho Thanh Duc. Rutland, Vermont: Tuttle, 1967.

Tan Viet Dieu. "A Contribution to the Study of Kim Van Kieu, Our National Poem," in *Van-hoa nguyet-san* 11, no. 6 (1962), pp. 647–83.

Tran cuu-Chan. " 'Lu-van-tien': a Folk Poem of South Vietnam," in *Asian Pacific Quarterly of Cultural and Social Affairs* 3, no. 2 (Autumn 1971), pp. 70–79.

Tran dien Van. "Artistic and Literary Life in the Liberated Zones of South Vietnam," in *Vietnamese Studies*, no. 14 (1967), pp. 11–23.

Vu Dinh Lien. "Nguyen Dinh Chieu: The Bard of South Vietnam, 1822–1888," in *Vietnamese Studies*, no. 1 (1964), pp. 263–78.

War Wife, The: Vietnamese poetry selected and translated by Keith Bosley. London: Allison & Busby, 1972.

Weiss, Peter. *Notes on the Cultural Life of the Democratic Republic of Vietnam* (trans. from the German). London: Calder & Boyars, 1970.

BIBLIOGRAPHY

FRENCH AND ENGLISH TRANSLATIONS OF MODERN VIETNAMESE WRITING

French

Chanson des deux rives, La. Poems translated by Georges Boudarel, Le Van Chat, and P. Gamarra. Hanoi, 1963.

Corrèze, Françoise. *Le chant continu: poèmes d'enfants vietnamiens.* Translated by Xuan Dieu, Nguyen Khac Vien and Huu Ngoc; adapted and with preface by Françoise Corrèze. Paris: Les Éditeurs français réunis, 1971.

Dong Ho. "Quelques poèmes tirés du *Trinh trang* (Virginité)," translated in *Van Hoa* ("Culture"), no. 83. Saigon.

Nam Cao. *Chi Pheo et autres nouvelles,* translated by Le Van Lap and Georges Boudarel. Hanoi, 1960.

Nguyen Vy. "Quelques poèmes tirés du *Hoang Vu,*" translated in *Pho Thong,* nos. 100 and 103 (April and May 1963).

Vi Huyen Dac. *Gengis Khan* (play), French version. Saigon, 1962.

Vu Hoang Chuong. *Tam tinh nguoi dep* ("Les 28 étoiles"), poems translated by Simone Kuhnen de la Coeuillerie. Saigon: Éditions Nguyen Khang, 1961.

——*Thi tuyen* ("Poèmes choisis"), translated by Simone Kuhnen de la Coeuillerie. Saigon: Éditions Nguyen Khang, 1963.

English

Anh Duc. *Hon Dat* (novel), English edition. Hanoi: Foreign Languages Publishing House, 1969.

"From an Anthology of Vietnamese Poetry," in *Quadrant 65,* vol. 14, no. 3 (May–June 1970), pp. 93–96.

Huu Mai et al. *The Beacon Banner: Short Stories about the War of Resistance in Vietnam.* Hanoi: Foreign Languages Publishing House, 1964.

Le Kim Kien. *"Tu Uyen:* a Vietnamese Short Story," in *Hemisphere* 12 (April 1968), pp. 34–36.

Ngo Tat To. *When the Light is Out.* Hanoi, 1960.

Nguyen Dinh Thu. *"Under fire:* A North Vietnamese Novel," translated from *Innostrannaia literatura* in *Atlas,* no. 5 (November 1966), pp. 10–13, 55–62.

Nguyen Ngoc Bich. "War Poems from the Vietnamese," in *Hudson Review* 20 (Autumn 1967), pp. 361–68.

[199]

Nguyen Sen. *Diary of a Cricket,* translated from the Vietnamese by Dang The Binh, with illustrations by Truong Qua. Hanoi: Foreign Languages Publishing House, 1963.

Nhat Hanh. *Thich: The Cry of Vietnam,* poems translated by the author with Helen Coutant, with drawings by Vo Dinh. Santa Barbara, California: Unicorn Press, 1968.

Nhat Linh. *"The Return Path of Thoughts,* excerpts from a novel," translated by Vo Dinh in *Unicorn* 3 (1969), pp. 17–36.

——*The Eraser,* translated by Harrison L. Shaffer, Jr., from Nghiem Xuan Viet's French translation, in *Viet my* 9, no. 2 (June 1964), pp. 9–16.

Poems and Short Stories, Vietnam P.E.N. Center. Saigon: Éditions Tin Sach, 1966.

The Phong. "Poems," translated from the Vietnamese by XH in *Tenggara* (Kuala Lumpur) 2, no. 1 (April 1968), pp. 3–12.

——"From a Writer's Diary," translated from the Vietnamese by Dam Xuan Can in *Tenggara* 2, no. 2 (October 1968), pp. 52–57.

To Huu. *Poems,* translated by Aileen Palmer. Hanoi, 1959.

——*Poems,* translated by Pham Huy Thong. Hanoi, 1961.

"Vietnamese poetry by To Huu, Ho Chi Minh, Nguyen Kim Ngan, Truong Quoc Khanh, and Ly Phuong Lien," translated by Norman Peagan and Nguyen Hoi Chan in *Bulletin of Concerned Asian Scholars* 4, no. 4 (December 1972). Stanford, California.

Vu Hoang Chuong. *Communion* (poems), translated with drawings by Ysabelle Baes. Saigon: Éditions Nguyen Khang, 1960.

Xuan Thieu et al. *The White Buffalo* (short stories). Hanoi: Foreign Languages Publishing House, 1962.

INDEX

AFIMA (Association pour la Formation
  Intellectuelle et Morale des
  Annamites), 91*n* 4, 118
AFIMA Bulletin, 192
AFIMA Dictionary, 22
Aí Lan, 132
Amaral, Fr. de, 18
Amphitryon legend, 32
An-dương-vương, xi, 4, 5*n* 6
An-nam tạp-chí, 157
Anh Đức, 144
Anh Nga, 123, 169
Anh Thơ, Mme, 123, 135, 169
Anh Tuyên, 137, 143
Annam, 26, 43
Arahat, 32*n* 5
Âu-Cơ, 2–3
Âu-lạc, xi, 2*n* 1, 4
August Revolution, xii, 108, 128, 130
Aymonier, Étienne, 23

Bà Đen, Mount, 32
Bá Di (Ch. Po Yi), 59*n* 2, 97*n* 5
Bà huyện Thanh-quan, vii, 100–1
Ba-Thục (Ch. Pa-chou), 3*n* 4
Babut, 156
Bạc-Bà, 87
Bắc-ninh, 10, 102
Bắc-sơn, 131
Bạch-đằng, River, 66
Bạch-hạc, 3, 4, 79
Bạch-hạc đình, 130
Bạch Hải, 185
Bạch Hoa, 97
Bạch-Nga, 169

Bách nhẫn ngâm, 60
Bạch-vân quốc-ngữ thi, 71
Balzac, Honoré de, 124
Băn Khoăn (or *Thanh đức*), 189
Ban tiệp-dư, 83*n* 3
Bằng, 168
Bàng Bá-Lân, 123, 130, 137, 169
Bang Bạnh, 162
Bang Viêt, 153
Bảo Đại, Emperor, 76, 108, 130
Bảo-thủ movement, 101
Barbosa, Fr., 18
Barbusse, Henri, 124
Bát-Nhẫn, 33
Bédier, Joseph, 94
Bernanos, Georges, 180
Bích Khê, 130
Biểu nhất lãm văn-học cận-đại, 21
Bình Nguyên-Lộc, 137, 143
Black Flags, 18*n* 18
Blue River, 2, 4
Book of Poetry, 7
Buck, Pearl, 128
Buddha, Buddhism, and Buddhists,
  8–11, 17, 30, 32–37, 50, 61, 121, 127,
  183–4, 188
Bùi Công-Trừng, 120
Bùi Đức Aí, 149
Bùi Giáng, 137
Bùi Hiền, 179
Bùi Hữu-Nghĩa, 110
Bùi Huy-Phồn, see Đỗ Phồn
Bùi Khánh-Đản, 136
Bùi Kỷ, 53, 121, 179
Bửu Cầm, 136

Bửu Đình, 118
Bửu Tiên, 135

Ca dao (folksongs), 46–50, 99
Cadière, Léopold, 23
Cạm bẫy người ('Man-trap'), 121
Cảm súc, 171
Cần Lao, 138
canard enchâiné, Le, 119, 162
Canh-tân movement, 101
Cao Bá-Đạt, 103
Cao Bá-Nhạ, 103–4
Cao Bá-Quát, 102–3
Cao Bằng, 75
Cao Daism, 127
Cartoons, satirical, 119, 161, 162
Caspar, 21
Catholic missionaries, 17
Catroux, General, 125
Cây đàn muôn điệu, 170
Céline, Louis, 180
Censorship, press, 122, 125
Champa, xi, xii, 3n 5, 51
Chams, the, 51, 76
Chàng Lía, 36
Châteaubriand, François-René de, 92
Chế Lan-Viên, 122, 131, 133, 135, 170
Chén thuốc độc, 118
Chéon, Jean Nicolas, 23
Chiang Kai-shek, General, 125
Chiêu tụng Tây-hồ phú, 80
Chiêu Hồ, 98
Chiêu Quân (Vương Tường), 56, 66
China, colonization of Vietnam by, 6–7, 14
China, cultural influence of, 6–8, 12, 25–8, 113
Chinese classics, 7–8, 52, 77
Chinese *genres*, adaptation of, 77–80
Ch'in Shih-huang-ti, Emperor, 104
Chính khí ca, 57
Chinh-phụ ngâm, 81–2
Chinh-phụ ngâm bị-khảo, 81
Chớp bóng, 157
Chou (dynasty), 59n 2, 97n 6 and 9

Christianity, introduction of into
  Vietnam, xii, 76, 123
Christians, 18n 18
Chu An, 51
Chu Mạnh-Trinh, 110
Chu Thiên, 129
Chu Tử, 140
Chu Tử Đán, 13
Chu Văn, 149
Ch'ü Yüan (Viet. Khuất Nguyên), 66
Chương dân thi thoại, 170
Cinderella theme, 29, 38
Claudel, Paul, 169
Cồ Bu, 36
Cô dầu Yên, 121
Cô đốc Minh, 121
Cờ kim nữ sử (Ch. *Ku-chin nü-shih*), 84
Cổ-loa, 4, 5n 7, 6n 9
Cổ phong, 169
Cochin-China, 23, 26, 76, 109, 121, 156, 177
Con Co, 145
Con đường sáng, 164
Concubines, abandoned, 81–3
Confucians, 17–8, 52, 59, 71, 89, 91, 109, 110, 111, 116, 119, 163, 165, 178
Confucianism, xii, 8, 61, 113, 162
Confucius, 59n 3, 127
Corneille, Pierre, 28, 81, 118
Council for the Advancement of Native
  Education: recommendations for
  spelling reform, 24
Court life, influence of, 11 ff, 69
"Courtly romances,", 177
Cung oán ngâm khúc, 81–3
Cung Trầm Tưởng, 137, 172
Cung từ bách thủ (Ch. *Kung tz'u po shou*), 82
Cuội, 64
Cương mục, 12, 135
Cửu Long, 143, 144

Dạ Lang (Ch. Ye-lang), 2
Đái Đức Tuấn, see Tchya
Đại-Nam đồng-văn nhật báo, 156
Đại Nam quốc-âm tự-vị, 22, 110

INDEX

Đại Nam quốc-sử diễn-ca, 22
Đại Thánh, 34–5
Đại-Việt, 126
Đại Việt sử ký toàn thư, 12
Đại-Việt tân-báo, 156
Đại-Việt tạp-chí, 157
Đại Vương Hải, 36
Đạm Tiên, 93
Đăng-cổ tùng-báo, 157
Đặng Huyền Quang, 9
Đặng Thái-Mai, 128, 129, 131, 133, 145
Đặng Trần Côn, 81
Đào Duy-Anh, 92, 121, 127
Đào Nguyên-Phổ, 156
Đào Trinh-Nhất, 112, 132
Đào Vũ, 135, 149
Đất nước đứng lên, 135
Decoux, Admiral, 125
Đêm sầu về, 172
Đêm sông Hương, 121
Đêm trinh, 172
Descartes, René, 28
Dhammapada, the, 34
Dialectical materialism, 129, 131
Dickens, Charles, 124
Dictionaries, Vietnamese, 18–9, 22, 110
Didactic poetry, 60–4
Diderot, Denis, 113
Diêm Vương, 32
Diễn-ca, 77
Điêu Tàn, 170
Đinh (dynasty), xii, 9
Đinh Gia-Trinh, 128
Đinh Hùng, 137, 141
Đinh Quang Nhã, 144
Đinh Tiên Hoàng, Emperor, 13, 43
Đỗ Đức-Dục, 128
Đỗ Đức-Thu, 128
Đỗ Phồn (Bùi Huy-Phồn), 129, 179
Đồ-sơn, 96
Đỗ Thúc Vinh, 140
Đỗ Trọng Huê, 141
Doan, 190
Đoàn Giới, 149
Đoàn Phú-Tứ, 124, 130

Đoàn Quan Tân, 143
Doãn Quốc-Sỹ, 137, 140
Đoàn Thêm, 137
Đoàn Thị-Điểm, 81
Đoạn tuyệt, 162, 164, 180–1, 190
Đoàn Văn-Cừ, 122
Đoàn Văn-Khâm, 11
Documentary writing, 108, 120–1, 123, 179
Đôi Bạn, 181–2, 190
Đời mưa gió, 189
Đời nay, 161
Đổng bệnh, 189
Động Đình (Ch. Tong-t'ing), 2, 3
Đông dương tạp-chí, 25, 109, 114, 117, 156–60, 177
Đông Hồ (Lâm Tần-Phác), 115, 116, 117, 120, 137, 141, 143
Đông-kinh nghiã-thục movement, 109, 111–3
Đông Tây, 119
Dostoyevsky, Fyodor, 124, 180
Dress reform, 119, 163
Dũng, 180–2, 190
Dương Bá-Trạc, 115, 127
Dương Bạch-Mai, 125
Dương Đức-Hiền, 128
Dương Khuê, 110
Dương-Lễ, 98
Dương Quảng-Hàm, 115, 178
Dương Thị Minh Hương, 144
Duvernois, Henri, 124

Enigmas, prophetic, 73–4
Epictetus, 28
Eroticism, 140
Etiological myths, 4, 29–31
Existentialism, 137, 141, 168

Fashion, women's, 119, 163
Feng shen, 177
Finot, Louis, 23
Flaubert, Gustave, 124
Folksongs (*ca dao*), 46–50, 99
Folktales, 29–45

Fort, Paul, 168
French colonization, xii, 25–6, 76, 96, 107
Gái nhờ thì phú, 79
Gái quê, 170
Gánh hàng hoa, 189
Gargantua-Pantagruel theme, 36
Gaspardone, Émile, 12, 58
Gauthier, Mgr., 21*n* 21
Geneva agreements, xii–xiii, 1, 108, 109, 134
Gengis Khan, 141
Génibrel, 21
Gia-đình, 110
Gia-định báo, 22*n* 23, 110, 156
Gia huấn ca, 22, 60–4
Gia Long, Emperor (Nguyễn Ánh), 14, 76
Giác-Duyên, 87
Giác-Hải, 10
Giản Chi, 141
Giảng văn Chinh-phụ ngâm, 133
Giát Hải, 32
Gide, André, 124
Giòng nước ngược, 120
Giọt lệ thu, 117
Goethe, Johann Wolfgang von, 124
Golden Turtle, 4, 5*n* 7, 6
Grand Lac, Hanoi, 80, 178
Greene, Graham, 180
Guitry, Sacha, 124

Hà-đông, 101, 103
Hà-nam, 105
Hà Sĩ Hiệp, 47
Hà Tịnh, 21*n* 21
Hà Tôn-Quyền, 91
Hải Thanh, 120
Hai tối tân hôn, 118
Hải Triều, 119, 120
Han (dynasty), 7, 56, 57*n* 5, 168
Han Cao-To, 66
Han Ch'eng, 83*n* 3
Han Kao-tsu, 57*n* 5

Han Kuang Wu-ti, 97*n* 10
Hàn Mặc-Tử (Nguyễn Trọng-Trí), 123, 130, 170
Hàn Thuyên (or Nguyễn Thuyên), 51
Hàn Thuyên (group), 109, 128, 129
Hàn Tín, 66
Hạng Võ/Vũ (Ch. Hsiang Yü), 57*n* 5, 66
Hậu-bổ, 92 and *n* 6
Heidegger, Martin, 137
Hemingway, Ernest, 180
Hiếu Chân (Nguyễn Hoạt), 136
Highlands of Vietnam, 103, 125, 126, 132
Hồ (dynasty), xii, 51
Hồ Biểu-Chánh (Hồ Văn-Trung), 117–8, 132, 143, 177
Hồ Chí-Minh (Nguyễn Aí-Quốc), 126, 128, 154–5
Hồ Hữu-Tường, 129, 140
Hồ Huyền Qui, 52
Hồ Phương, 146, 149
Hồ Qúy Ly, Emperor, 51, 52–3
Hồ Sinh, 52
Hồ Tôn Tinh, 3
Hồ Trọng-Hiếu, see Tú Mỡ
Hồ Văn-Hảo, 132
Hồ Văn-Trung, see Hồ Biểu-Chánh
Hồ Xuân Hương, vii, 91, 98–100
Hoa-tien, 77, 83–4
Hoài Thanh, 120, 131, 133
Hoài Vũ, 143, 144
Hoạn Thư, 87, 89–90
Hoàng Cao-Khải, 110
Hoàng Đạo, 123, 126, 161, 179
Hoàng Đế (Ch. Huang Ti), Emperor, 2 and *n* 2
Hoàng Đinh Phương, 140
Hoàng-giang, River, 68
Hoàng Hạc, 149
Hoàng Ngọc-Phách, 115, 117, 178
Hoàng Như Mai, 129, 144
Hoàng Thúc-Trâm, 127
Hoàng Tích-Chù, 25, 112, 119
Hoàng Trừ, 95, 98

Hoàng Trùng, 56
Hoàng Trung Thông, 153
Hoàng Vũ Thuật, 154
Hoàng Xuân Hãn, 82, 128
Học-Báo, 157
Học Phi, 135
Hội Khai trí tiến đức: Việt-nam tự điển (the AFIMA Dictionary), 22
Hồn bướm mơ tiên, 162, 182–4, 188
Hon dat, 144
Hồng Bàng (dynasty), xi
Hồng Đức period, 12
Hồng Đức quốc-âm thi-tập, 28, 60, 66–9, 71
Hồng-môn, 57*n* 5
Housewife, life of in eighteenth-century Vietnam, 48–9
Hsiung-nu, 56, 98
Hua-chien chi, 84
Hứa Do (Ch. Hsü Yü), 97 and *n* 4
Hugo, Victor, 117
"Hundred Flowers" period, 134
Hùng Vương (dynasty), 3–4
Hùng Vương pagoda, 96
Hưng Yên, 13
Hu-pei, 97*n* 11
Hữu Thanh tạp-chí, 25, 157
Huy, 184–5
Huy Cận, 120, 122, 135, 152, 163, 170
Huy Phương, 149
Huyền Chi, 132
Huỳnh Thúc Kháng, 91
Huỳnh Tịnh Của (Paulus Của), 21, 22*n* 23, 24, 110
Huỳnh Văn-Phương, 125

I-ching, 71
Illiteracy, elimination of, 15
Individualism, 140
Indochina war, first, xii, 131–2, 134, 148
Indochina war, second, 138, 145

Jade Emperor, 31
Japanese, occupation of Indochina by, 125–6

Jātakas, 29*n* 1
Jésus-Christ, 130

Kahn, Gustave, 168
K'ang Yu-wei (Viet. Khang Huu-Vi), 26, 113
Karlgren, Bernard, 16
Karr, Alphonse, 183
Kẻ trộm quân-tử, 36
Khái Hưng, 121, 123, 161, 164, 179, 182–191
Khai trí tiền đức (AFIMA), 91*n* 4, 118
Khâm định Việt sử thông giám cương mục, 12, 135
Khánh, 182
Khánh-Đàm, 187
Khảo luận về Kim Vân Kiều, 92
Kho, 38
Khoa-học phổ-thông, 157
Khổng Lồ, 32
Khổng Lộ Quảng Trí, 11
Không một tiếng vang, 121
Kiến văn tiểu lục, 10, 13
Kiều Thanh-Quế, 178
Kim-Sơn pagoda, 96
Kim tiền, 124
Kim Trọng, 86–90, 93
Kim Vân Kiều (truyện), 15, 22, 77, 83–4, 86–94, 95
Kin Ch'eng t'an (Viet. Kim Thánh-Thán), 88
Kinh Kha, 123
Kinh nghĩa, 77, 78, 79
Kuhnen de la Coeuillerie, Simone, 171
Kwangtung, 4
Kỹ nghệ lấy Tây, 121
Kỳ Văn Nguyen, 140

La dame aux camélias, influence of, 117, 178
La lutte, 125
Lạc Long Quân, 2–3
Lâm Tân-Phác, see Đông Hồ
Lamartine, Alphonse de, 92

INDEX

Lan, 183–4
Lãng Nhân, see Phùng Tất-Đắc
Lankā, Mount, 10*n* 12
Lankāvatāra sutra, the, 10*n* 12
Lao Động, 133, 134
Lấy chồng cho đáng tấm chồng, 79
Lê (dynasty), xii, 9, 12, 45, 59, 61, 70,
    71, 73, 74, 75, 77, 80, 92, 186
Lê Anh Xuân, 153
Lê Báo, 186
Lệ chi viên, 130
Lê Chiêu Tông, Emperor, 70
Lê Dư, 115, 121, 179
Lê Duy-Cử, 102
Lê Duy Phương, 154
Le Grand de la Liraÿe, Abbé, 21
Lê Hi, 12
Lê Khâm, 149
Lê Lợi, see Le Thai To
Lê Nại, 36
Lê Ngọc Trụ, 136, 141, 142, 143
Lê Như Hồ, 36
Lê Phương, 149
Lê Qúi Đôn, 10, 13, 53, 78–9, 135
Lê Tất Diệu, 140, 143
Lê Thái Tổ, Emperor, xii, 59, 65, 75
Lê Thái Tong, Emperor, 52, 59
Lê Thăng, 115
Lê Thanh, 178
Lê Thánh Tông, Emperor, 12, 65–9, 75
Lê Tràng-Kiều, 120
Lê Văn Hòe, 83, 127
Lê Văn Hưu, 12
Lê Văn Siêu, 129
Lê Vĩnh Hòa, 140, 144
Légendes des terres sereines, 68
Li Po (Li T'ai-po), 82, 168
Liang Ch'i-ch'ao (Viet. Luong Khai
    Sieu), 26, 113
Lịch triều hiến chương loại chí, 28
Liễu Hạnh, 44
Linh Bảo, Mme, 137
Lĩnh-nam trích quái, 2, 29
Linh Phượng, 117
Literary examinations, 7, 11–12, 48, 96,
104, 112; abolished by the French, 15
Literary criticism, 108, 136
Literary prizes in modern Vietnam, 134,
    137, 142–4
Lỡ bước sang ngang, 170
Loa Thành, 6 and *n* 9
Loan, 180–2
Lộc, 184–5, 189
Long-giáng Pagoda, 183
Long Khánh period, 53
Long-vân Pagoda, 183
Lü Ch'i, 96
Lửa thiêng, 170
Lục-bát verse, 46, 53, 61, 77, 95, 98
Lục-tỉnh tân-văn, 157, 158
Lục Vân Tiên, 22, 95, 96–7
Luen yu, 127
Lương Đức-Thiệp, 129
Lương Thị Vinh, 151
Lương Văn-Can, 111
Lương Văn Đạt, 18*n* 18
Lưu-Bính Dương-Lễ, 98
Lưu Nghi, 101
Lưu Trọng-Lư, 120, 122, 133, 135, 152,
    169, 170
Lý (dynasty), xi–xii, 7, 8, 10, 74
Lý-công truyện, 95, 97
Lý Nguyên Cát, 13
Lý Nhân Tông, Emperor, 9, 10
Ly-tao (Ch. *Li sao*), 66
Lý Toét, 119, 162

Mã Giám-Sinh, 87
Mạc (dynasty), 70–1, 75, 78
Mạc Đăng Dung, Emperor, 70
Mai, 184–6
Mai Trung Tĩnh, 143
Mallarmé, Stéphane, 130
Malot, Hector, 117
Mạnh Mẽ, 38
Mạnh Phú-Tư, 131
Mảnh trăng thu, 118
Marillier, Fr. André, 19
Martin du Gard, Roger, 180
Marty, Louis, 115, 159

INDEX

Marxism, 109, 129, 131; split between
 III and IV internationals, 125
Maugham, Somerset, 128
Mây vẫn thơ, 120, 169
Mẹ ơi con muốn lẫy chồng, 79
Mèo (Miao), 31 and *n* 3
Mị Châu, 4–6
Mill, John Stuart, 27
Ming (dynasty), xii, 65, 84
Mình Đồng Gan Sắt, 38
Minh Đức, Mme, 137
Minh Huy, 137
Minh Mệnh, Emperor, 91, 92
Molière, Jean-Baptiste Poquelin de,
 118
Mongols, struggles against, xii, 51
Montesquieu, Charles Louis, Baron de,
 27, 113
Một nền văn-hóa mới, 131
Musset, Alfred de, 124
Mỵ Ê, 66

Nam Cao, 131, 133, 145, 147
Nam Hải, 3
Nam Phong tạp-chí, 25, 28, 90–1, 109,
 112, 114–5, 117, 118, 156, 157,
 159–61, 177
Nam Trân, vii
Nam xương, 68
Narrative poems, 77, 81, 83–98
"New Culture" (China), 113
"New Poetry" (*Thơ mới*), 109, 116, 119,
 120, 122, 163, 165–76
New Year, celebration of, 66–7, 105,
 117, 160
Ngã Ba-Hạc phú, 79
Ngâm, 81
Nganh, 55
Ngày nay, 124, 156, 157, 161, 189
Ngày xưa, 169
Nghệ An, 21*n* 21, 46, 56
Nghĩa sĩ truyện, 56
Nghiêm-Lăng, 97 and *n* 10
Nghiêm Toản, 136, 143
Nghiêm Xuân Hồng, 141

Nghiêm Xuân-Yêm, 128
Nghiêu (Ch. Yao), Emperor, 67*n* 1,
 96*n* 1
Ngô (dynasty), xii
Ngọ Báo, 119
Ngô Chân Lưu, 9
Ngô Đình Diệm, xiii, 138–9
Ngo Dinh Nhu, 138
Ngô Đức Kê, 91
Ngô Sĩ Liên, 12
Ngô Tất-Tố, 123, 130, 133, 179
Ngô Văn-Triện, 130
Ngọc, 183
Ngọc-Hoa, 95, 98
Ngọc Linh, 137
Ngu I, 136, 137
Người sơn nhân, 169
Nguyễn, Lords, 48, 75–6, 78
Nguyễn (dynasty), xii, 12, 14, 74, 98,
 108
Nguyễn Ái-Quốc, see Hồ Chi-Minh
Nguyễn Ánh, see Gia Long, Emperor
Nguyễn Ba-Học, 115, 118, 177
Nguyễn Bá Lân, 79
Nguyễn Bá-Trác, 115
Nguyễn Bách-Khoa, see Trương Tửu
Nguyễn Bạt-Tụy, 136
Nguyễn Biểu, 56
Nguyễn Bính, 122–3, 170
Nguyễn Bỉnh Khiêm, 13, 44, 59, 70–4,
 101
Nguyễn Bui Voi, 154
Nguyễn Can-Mộng, 115
Nguyễn Cát-Tường, 119, 161, 163
Nguyễn Công-Hoan, 123, 135, 145, 146,
 179
Nguyễn Công Trứ, 90–1, 101
Nguyễn Đạt, 98
Nguyễn-Đạt Nguyễn-Sinh, 98
Nguyễn Đình-Chiểu, 14, 96, 110, 132,
 144
Nguyễn Đình-Chiểu literary prize,
 143–4
Nguyễn Đình-Hòa, 136
Nguyễn Đình-Lạp, 123, 129

Nguyễn Đình-Thi, 131, 133, 145, 148
Nguyễn Đỗ-Cung, 129
Nguyễn Đỗ-Mục, 114, 158
Nguyễn Đôn-Phục, 25, 112, 115
Nguyễn Đồng-Chi, 129
Nguyễn Dữ, 86, 88, 90, 92–4
Nguyễn Du và truyện Kiều, 129
Nguyễn Đức-Quỳnh, 129
Nguyễn Duy-Can, 136
Nguyễn Gia Thiều, 82–3
Nguyễn Gia-Trí, 161
Nguyễn Hiến Lê, 24, 136, 143
Nguyễn Hoạt, see Hieu Chan
Nguyễn Hồng, 123, 131, 145, 179
Nguyễn Huệ, Emperor, 14, 186
Nguyễn Hung, 135
Nguyễn Hữu Chỉnh, 79
Nguyễn Hữu Tiến, 25, 112, 115, 160
Nguyễn Huy Lượng, 80
Nguyễn Huy Tự, 83–4
Nguyễn Huy-Tưởng, 131, 133, 135,
    145, 152
Nguyễn Khắc-Hiếu, see Tản Đà
Nguyễn Khải, 135, 146, 149
Nguyễn Khoa Diêm, 143, 144, 153
Nguyễn Khuyến (Tam-Nguyên Yen-
    Đỗ), 104–6, 110
Nguyễn Kiên, 149
Nguyễn Kim, 70, 75
Nguyễn Ly, 101
Nguyễn Mạnh-Bảo, 136, 143
Nguyễn Mạnh-Bổng, 115
Nguyễn Mạnh Côn, 140
Nguyễn Minh Châu, 146
Nguyễn Ngọc, 135, 146, 149
Nguyễn Nhược-Pháp, 120, 169
Nguyễn Quyên, 111
Nguyễn Sa, 137, 141
Nguyễn Sĩ Cố, 51
Nguyễn Sinh, 98
Nguyễn Tây Sơn (dynasty), see Tây
    Sơn
Nguyễn Thị Cẩm Thành, 149
Nguyễn Thị-Lưu, 125
Nguyễn Thị Thuy Vũ, 140

Nguyễn Thị-Vinh, Mme, 137
Nguyễn Thiện, 84
Nguyễn Thiệu-Lâu, 128
Nguyễn Thuyên, see Hàn Thuyên
Nguyễn Tiên-Lãng, 115, 160, 167
Nguyễn Trãi, 13, 43, 52, 58–64, 65, 69,
    72, 101, 135
Nguyễn Trãi gia huấn, 60–4
Nguyễn Triệu-Luật, 115, 129–30
Nguyễn Trọng-Phan, 128
Nguyễn Trọng-Thuật, 115, 117, 177–
    8
Nguyễn Trọng-Trí, see Hàn Mặc-Tử
Nguyễn Trường Tộ, 21–2
Nguyễn Tuân, 122, 126, 129, 131, 145,
    147, 179
Nguyễn Tường-Phượng, 127
Nguyễn Tường-Tam, see Nhất Linh
Nguyễn Văn Bông, 145, 148, 149
Nguyễn Văn-Giai, 110
Nguyễn Văn Ngọc, 45, 121, 179
Nguyễn Văn-Nguyên, 125
Nguyễn Văn-Tạo, 125
Nguyễn Văn Thiệu, 139, 142
Nguyễn Văn-Tố, 114, 121, 127, 128,
    163, 179
Nguyễn Văn-Trung, 136
Nguyễn Văn Vinh, 24, 28, 86, 111,
    114–5, 117, 118, 151, 157, 158, 159,
    160, 163
Nguyễn Vỹ, 137, 170, 172
Nguyễn Xuân-Sanh, 130
Nhã Ca, 141, 143
Nhạc-phủ (Ch. *yüeh-fu*), 81, 168
Nhan Tử (Ch. Yen Yuan), 59
Nhất Linh (Nguyễn Tường-Tam), 121,
    123, 126, 132, 137, 161, 164, 179,
    180–2, 187, 189–91
Nhật Tiến, 137
Nhật tinh ngâm, 60
Nhị độ mai (Ch. *Erh tu mei*), 95, 96
Nhị Nương, 186
Như Mai, see Hoàng Như Mai
Những bức thư tình, 124
Những người ở lại, 133

Nhượng Tống, 118
Nôm, 8, 11, 13, 15–17, 22, 28, 51, 52, 53, 56, 57, 60, 71, 73, 75–85, 86, 88, 95–106, 107, 110
Nông cổ mín đàm, 156
Nòng Minh Châu, 149
Novel, development of the, 109, 117–8, 137, 177–91
Nửa chừng xuân, 162, 164, 184–6, 189

Obscene double meanings, 98–100
Ông Ký Cóp, 124
Ông Ở, 36
Opium War, the, 25
Otium, pleasures of, 58–9, 71–3, 101–2

Pai-hua (Viet. bạch thoại), 26
Parenthood, labors of, 50
Pascal, Blaise, 124
Pasternak, Boris, 180
Pelliot, Paul, 23
PEN club of Vietnam, 136
Perse, Saint-John, 137
Phạm-công Cúc-hoa, 95, 98
Phạm Công Trứ, 12
Phạm Đình-Hồ, 98
Phạm Đình-Tân, 132, 137
Phạm Duy Khiêm, 68
Phạm Duy-Tốn, 111, 118, 177
Phạm Huy-Thông, 122, 163, 169
Phạm Ngọc-Khuê, 129
Phạm Quỳnh, 25, 28, 90–1, 115, 117, 118, 151, 159–61
Phạm Thái, 80, 95, 186–7
Phạm Tiến Duật, 153
Phạm Trọng Điểm, 58
Phạm Van Giao, 73
Phạm Van-Hạnh, 130
Phan Anh, 128
Phan Bội-Châu, 111
Phan Chu-Trinh, 111, 181
Phan Huy Chú, 28, 53, 135
Phan Huy Ích, 81
Phan Kế Bính, 25, 114, 157, 158, 177

Phan Khắc-Khoan, 124
Phan Khóai, 57n 5
Phan Khôi, 119–20, 165–6, 169
Phan Nhuận, 154
Phan Sinh, 85
Phan Thanh, 178
Phan Thanh Giản, 22n 22
Phan Thị Thanh Nhàn, 153
Phan Trần, 22, 83, 84–5
Phan Trần-Chúc, 130
Phan Van-Hùm, 125, 132
Phan Văn Trị, 14
Pháp Vân Pagoda, 10
Phật Tích, Mount, 66
Phép giảng tám ngày cho kẻ etc., 19–20
Phó Duyệt (Ch. Fu Yüeh), 97
Phổ-thông, 169
Phong, Mount, 3
Phong Hóa, 119, 120, 121, 156, 157, 161–4, 165
Phú, 77, 78–80
Phú Đông-Hồ, 117
Phụ-nữ tân-văn, 157, 165
Phụ-nữ thời-đàm, 157
Phú Xuân, 76
Phùng Tất-Đac (Lãng Nhân), 122, 136, 141, 179
Phượng Giang, 122
Po Chü-i, 58, 168
Popular Front in France, 119, 122, 178, 187, 190
Pornography, 140
Prévert, Jacques, 168
Proust, Marcel, 180
Proverbs and sayings, 45–6

Quả dưa đỏ, 117, 177–8
Quách Tấn, 130, 137
Quách Thoại, 137
Quan-Âm (Ch. Kuan-yin), 34–6
Quang Binh, 145
Quang Ngọc, 186
Quốc-âm thi-tập, 58–9
Quốc-ngữ, 8, 17–25, 27–8, 100, 107–12, 117, 130, 136, 156, 157, 159, 178

Quốc-oai, 102
Quyền sống con người trong truyện Kiều, 133

Racine, Jean, 81
Radcliffe, Anne, 179
Realism, 109, 117, 120–4, 179, 188
Red River, 51, 68, 79
Resistance literature, 132–5, 143–8
Rhodes, Fr. Alexandre de, 18–20
Riêng chung, 135
Rolland, Romain, 124
Romanization of Vietnamese, 17–25
Romanticism, 108–9, 140, 157, 178–9
Rosario, Fr. Philippe de, 20
Rousseau, J-J. 27, 113

San kuo che yen yi, 117, 177
Sào-Phủ (Ch. Ch'ao Fu), 97n 3 and 4
Sapek, 63n 4
Sartre, Jean-Paul, 137
Sayings and proverbs, 45–6
Schneider, 114, 158
Shākyamuni, 10n 12, 35–6, 188
Shang emperors, 59n 2, 97n 7
Shih ching (Viet. *Thi kinh*), 52, 57n 3 and 4
Short story, development of the, 118, 179, 189
Shu ching (Viet. *Thu kinh*), 52
Sở Khanh, 87
Sư kính tân trang, 95
Socialist realism, 109, 131, 133, 135, 179
Sơn Nam, 137
Sơn Tây, 3, 18n 18, 102
Sơn Trà, 120
Sông Đà, River, 79
Sông Lô, River, 79, 148
Sông Nhị, 132
Spelling reform in *quốc-ngữ*, 23–4
Spencer, Herbert, 27
Spirit world, intermingled with real world, 6, 32
Spring and Autumn, 7
Ssuma Hsiang-ju, 82
Sun Yat-sen, 113

Sung (dynasty), 58
Symbolist poetry, influence of, 130

Tạ Thu-Thâu, 125
Tạ Ty, 140
Taberd, Mgr., 20
Tài tử da cùng phú, 102
Tấm and Cám, 38–42
Tam Lang (Vũ Đình-Chí), 121, 122, 136, 137, 179
Tam-Nguyên Yên-đổ, see Nguyễn Khuyến
Tản Đà (Nguyễn Khắc-Hiếu), 25, 116–7, 123, 124, 157, 163, 166–7, 169
Tân-dân, 130
Tấn ngọc, 170
Tân Việt, 132
T'ang (dynasty), 7, 35, 56, 58, 78, 82, 96, 116, 123, 165, 168
Tang Bạt-Hồ, 111
Tao Đàn, 12, 65
Taoism, 71, 127
Tập thơ đầu, 169
Tây du ký (Ch. *Hsi yü chi*), 34, 117
Tây Kết, 13
Tây Sơn (dynasty), xii, 74, 76, 78, 80, 92, 186
Tchya (Dai Duc Tuan), 137
Tế Hanh, 131, 153
Teh-tsung, Emperor, 96
Thạch Lam, 123, 126, 161, 179
Thạch Sùng, 36–7
Thái Công, 97n 9
Thân, 180–1
Thần Nông, Emperor, 1
Than Van, 142
Thăng Long (ancient Hanoi), 75, 101
Thanh Hóa, 46, 71, 75
Thanh Lãng, Professor, 21, 136, 143, 178
Thanh-Minh, 93
Thanh nghị, group, 109
Thanh nghị, weekly paper, 128
Thanh tâm tài nhân, 88n 2
Thanh Tâm Tuyển, 141

INDEX

Thành Thang (Ch. Sheng T'ang), Emperor, 97n 7

Thế Lữ, 120, 133, 161, 163, 165, 169, 170

The Uyen, 140

Theater, introduction of from China, 12–13

Theater, in modern Vietnam, 118, 121, 124, 130, 131, 133, 135, 136, 141–2, 149–52

Thiền uyển tập anh thư, 10

Thiết Vu, 68

Thiều Sơn, 115, 120, 130, 136

Thơ thơ, 170

Thuấn (Ch. Shun), Emperor, 66, 67n 1, 96n 2

Thục, 4

Thực-nghiệp dân-báo, 157

Thúc Sinh, 87, 89

Thượng Sỹ, 130, 136

Thủy hử (Ch. Shui hu), 88n 3

Thúy Kiều, 86–94

Thúy Vân, 86, 88

Tī-ni-da (Vinītaruci), 10

Tiền-phong, 131

Tiếng dân, 157

Tiếng địch sông Ô, 169

Tiếng sáo thiên-thai, 170

Tiếng thu, 170

Tiêu-sơn tráng-sĩ, 162, 186–7

Tiêu Tương, 66

Tin-mới, 130

Tình già, 165–6

Tình si, 171

Tinh-Việt, 19

Tô Hoài, 131, 133, 135, 145, 147, 179

Tô Hữu, 131, 133, 135, 152

Tô Ngọc-Vân, 161

Tố Tâm, 117, 178

Tô Thùy Yên, 141

Tô Vũ, 66

Toan Anh, 141

Toàn thư (Đại Việt sử ký toàn thư), 12

Tôi kéo xe, 121

Tối tăm, 190

Tolstoy, 124

Tôn Thọ-Tường, 110

Tổng biệt, 166–7

Tonkin, 4, 9, 14, 18, 26, 75, 105, 184

Tourane, 14n 6

Trắc, 168

Trần (dynasty), xii, 9, 12, 13, 51, 52, 53, 61, 74

Trần Bạch Đằng, 143

Trần Bình-Lộc, 161

Trần Đăng, 133, 145

Trần Diệu Thường, 85

Tran Đoàn (Ch. Ch'en T'uan), 97n 11

Trần Hưng Đạo, General, 14, 51

Trần Lê Nguyễn, 141, 143

Trần Nguyễn, 154

Trần Tế Xương, 104, 110

Trần Thanh Mại, vii

Trần Thi Nha Ca, 140

Trần Tiêu, 179

Trần Tình văn, 103

Trần Trọng-Kim, 115, 121, 128, 132, 179

Trần Tuấn-Khải, 116, 143

Trần Văn Giáp, 58, 127, 128, 179

Trần Văn-Trạch, 125

Trạng Ếch, 44

Trạng Hiền, 44

Trạng-nguyên, 31n 4, 37, 43–4, 67

Trạng Quỳnh, 44

Trạng Trình, see Nguyễn Bỉnh-Khiêm

Trạng Trình, thân thế, sự nghiệp etc., 73

Transformation, in folktales, 36–7, 38 ff.

Trê cóc (truyện), 53–5, 61

Tri-tân, 109, 127

Tri-tân tạp-chí, 128

Triệu (dynasty), xi

Triệu Đà (Ch. Ch'ao T'o), 4–6

Triều Đẩu, 55

Trịnh, Lords, 48, 70, 75–6, 78, 83n 2

Trịnh Kiểm, 70, 75

Trịnh Như-Tấu, 127

Trình quốc-công sấm, 73

Trịnh Sâm, 80

Trinh thử (truyện), 52–3, 61

INDEX

Trình tiên-sinh quốc-ngữ, 73

Trình trạng-nguyên sấm ký diễn ca, 73

Tristan and Iseult, 94

Trọng Lang, 123, 136, 179

Trọng Thủy, 4–6

Trúc, 181

Trưng sisters, xi, 13, 43

Trung-Bắc tân-văn, 157, 158

Trước đèn, 122

Trương Lương, 66

Trương Phụ (Ch. Chang Fu), General, 56

Trương Quỳnh-Như, 95, 186–7

Trương Tử (alias Nguyen Bach-Khoa), 128, 129, 179

Trương Vĩnh-Ký (Petrus Ký), 21, 22*n* 22, 24, 110, 111

Truyện anh Lực, 135

Truyện giải buồn, 22

Truyện giải buồn cuốn sau, 22

Truyền kỳ mạn lục, 29

Ts'ao Yu, 128

Tsien-tang, River, 88

Tú Bà, 87

Từ Đạo Hạnh, 9

Tự Đức, Emperor, 21*n* 21, 53, 58, 91, 103

Từ Hải, 87, 89

Tự-lực văn đoàn, 25, 109, 118, 120, 121, 122, 123, 124, 126, 127, 129, 132, 137, 161–5, 178, 179, 180–191

Tú Mỡ (Hồ Trọng-Hiếu), 119, 120, 133, 161

Tự tình khúc, 103

Tuần Lan, 154

Tục lụy, 189

Tục-ngữ phong-dao, 45

Tuệ Mai, 143

Tứng Chou lieh-kuo, 177

Tụng Tây-hồ phú, 80

Tương-lai, 124

Tương-lai văn-nghệ Việt-nam, 129

Tương Phổ, Mme, 115, 116, 117, 137

Tùy bút, 179

Túy Hồng, 140

Tuyên phu ngộ phối tân truyện, 98

Tuyết hồng lệ sử, 178

Ức-Trai di-tập, 58

"Uncommitted" novelists in S. Vietnam, 179–80

Underworld, in Chinese mythology, 31–2

Union of Vietnamese Writers and Artists, 145

Ướt, 38

Uyên ương, 118

Valéry, Paul, 130

Vân Đài, Mme, 135

Vạn Hạnh, 10

Văn-hóa cứu quốc, 131

Văn-học khái-luận, 129

Văn-học tạp-chí, 157

Văn lan nhật ký, 178

Văn Lang, xi, 2 and *n* 1, 3, 4

Văn mới, 129

Văn mới tuổi xanh, 129

Văn sách, 77, 78

Vang bóng một thời, 122

Vị (Ch. Wei), River, 97 and *n* 9

Vi Huyền-Đắc, 118, 121, 124, 129, 130, 136, 141, 143

Vì sao, 171

Viên Phương, 140, 143, 144

Việt-điện u linh tập, 29

Việt-Minh, 126, 130

Việt-nam cổ-văn học-sử, 129

Vietnam, legendary origins of, 1–4

Vigny, Alfred de, 92

Vinītaruci, 10

Võ Đắt, 132

Võ Huy Tâm, 135, 145, 148

Võ Phiến, 137, 140, 143

Võ Thành An, 154

Võ Tùng-Linh, 135

Vội vàng, 171

Voltaire, François-Marie Arouet de, 113

Vũ Bằng, 121, 122, 136, 137, 179

Vũ Đãi Vân, 84

INDEX

Vũ Đình-Chí, see Tam Lang
Vũ Đình-Hòe, 128
Vũ Đình-Long, 115, 118
Vũ Hanh, 140
Vũ Hoàng-Chương, 126, 130, 137, 141, 143, 171, 172
Vũ Khắc-Khoan, 136, 142, 143
Vũ Ngọc Phan, 178
Vũ Qùynh, 36
Vũ Thị Thương, 146
Vũ Trọng-Phụng, 121, 122, 124, 179
Vũ trung tùy bút, 98
Vũ Văn-Cần, 128
Vũ Văn-Hiền, 128
Vương Hồng-Sển, 136, 141, 143
Vuong Hong Xen, 141
Vương Tường, see Chiêu Quân
Vương Tường truyện, 55–6, 66

Walpole, Horace, 179
Wang Kien, 82
Warring States period, 66
Water King, Kingdom, 2, 31–2
Water Palace, 2, 68
Wen-wang, Emperor, $97n\ 9$
West, influence of on Vietnamese
literature, 25–8, 107–8, 113, 119, 182
Wu Ting, Emperor, $97n\ 8$
Wu-Wang, Emperor, $97n\ 6$

Xã Xệ, 162
Xiềng xích, 189
Xuân Cung, 149
Xuân Diệu, 120, 122, 131, 133, 135, 152, 163, 170, 171
Xuân Quỳnh, 153
Xuân thu Nhã tập, 109, 130
Xuân Xanh, 135

Y Doãn (Ch. Yi Yin), $97n\ 7$
Yang, 3
Yên-Đổ, see Nguyễn Khuyển
Yên-tử, Mount, 96
Yêu dương, 169
Yin (dynasty), $97n\ 8$
Yin, 3
Yüeh-fu, see *nhạc phủ*
Yü-tsan chi, 84
Yuan (dynasty), 13, 44

Zen (*dhyāna*), $9n\ 10$, 10